NUMBERS 0-12

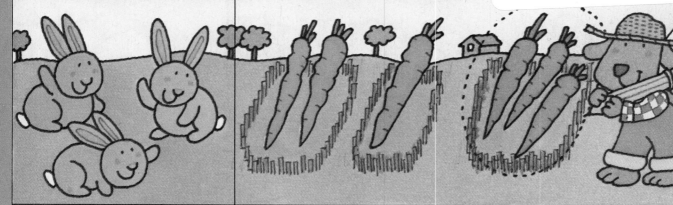

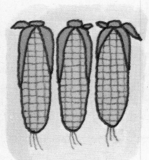

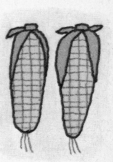

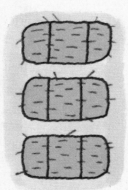
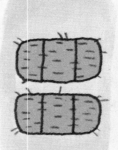

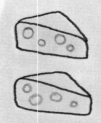
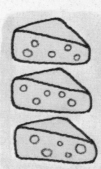

Same number

(one) 1

one   two

(1)   2   1   (2)

How many are there?

1   2

1   2

1   2

1   2

Numbers 1 and 2   (three) **3**

Write.

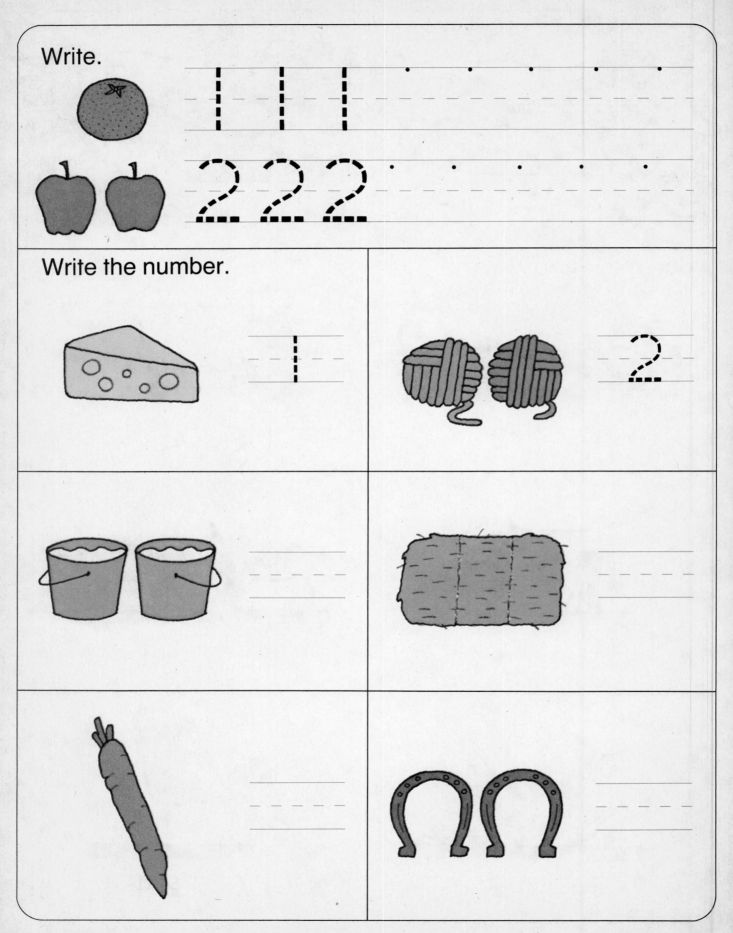

Write the number.

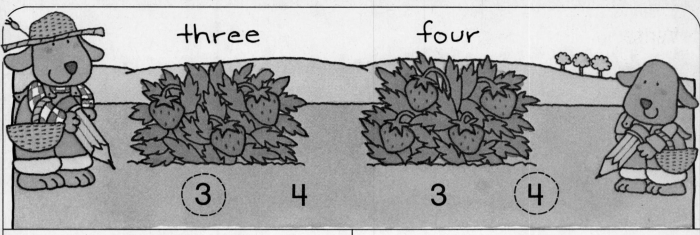

three   four

3   4   3   4

How many are there?

3   4

3   4

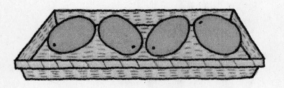

3   4

3   4

3   4

3   4

Numbers 3 and 4

(five) **5**

Write.

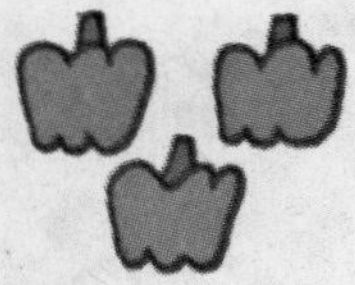

3 3 3 · · · · ·

4 4 4

Write the number.

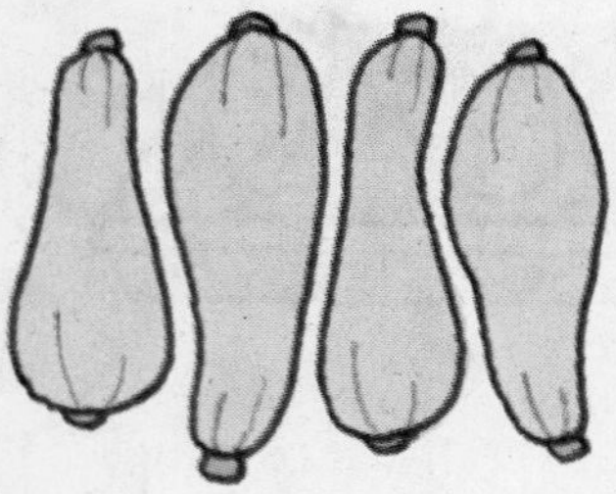

4

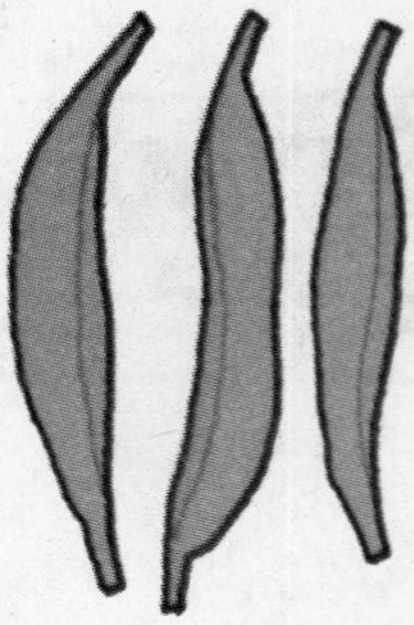

3

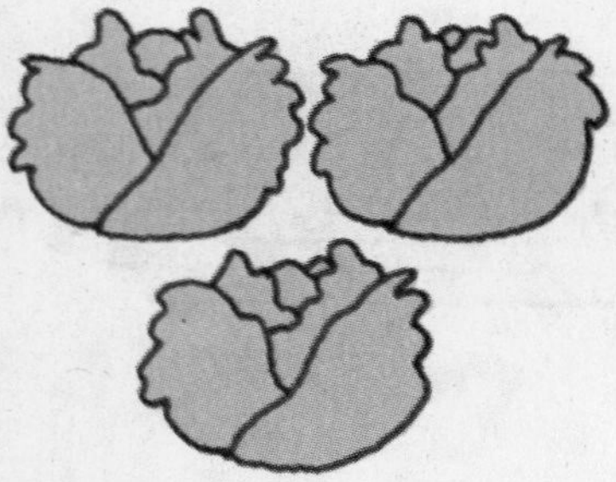

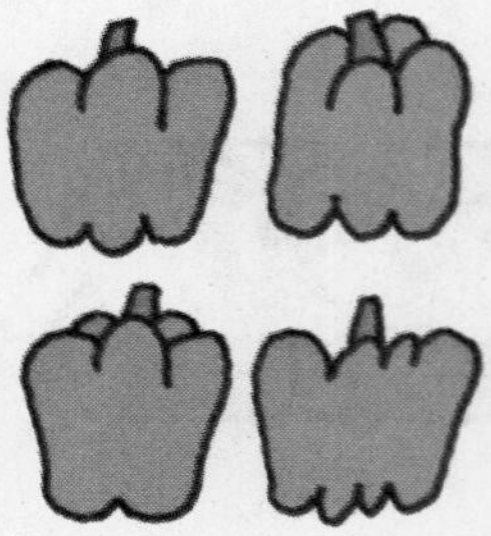

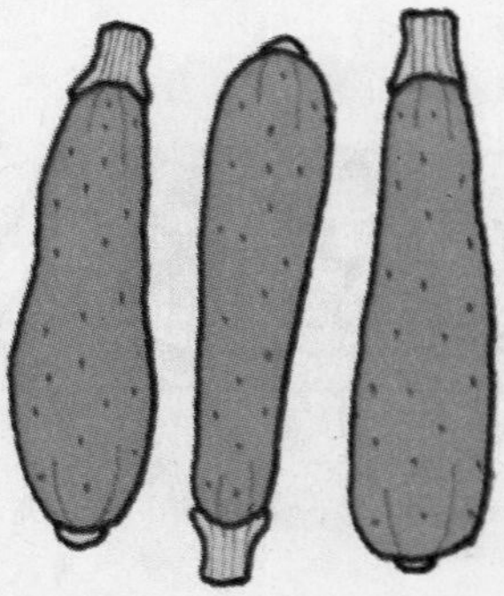

6 (six)

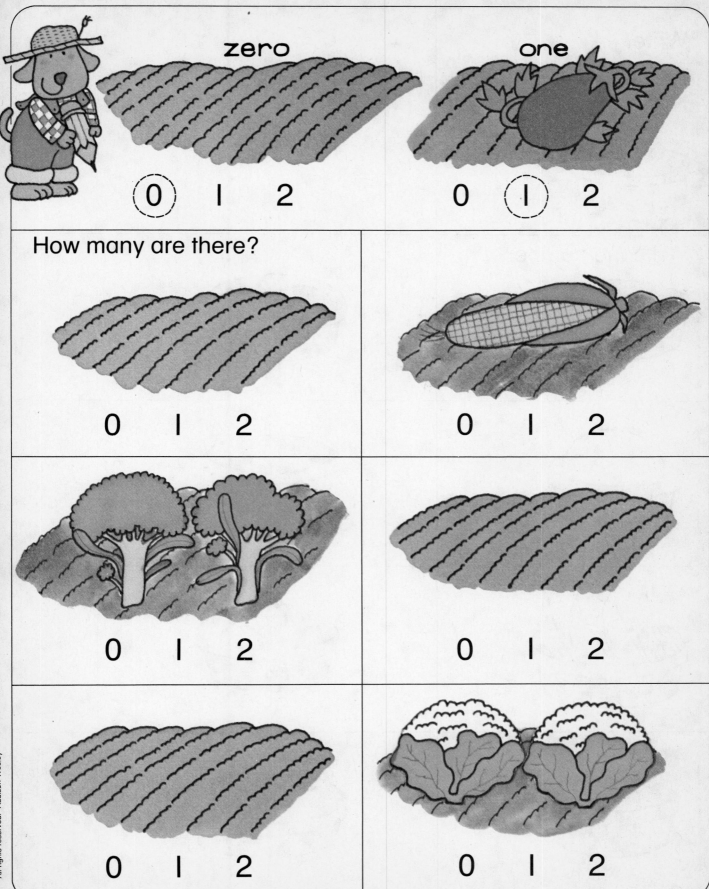

zero

one

(0)   1   2

0   (1)   2

How many are there?

0   1   2

0   1   2

0   1   2

0   1   2

0   1   2

0   1   2

Write.

O O O . . . . .

Write the number.

0

Write the numbers in order.

Color.

0   1   2   3   4

Color.

Name _____

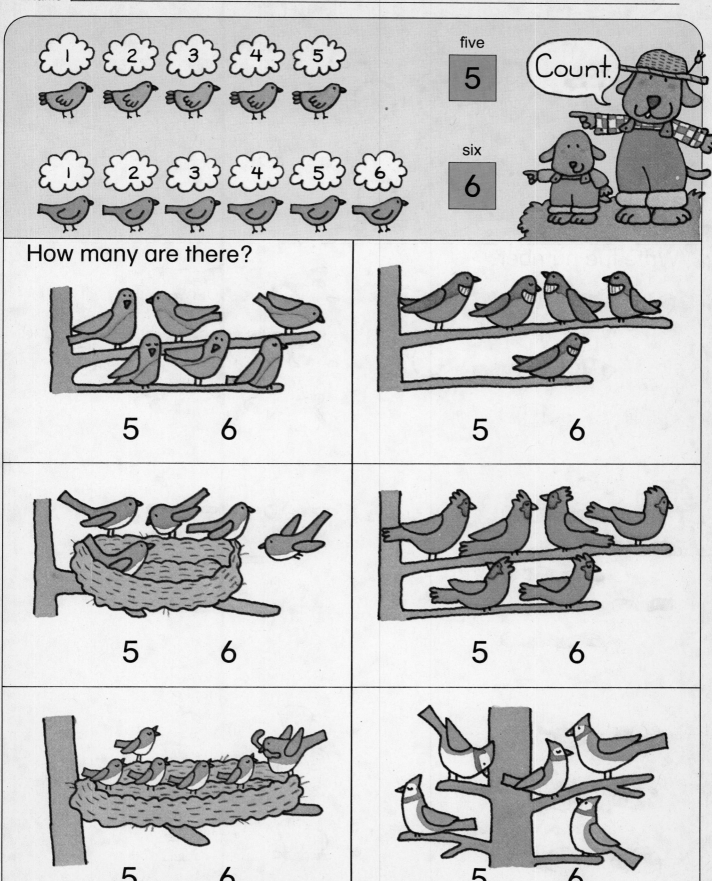

five

5

six

6

Count.

How many are there?

5   6

5   6

5   6

5   6

5   6

5   6

Write.

5 5 5 . . . . .

6 6 6 . . . . . .

Write the number.

5

6

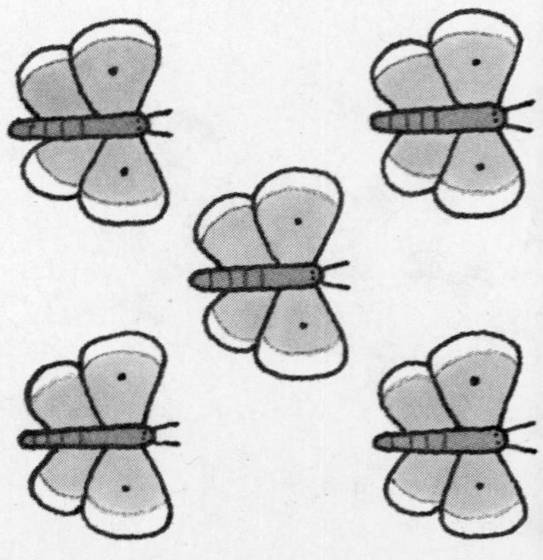

_ _ _

_ _ _

_ _ _

_ _ _

seven

7

eight

8

Count.

How many are there?

7   8

7   8

7   8

7   8

 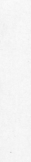

7   8

7   8

Write.

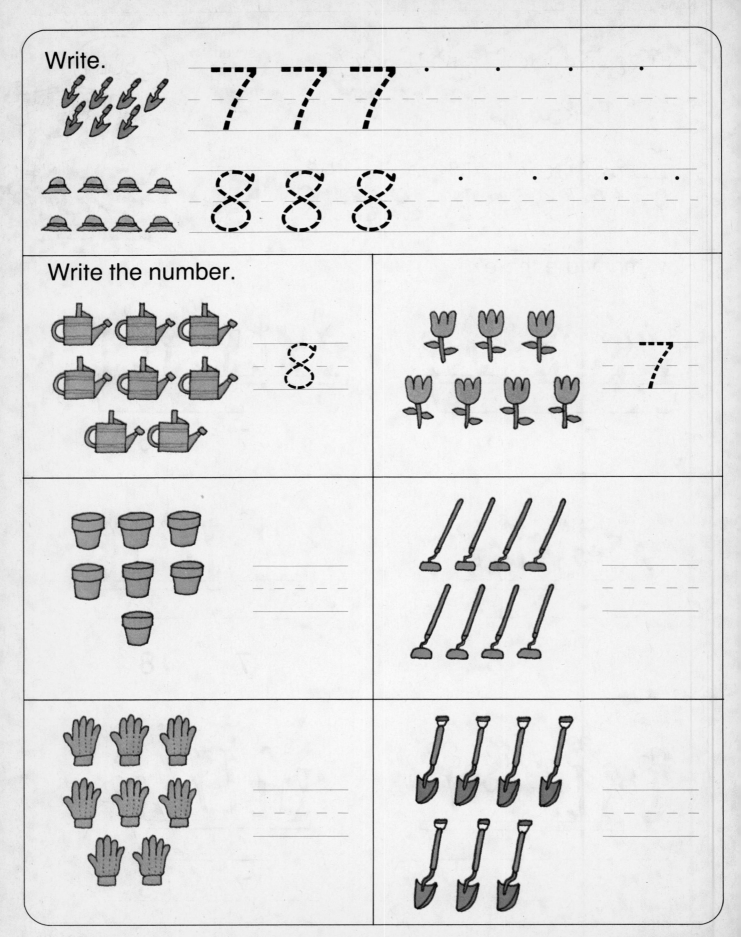

7 7 7 . . . .

8 8 8 . . . .

Write the number.

8

7

Write the numbers in order.

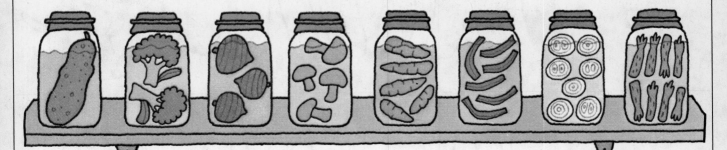

1 2 3 _ _ _ _ _

1 2 _ _ _ _ _ _

_ _ _ _ _ _ _ _

1 2 _ _ _ _ _ _

Color.

6

7

8

Order and practice

(fifteen) 15

Color.

5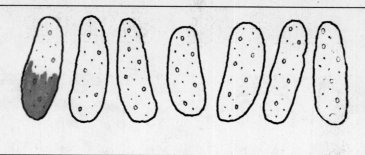

6

4

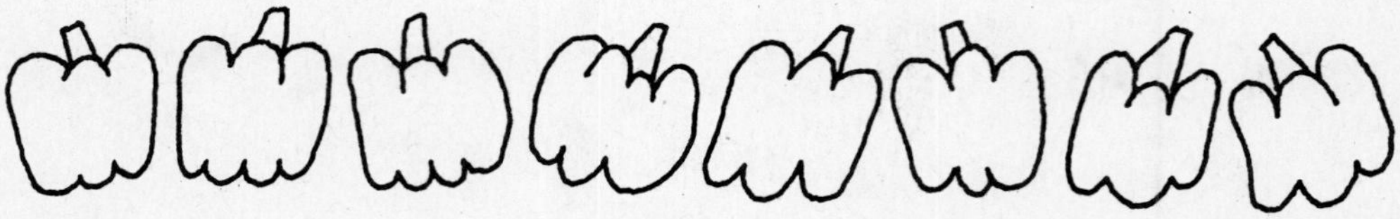

5

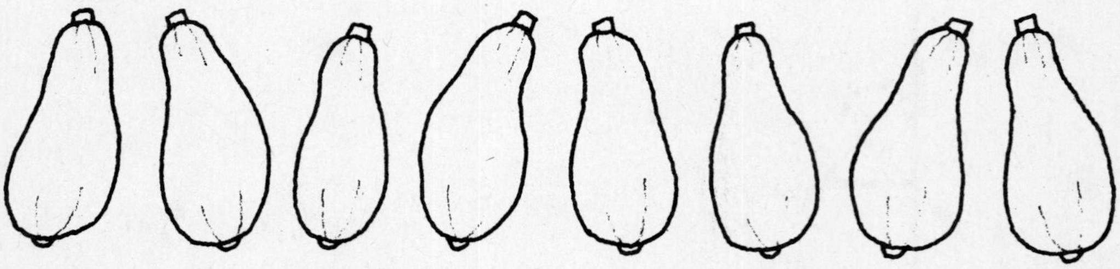

8

7

Practice

Name _____

nine

9

ten

10

Count.

How many are there?

9   10

9   10

9   10

9   10

Numbers 9 and 10

(seventeen) **17**

Write.

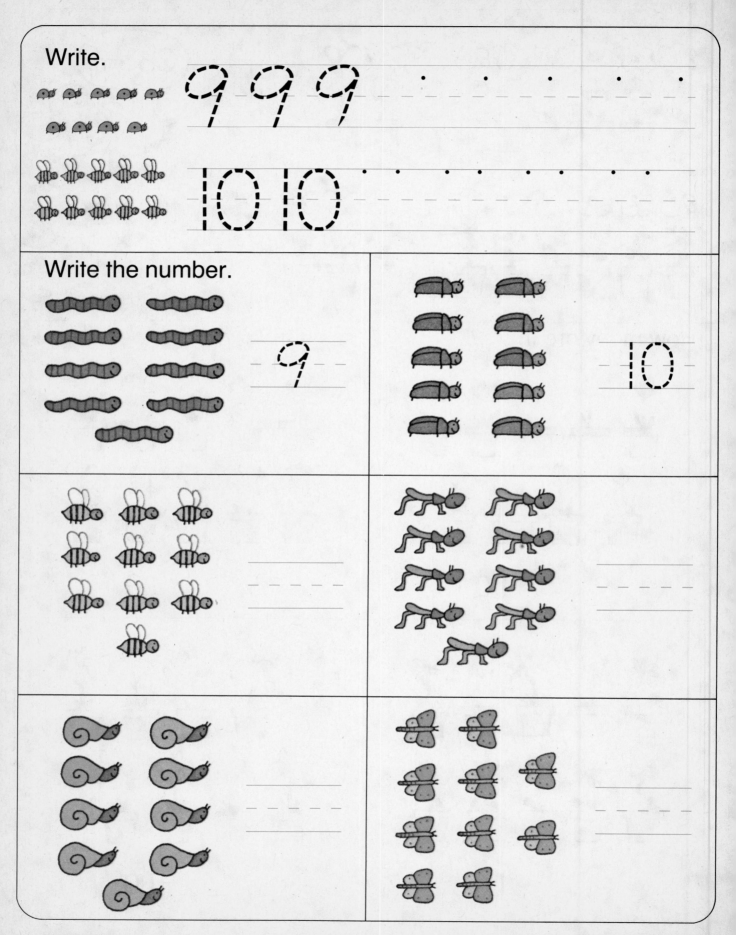

9 9 9 . . . . .

10 10 10 . . . .

Write the number.

9

10

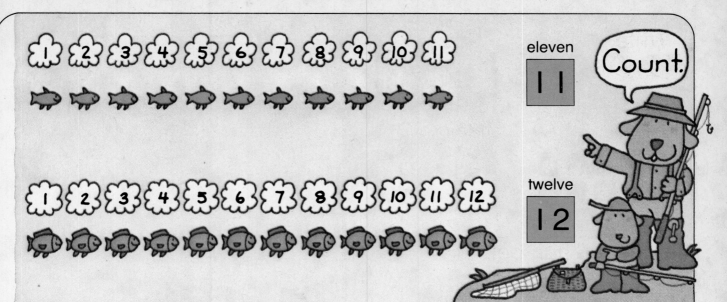

eleven
11

twelve
12

Count.

How many are there?

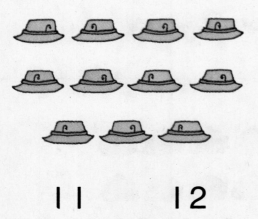

11   12

11   12

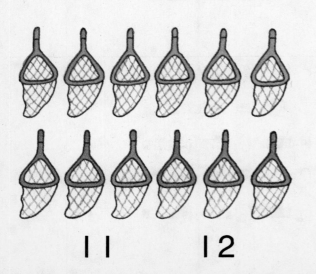

11   12

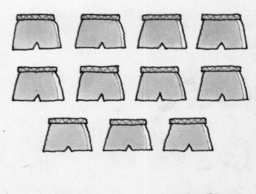

11   12

Numbers 11 and 12

(nineteen) 19

Write.

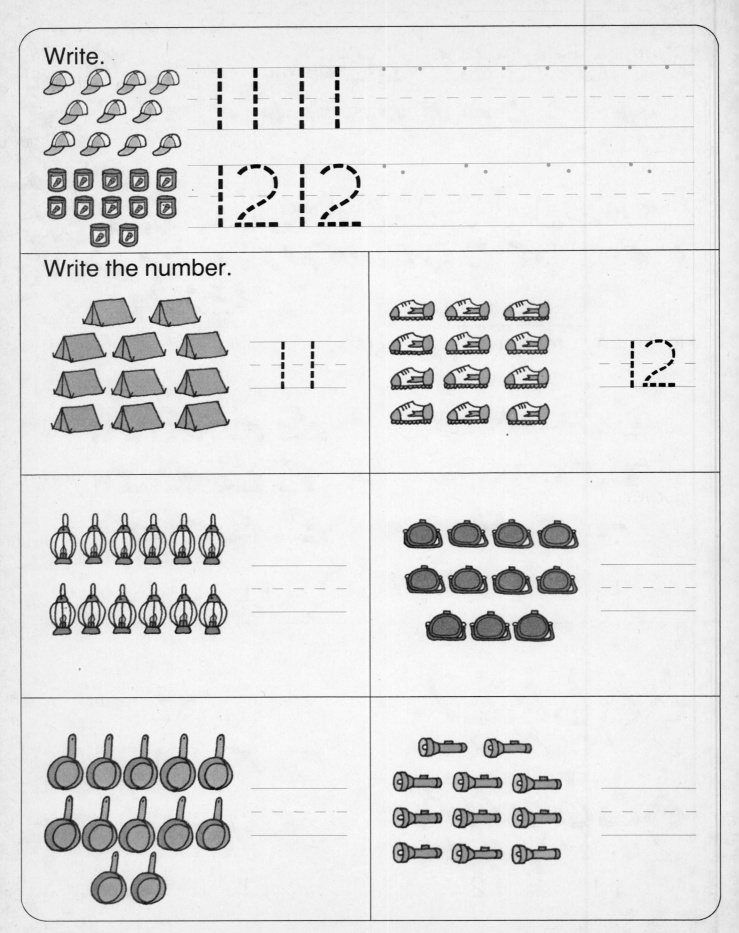

Write the number.

Write the numbers in order.

_____ _____ _____ _____ _____ _____

_ _ _ _ _ _ _ _ _ _ _ _ _ _ _ _ _ _ _ _ _ _ _ _

_____ _____ _____ _____ _____ _____

_ _ _ _ _ _ _ _ _ _ _ _ _ _ _ _ _ _ _ _ _ _ _ _

Color.

8

9

10

11

12

How many are there?

Color the graph.

	1	2	3	4	5	6	7	8	9	10	11	12
	1	2	3	4	5	6	7	8	9	10	11	12

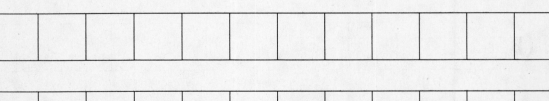
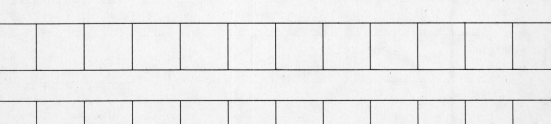

Bar graph

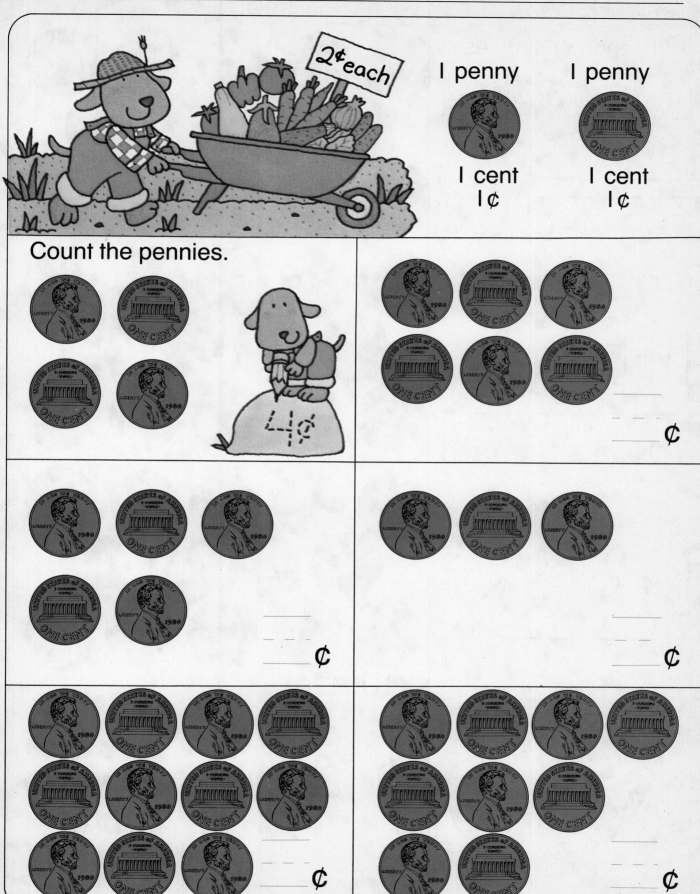

Name _____

2¢ each

I penny · I cent · I¢

I penny · I cent · I¢

Count the pennies.

4¢

_____ ¢

_____ ¢

_____ ¢

_____ ¢

_____ ¢

Counting pennies

(twenty-three) 23

Ring enough pennies.

8¢

11¢

9¢

SKILLKEEPER

Count.

Counting pennies

Name _____

What number comes next?

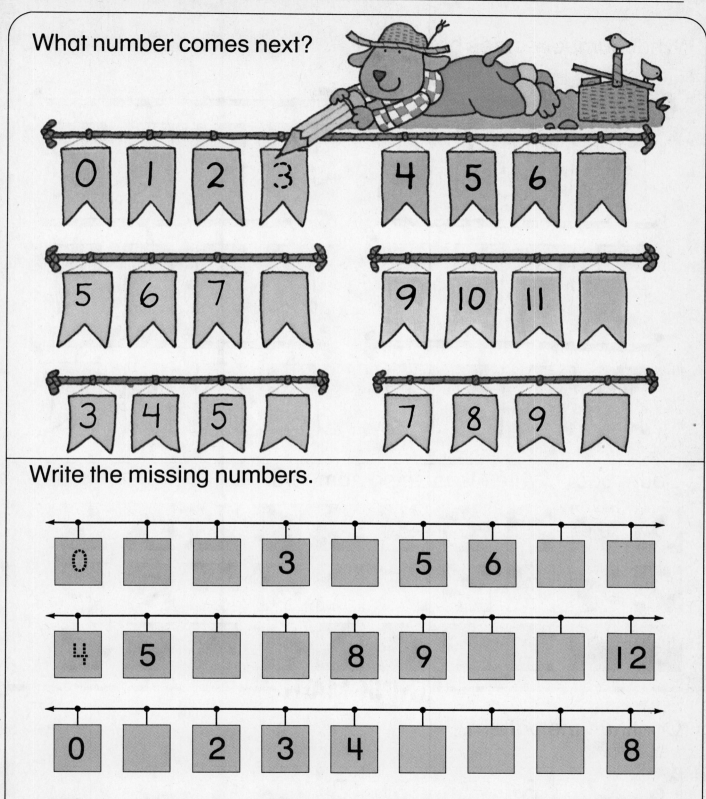

| 0 | 1 | 2 | 3 | | 4 | 5 | 6 | |

| 5 | 6 | 7 | | | 9 | 10 | 11 | |

| 3 | 4 | 5 | | | 7 | 8 | 9 | |

Write the missing numbers.

| 0 | | | 3 | | 5 | 6 | | |

| 4 | 5 | | | 8 | 9 | | | 12 |

| 0 | | 2 | 3 | 4 | | | | 8 |

| 4 | | 6 | 7 | 8 | | | | 11 |

What comes next—counting on number

What number comes before?

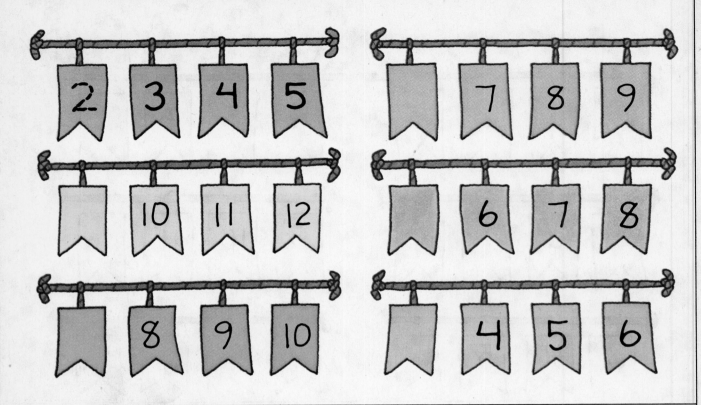

Count back. Write the missing numbers.

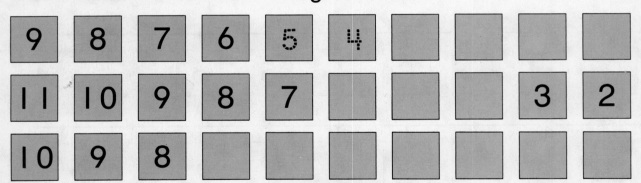

9	8	7	6	5	4				
11	10	9	8	7				3	2
10	9	8							

THINK MATH

Continue the pattern.

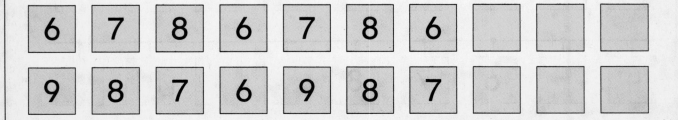

6	7	8	6	7	8	6			
9	8	7	6	9	8	7			

2   6

How many are there?
Ring the greater.

4   5

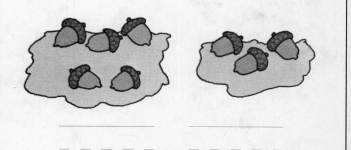

Ring the greater.

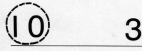 3   7   12   9   10

5   8   11   7   3   11

7   5

How many are there?
Which is less?

6   7

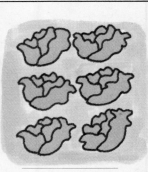

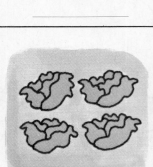

Which is less?

3   5   7   4   12   10

11   12   10   9   7   11

Name _____

CHAPTER REVIEW/TEST

Write the number.

1.

_ _ _ _ _ _

2.

_ _ _ _ _ _

Count.

3.

_ _ _ _ _ _

_ _ _ _ _ _

4.

_ _ _ _ _ _

_ _ _ _ _ _

5. Count the pennies.

_ _ _ _ _ _ ¢

6. Write the missing numbers.

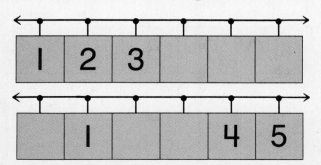

| 1 | 2 | 3 | | | |

| | 1 | | | 4 | 5 |

7. Ring the greater.

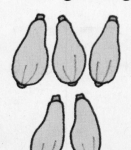

CUMULATIVE REVIEW

How many are there?

1.
   - ● 2
   - ○ 1
   - ○ 4

2.
   - ○ 6
   - ○ 4
   - ○ 0

3.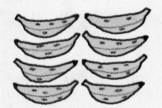
   - ○ 8
   - ○ 10
   - ○ 11

4.
   - ○ 9
   - ○ 5
   - ○ 7

5.
   - ○ 2
   - ○ 4
   - ○ 5

6.
   - ○ 5
   - ○ 6
   - ○ 7

7. **What comes next?**

| 4 | 5 | 6 | |
   - ○ 7
   - ○ 3
   - ○ 8

8.

| 9 | 10 | 11 | |
   - ○ 8
   - ○ 7
   - ○ 12

Count back.

9.

| 6 | 5 | 4 | |
   - ○ 1
   - ○ 3
   - ○ 2

10.

| 10 | 9 | 8 | |
   - ○ 7
   - ○ 11
   - ○ 12

ANOTHER LOOK

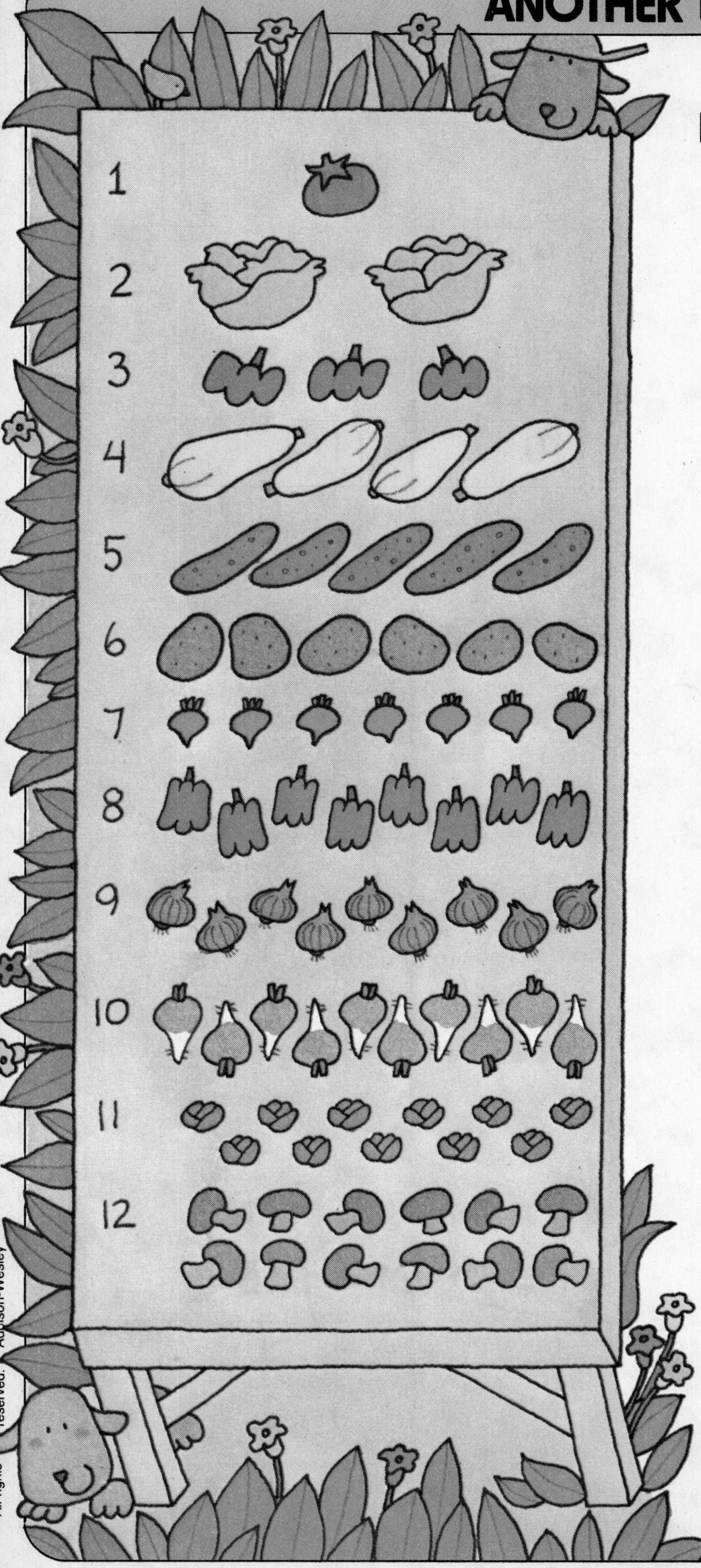

1	
2	
3	
4	
5	
6	
7	
8	
9	
10	
11	
12	

How many are there?

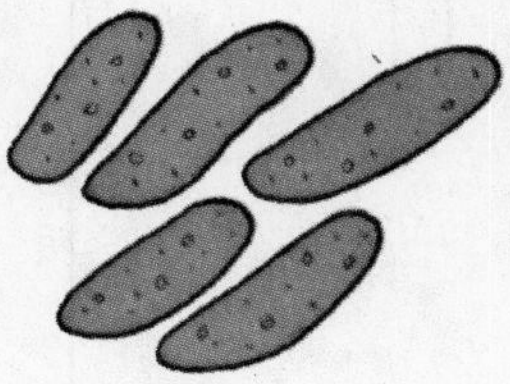

5

4 (5) 6

7 8 9

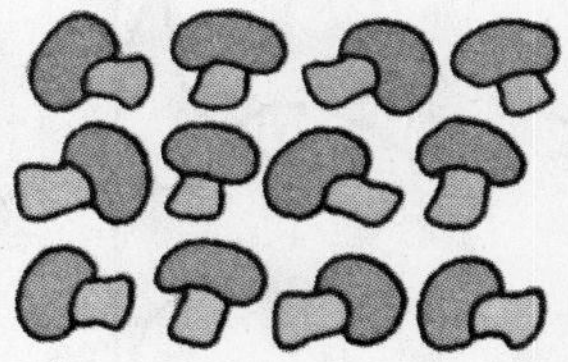

10 11 12

7 8 9

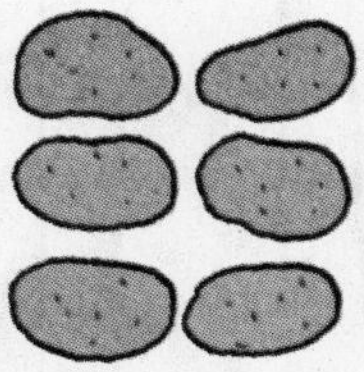

5 6 7

Give the missing tallies.

I	II			⳾⳾⳾⳾	⳾⳾⳾⳾ I
1	2	3	4	5	6

⳾⳾⳾⳾ II			⳾⳾⳾⳾ ⳾⳾⳾⳾		
7	8	9	10	11	12

Connect the dots.

Enrichment—using tally marks

SUMS TO 5

Use counters.

1.

Put in
1

Put in
3

4
_____
in all

2.

Put in
2

Put in
3

_____
in all

3.

Put in
2

Put in
1

_____
in all

4.

Put in
4

Put in
1

_____
in all

Addition concept—sums to 5

How many are there?

1.

3   1   4
_____   _____   _____
in all

2.

_____   _____   _____
in all

3.

_____   _____   _____
in all

4.

_____   _____   _____
in all

Addition concept—sums to 5

Tell a story. How many are there?

1.

$$\underline{\quad 2 \quad} + \underline{\quad 1 \quad} = \underline{\quad 3 \quad} \leftarrow \text{Sum}$$

in all

2.

$$\underline{\qquad} + \underline{\qquad} = \underline{\qquad}$$

in all

3.

$$\underline{\qquad} + \underline{\qquad} = \underline{\qquad}$$

in all

4.

$$\underline{\qquad} + \underline{\qquad} = \underline{\qquad}$$

in all

Addition equations—motion pictured

(thirty-five) **35**

How many are there in all?

1.

$2 + 1 = \underline{\quad 3 \quad}$
in all

2.

$1 + 3 = \underline{\qquad}$
in all

3.

$2 + 2 = \underline{\qquad}$

4.

$1 + 2 = \underline{\qquad}$

5.

$3 + 1 = \underline{\qquad}$

6.

$1 + 1 = \underline{\qquad}$

7.

$2 + 3 = \underline{\qquad}$

8.

$1 + 4 = \underline{\qquad}$

Addition equations—motion pictured

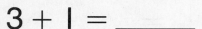

Name _____

How many are there?

1.

___1___ + ___4___ = ___5___
                        in all

2.

___2___ + ___1___ = ___3___
                        in all

3.

1 + 2 = _____

4.

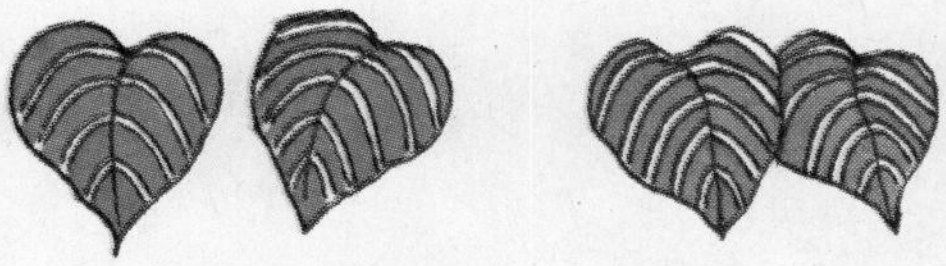

2 + 2 = _____

5.

4 + 1 = _____

6.

2 + 3 = _____

7.

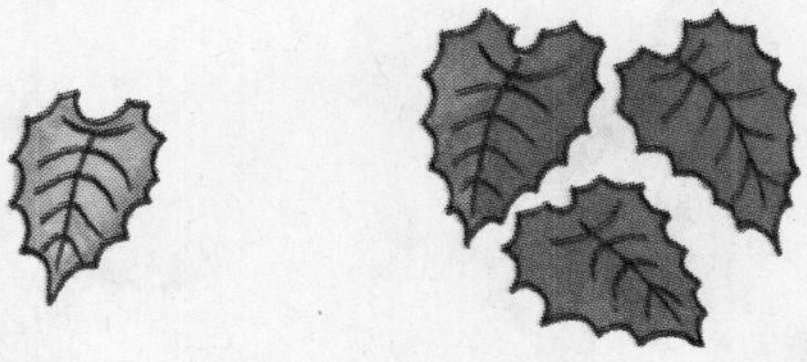

1 + 3 = _____

8.

3 + 2 = _____

Draw your own.
How many are there in all?

1.

$$3 + 1 = \underline{4}$$

2.

$$1 + 2 = \underline{3}$$

3.

$$2 + 2 = \underline{\hphantom{00}}$$

4.

$$1 + 1 = \underline{\hphantom{00}}$$

5.

$$3 + 2 = \underline{\hphantom{00}}$$

6.

$$1 + 4 = \underline{\hphantom{00}}$$

SKILLKEEPER

Match.

5   3   2   7

Addition equations—draw your own models

These have the same sum.

$2 + 1 = \text{3}$ $1 + 2 = \text{3}$

Add.

1.

$3 + 0 = \text{3}$

2.

$0 + 3 = \underline{\hspace{2em}}$

3.

$2 + 3 = \underline{\hspace{2em}}$

4.

$3 + 2 = \underline{\hspace{2em}}$

5.

$0 + 2 = \underline{\hspace{2em}}$

6.

$2 + 0 = \underline{\hspace{2em}}$

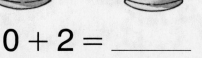

Add.

1.

$2 + 1 = 3$

2.

$3 + 2 = \underline{\qquad}$

Add.

3. $4 + 1 = \underline{\qquad}$ $1 + 1 = \underline{\qquad}$ $1 + 3 = \underline{\qquad}$

4. $0 + 5 = \underline{\qquad}$ $1 + 2 = \underline{\qquad}$ $2 + 3 = \underline{\qquad}$

5. $2 + 2 = \underline{\qquad}$ $0 + 4 = \underline{\qquad}$ $2 + 0 = \underline{\qquad}$

6. $1 + 4 = \underline{\qquad}$ $0 + 0 = \underline{\qquad}$ $3 + 1 = \underline{\qquad}$

7. $2 + 0 = \underline{\qquad}$ $3 + 0 = \underline{\qquad}$ $3 + 2 = \underline{\qquad}$

THINK MATH

How many are there in all? 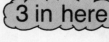 3 in here

$\underline{\qquad}$
In all

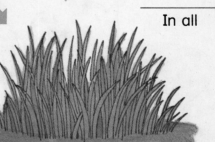

Practice the facts

$3 + 2 = \underline{5}$

$$\begin{array}{r} 3 \\ +2 \\ \hline 5 \end{array}$$

Add.

1.

$2 + 1 = \underline{3}$

$$\begin{array}{r} 2 \\ +1 \\ \hline 3 \end{array}$$

2.

$2 + 2 = \underline{}$

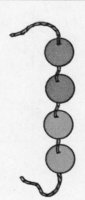

$$\begin{array}{r} 2 \\ +2 \\ \hline \end{array}$$

3.

$1 + 3 = \underline{}$

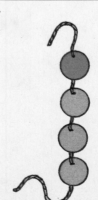

$$\begin{array}{r} 1 \\ +3 \\ \hline \end{array}$$

Vertical notation

Write the problems. Add.

1.

$$\begin{array}{r} 1 \\ +\ 2 \\ \hline 3 \end{array}$$

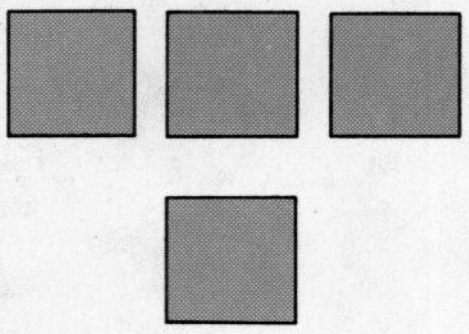

$$\begin{array}{r} 3 \\ +\ 1 \\ \hline 4 \end{array}$$

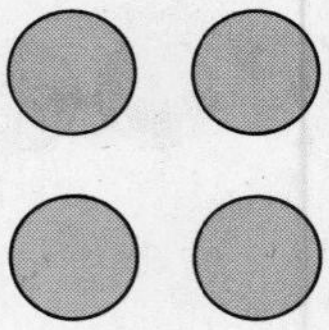

$$\begin{array}{r} 2 \\ +\ 2 \\ \hline 4 \end{array}$$

2.

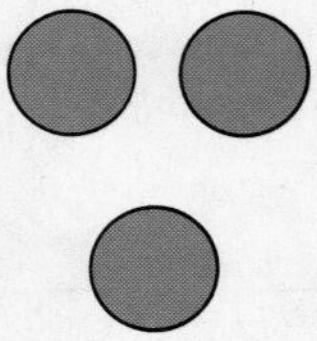

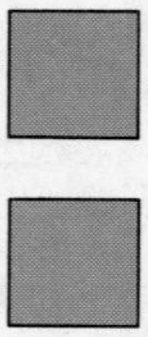

3.

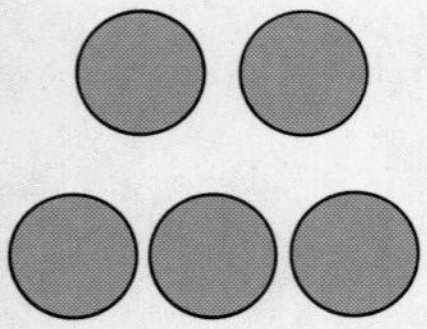

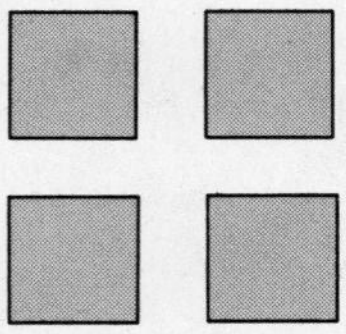

Vertical notation—copying problems

Add. Color the balloons.

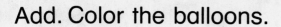

1 purple
2 yellow
3 green
4 red
5 blue

$$\begin{array}{r} 1 \\ +\ 2 \\ \hline \end{array}$$

$$\begin{array}{r} 2 \\ +\ 0 \\ \hline \end{array}$$

$$\begin{array}{r} 1 \\ +\ 4 \\ \hline \end{array}$$

$$\begin{array}{r} 2 \\ +\ 2 \\ \hline \end{array}$$

$$\begin{array}{r} 2 \\ +\ 1 \\ \hline \end{array}$$

$$\begin{array}{r} 1 \\ +\ 0 \\ \hline \end{array}$$

$$\begin{array}{r} 3 \\ +\ 2 \\ \hline \end{array}$$

$$\begin{array}{r} 2 \\ +\ 3 \\ \hline \end{array}$$

$$\begin{array}{r} 1 \\ +\ 3 \\ \hline \end{array}$$

$$\begin{array}{r} 3 \\ +\ 0 \\ \hline \end{array}$$

$$\begin{array}{r} 1 \\ +\ 1 \\ \hline \end{array}$$

$$\begin{array}{r} 4 \\ +\ 1 \\ \hline \end{array}$$

$$\begin{array}{r} 3 \\ +\ 1 \\ \hline \end{array}$$

Add.

1.

1	3	1	2	0
+4	+0	+3	+2	+2

2.

2	0	2	3	1	1
+1	+4	+3	+1	+2	+0

3.

4	0	4	3	5	2
+1	+1	+0	+2	+0	+1

4.

0	2	2	2	3	1
+3	+3	+0	+2	+1	+1

SKILLKEEPER

Write the missing numbers.

1 , 2 , ___ , ___ , ___ , 6 , 7 , ___ , ___ , ___

3 , 4 , 5 , ___ , ___ , ___ , 9 , 10 , ___ , ___

Practice the facts

Add.

1.

$3¢$
$+ 1¢$
$\underline{}$
$4¢$

2.

$2¢$
$+ 2¢$
$\underline{}$
$¢$

3.

$2¢$
$+ 3¢$
$\underline{}$
$¢$

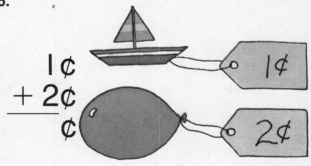

4.

$1¢$
$+ 3¢$
$\underline{}$
$¢$

Find the cost for both.

5.

$2¢$
$+ 1¢$
$\underline{}$
$3¢$

2¢

1¢

6.

$1¢$
$+ 2¢$
$\underline{}$
$¢$

1¢

2¢

7.

$3¢$
$+ 2¢$
$\underline{}$
$¢$

3¢

2¢

8.

$1¢$
$+ 1¢$
$\underline{}$
$¢$

1¢

1¢

Add.

1.

2	3	1	0	3
+2	+2	+0	+4	+1

2.

1	3	2	4	0	2
+4	+0	+3	+1	+0	+1

3.

4	0	3	1	2	0
+0	+1	+1	+3	+2	+5

4.

2	1	4	3	1	2
+0	+2	+1	+2	+1	+3

THINK MATH

Write the missing letter. Then write the number.

on⊕__ ___ _1_

t__o _____

fo__r _____

e   u

w   v

x   s

fi__e _____

si__ _____

__even _____

Practice the facts

Name _____

Tell a story. Answer the question.

1. How many are there in all?

_____
in all

2. How many are there in all?

_____
in all

3. How many are there in all?

_____
in all

4. How many are there in all?

_____
in all

5. How many are there in all?

_____
in all

6. How many are there in all?

_____
in all

Problem solving—tell a story

Cathy's Clothes

Color.
How many ways can you dress Cathy?

Problem solving strategy—make a list

CHAPTER REVIEW/TEST

Add.

1.

$3 + 1 =$ _____

2.

$2 + 3 =$ _____

3.

$1 + 2 =$ _____

4.

$2 + 2 =$ _____

Find the sums.

5.

4	2	3	3	2	3
$+1$	$+2$	$+0$	$+2$	$+1$	$+1$

6.

1¢	2	1¢	1¢	0	1¢
$+1$¢	$+3$	$+2$¢	$+3$¢	$+2$	$+4$¢
¢		¢	¢		¢

7. How many are there in all?

_____ in all

CUMULATIVE REVIEW

How many are there?

1.

- ○ 2
- ○ 3
- ○ 4

2.

- ○ 4
- ○ 5
- ○ 6

3. Count the pennies.

- ○ 8¢
- ○ 9¢
- ○ 10¢

4. What number is next?

6, 7, 8, ___

- ○ 8
- ○ 9
- ○ 10

Add.

5.

- ○ 3
- ○ 4
- ○ 5

$2 + 3 =$ ___

6.

- ○ 1
- ○ 2
- ○ 3

$1 + 1 =$ ___

7.

$$\begin{array}{r} 2 \\ + 0 \\ \hline \end{array}$$

- ○ 2
- ○ 3
- ○ 4

8.

$$\begin{array}{r} 1 \\ + 3 \\ \hline \end{array}$$

- ○ 2
- ○ 3
- ○ 4

9. How many are there in all?

- ○ 3
- ○ 2
- ○ 4

ANOTHER LOOK

$$\begin{array}{r} 2 \\ + 1 \\ \hline 3 \end{array}$$ ← In all

Add.

1.
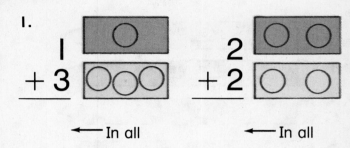

$$\begin{array}{r} 1 \\ + 3 \\ \hline \end{array}$$ ← In all

$$\begin{array}{r} 2 \\ + 2 \\ \hline \end{array}$$ ← In all

2.

$$\begin{array}{r} 0 \\ + 3 \\ \hline \end{array}$$ ← In all

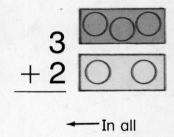
$$\begin{array}{r} 3 \\ + 2 \\ \hline \end{array}$$ ← In all

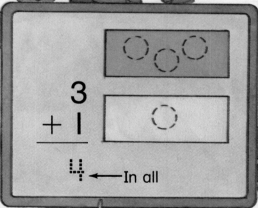

$$\begin{array}{r} 3 \\ + 1 \\ \hline 4 \end{array}$$ ← In all

Draw your own pictures.
Find the sums.

3.

$$\begin{array}{r} 2 \\ + 2 \\ \hline \end{array}$$ ← In all

$$\begin{array}{r} 1 \\ + 2 \\ \hline \end{array}$$ ← In all

4.

$$\begin{array}{r} 2 \\ + 3 \\ \hline \end{array}$$ ← In all

$$\begin{array}{r} 1 \\ + 4 \\ \hline \end{array}$$ ← In all

ENRICHMENT

Write the sums in the table. Color.

0 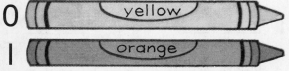 yellow
1 orange
2 red
3 blue
4 green
5 purple

+	0	1	2	3	4	5
0						5	← 0 + 5
1				4		
2						
3		4				
4						
5	5					

1 + 3

3 + 1

5 + 0

DIFFERENCES TO 5

3 Name _____

Use counters.

1.

Put in	Take out	
4	1	**3**
		_____
		are left

2.

Put in	Take out	
3	2	
		_____
		is left

3.

Put in	Take out	
5	3	
		_____
		are left

4.

Put in	Take out	
3	1	
		_____
		are left

Subtraction concept

(fifty-three) **53**

Fill in the blanks.

1.

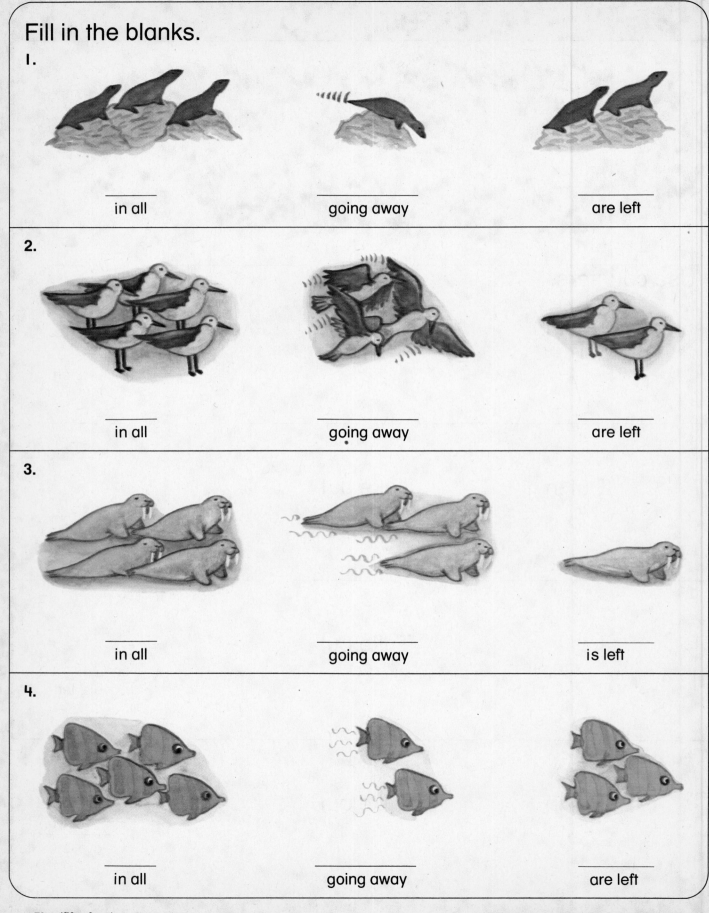

_____ in all   _____ going away   _____ are left

2.

_____ in all   _____ going away   _____ are left

3.

_____ in all   _____ going away   _____ is left

4.

_____ in all   _____ going away   _____ are left

     Subtraction concept—(three pictures)

Name _____

$$\underline{3}$$
in all

$$\underline{3} - \underline{2} = \underline{1}$$
in all   Difference

Tell a subtraction story. Write a number sentence.

1.

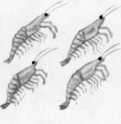 

$$\underline{4}$$
in all

$$\underline{4} - \underline{} = \underline{}$$
in all

2.

$$\underline{}$$
in all

$$\underline{} - \underline{} = \underline{}$$
in all

3.

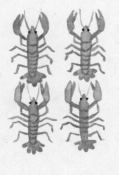 

$$\underline{}$$
in all

$$\underline{} - \underline{} = \underline{}$$
in all

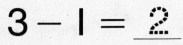

There are 2 left.

$3 - 1 = \underline{2}$

How many are left?

1.

$3 - 2 = \underline{1}$

2.

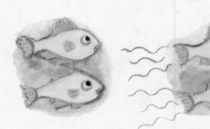

$4 - 2 = \underline{}$

3.

$4 - 3 = \underline{}$

4.

$2 - 1 = \underline{}$

5.

$5 - 2 = \underline{}$

6.

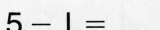

$5 - 1 = \underline{}$

Subtraction concept—one picture

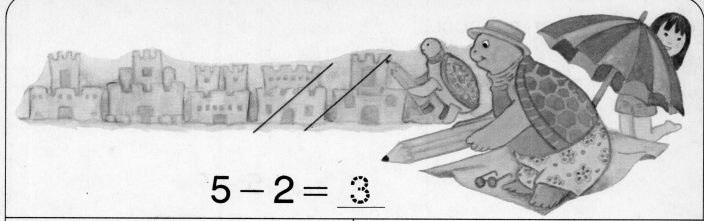

$$5 - 2 = \underline{3}$$

Cross out. Then subtract.	
1. 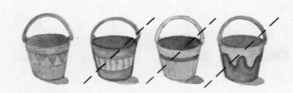 $$4 - 3 = \underline{1}$$	**2.** 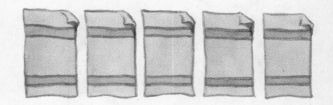 $$5 - 1 = \underline{}$$
3.  $$3 - 2 = \underline{}$$	**4.** 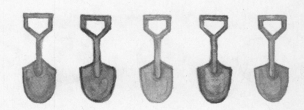 $$5 - 3 = \underline{}$$
5.  $$4 - 2 = \underline{}$$	**6.**  $$3 - 1 = \underline{}$$

Subtraction concept—static model

Cross out. Then subtract.

1.

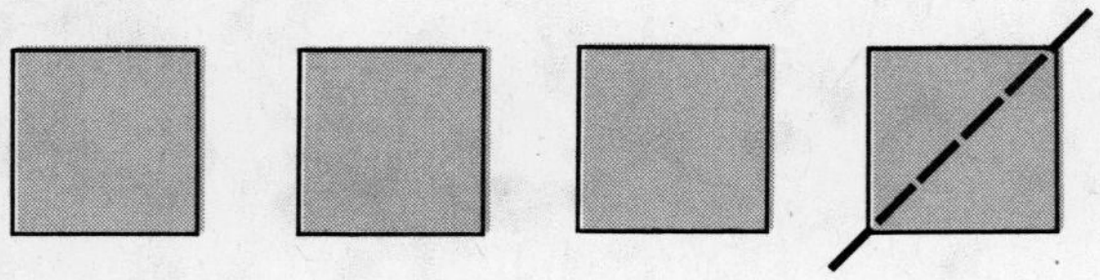

$$4 - 1 = \underline{\quad}$$

2.

$$5 - 2 = \underline{\quad}$$

3.

$$3 - 2 = \underline{\quad}$$

4.

$$4 - 2 = \underline{\quad}$$

5.

$$3 - 1 = \underline{\quad}$$

6.

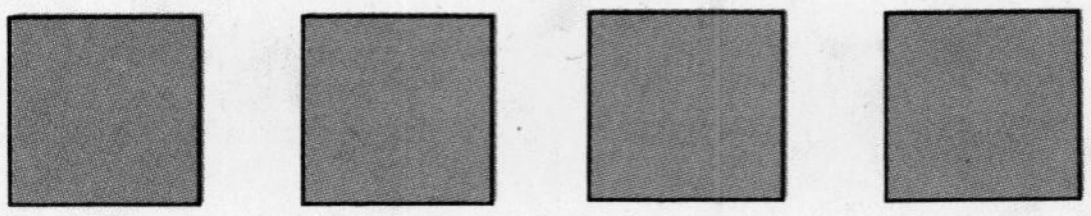

$$4 - 3 = \underline{\quad}$$

7.

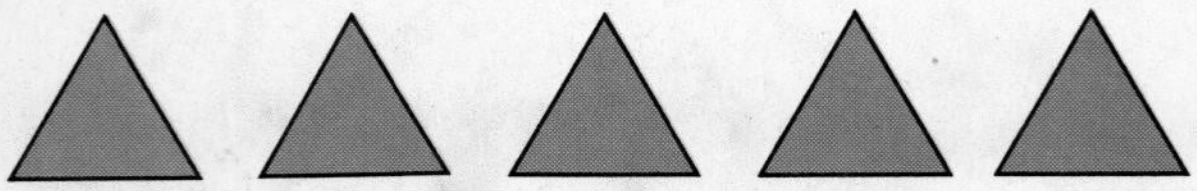

$$5 - 3 = \underline{\quad}$$

8.

$$5 - 1 = \underline{\quad}$$

Subtraction concept—static model

$2 - 2 = \underline{0}$

$4 - 0 = \underline{4}$

Subtract.

1.

$3 - 3 = \underline{}$

2.

$2 - 0 = \underline{}$

3.

$5 - 0 = \underline{}$

4.

$4 - 4 = \underline{}$

5.

$3 - 0 = \underline{}$

6.

$5 - 5 = \underline{}$

Zero in subtraction

Subtract.

1.

$4 - 1 = \underline{}$

2.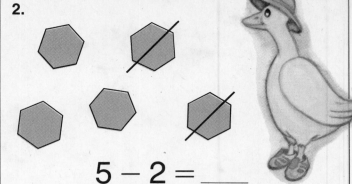

$5 - 2 = \underline{}$

3. $2 - 1 = \underline{}$ $5 - 1 = \underline{}$ $4 - 2 = \underline{}$

4. $1 - 1 = \underline{}$ $4 - 4 = \underline{}$ $2 - 2 = \underline{}$

5. $5 - 3 = \underline{}$ $3 - 0 = \underline{}$ $3 - 2 = \underline{}$

6. $2 - 0 = \underline{}$ $5 - 0 = \underline{}$ $3 - 3 = \underline{}$

7. $4 - 1 = \underline{}$ $4 - 0 = \underline{}$ $5 - 4 = \underline{}$

THINK MATH

How many are hiding? $\underline{}$

5 in all

Practice the facts

$5 - 3 = \underline{2}$

$$\begin{array}{r} 5 \\ -3 \\ \hline 2 \end{array}$$

Cross out. Subtract.

1.

$4 - 1 = \underline{3}$

$$\begin{array}{r} 4 \\ -1 \\ \hline 3 \end{array}$$

2.

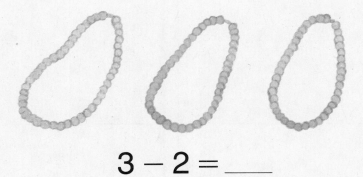

$3 - 2 = \underline{}$

$$\begin{array}{r} 3 \\ -2 \\ \hline \end{array}$$

3.

$5 - 2 = \underline{}$

$$\begin{array}{r} 5 \\ -2 \\ \hline \end{array}$$

Vertical notation

Write the problems. Subtract.

1.

$$3$$
$$- 2$$
$$1$$

2.

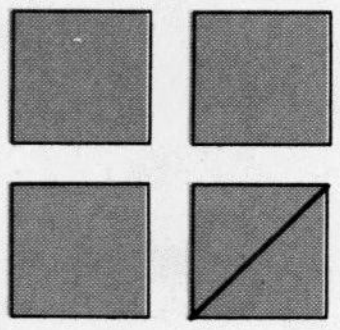

$$4$$
$$- 1$$
$$3$$

3.

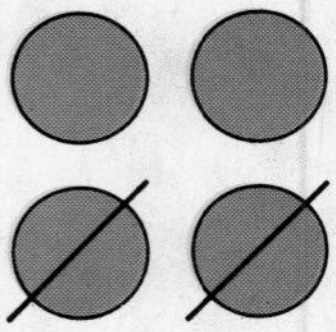

$$4$$
$$- 2$$
$$2$$

4.

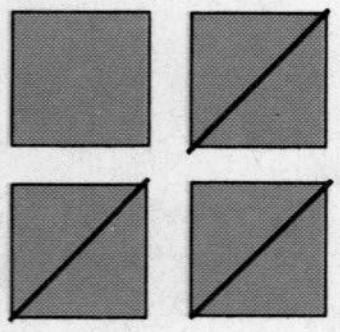

5.

6.

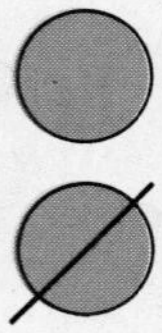

7.

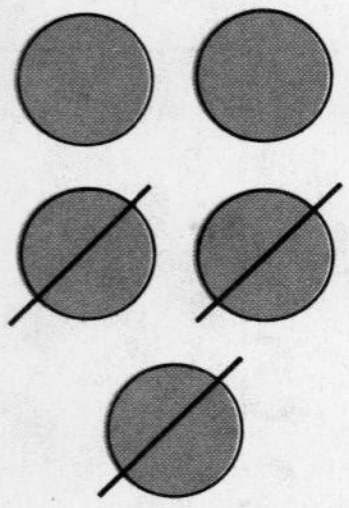

8.

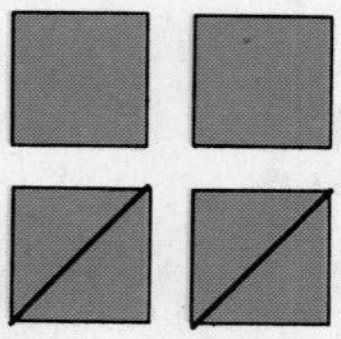

9.

Vertical notation—copying problems

Name _____

Color.

0 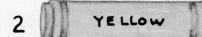 RED
1  ORANGE
2  YELLOW
3  GREEN
4  BLUE
5 PURPLE

$3 - 0 = 3$

$5 - 1 = \_\_\_$

$5 - 3 = \_\_\_$

$4 - 4 = \_\_\_$

$5 - 4 = \_\_\_$

$5 - 3 = \_\_\_$

$2 - 1 = \_\_\_$

$4 - 2 = \_\_\_$

$5 - 0 = \_\_\_$

$3 - 0 = \_\_\_$

$4 - 0 = \_\_\_$

Practice the facts

Subtract.

1.
$$\begin{array}{r} 2 \\ -0 \\ \hline \end{array}$$
$$\begin{array}{r} 3 \\ -1 \\ \hline \end{array}$$
$$\begin{array}{r} 1 \\ -0 \\ \hline \end{array}$$
$$\begin{array}{r} 5 \\ -3 \\ \hline \end{array}$$
$$\begin{array}{r} 2 \\ -1 \\ \hline \end{array}$$

2.
$$\begin{array}{r} 5 \\ -3 \\ \hline \end{array}$$
$$\begin{array}{r} 4 \\ -1 \\ \hline \end{array}$$
$$\begin{array}{r} 5 \\ -1 \\ \hline \end{array}$$
$$\begin{array}{r} 3 \\ -2 \\ \hline \end{array}$$
$$\begin{array}{r} 4 \\ -0 \\ \hline \end{array}$$
$$\begin{array}{r} 5 \\ -5 \\ \hline \end{array}$$

3.
$$\begin{array}{r} 1 \\ -1 \\ \hline \end{array}$$
$$\begin{array}{r} 5 \\ -2 \\ \hline \end{array}$$
$$\begin{array}{r} 4 \\ -3 \\ \hline \end{array}$$
$$\begin{array}{r} 4 \\ -2 \\ \hline \end{array}$$
$$\begin{array}{r} 3 \\ -0 \\ \hline \end{array}$$
$$\begin{array}{r} 5 \\ -0 \\ \hline \end{array}$$

4.
$$\begin{array}{r} 2 \\ -1 \\ \hline \end{array}$$
$$\begin{array}{r} 5 \\ -1 \\ \hline \end{array}$$
$$\begin{array}{r} 3 \\ -3 \\ \hline \end{array}$$
$$\begin{array}{r} 5 \\ -4 \\ \hline \end{array}$$
$$\begin{array}{r} 4 \\ -4 \\ \hline \end{array}$$
$$\begin{array}{r} 5 \\ -2 \\ \hline \end{array}$$

SKILLKEEPER

Add.

$$\begin{array}{r} 3 \\ +1 \\ \hline \end{array}$$
$$\begin{array}{r} 2 \\ +3 \\ \hline \end{array}$$
$$\begin{array}{r} 2 \\ +2 \\ \hline \end{array}$$
$$\begin{array}{r} 4 \\ +1 \\ \hline \end{array}$$
$$\begin{array}{r} 1 \\ +2 \\ \hline \end{array}$$
$$\begin{array}{r} 3 \\ +2 \\ \hline \end{array}$$

Practice the facts

Name _____

How much money is left?

1.
$$\begin{array}{r} 4¢ \\ -\ 1¢ \\ \hline 3¢ \end{array}$$

2.
$$\begin{array}{r} 3¢ \\ -\ 2¢ \\ \hline ¢ \end{array}$$

3.
$$\begin{array}{r} 5¢ \\ -\ 3¢ \\ \hline ¢ \end{array}$$

4.
$$\begin{array}{r} 4¢ \\ -\ 2¢ \\ \hline ¢ \end{array}$$

5.
$$\begin{array}{r} 4¢ \\ -\ 2¢ \\ \hline ¢ \end{array}$$

6.
$$\begin{array}{r} 5¢ \\ -\ 1¢ \\ \hline ¢ \end{array}$$
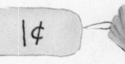

7.
$$\begin{array}{r} 5¢ \\ -\ 2¢ \\ \hline ¢ \end{array}$$
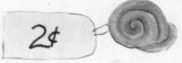

8.
$$\begin{array}{r} 4¢ \\ -\ 3¢ \\ \hline ¢ \end{array}$$

Subtracting pennies

Subtract.

1. $\begin{array}{r} 4 \\ -3 \\ \hline \end{array}$ $\begin{array}{r} 2 \\ -1 \\ \hline \end{array}$ $\begin{array}{r} 5 \\ -2 \\ \hline \end{array}$ $\begin{array}{r} 3 \\ -0 \\ \hline \end{array}$ $\begin{array}{r} 4 \\ -1 \\ \hline \end{array}$

2. $\begin{array}{r} 5 \\ -4 \\ \hline \end{array}$ $\begin{array}{r} 5 \\ -3 \\ \hline \end{array}$ $\begin{array}{r} 4 \\ -4 \\ \hline \end{array}$ $\begin{array}{r} 5 \\ -0 \\ \hline \end{array}$ $\begin{array}{r} 3 \\ -2 \\ \hline \end{array}$ $\begin{array}{r} 5 \\ -2 \\ \hline \end{array}$

3. $\begin{array}{r} 4 \\ -1 \\ \hline \end{array}$ $\begin{array}{r} 5 \\ -1 \\ \hline \end{array}$ $\begin{array}{r} 3 \\ -1 \\ \hline \end{array}$ $\begin{array}{r} 4 \\ -2 \\ \hline \end{array}$ $\begin{array}{r} 2 \\ -2 \\ \hline \end{array}$ $\begin{array}{r} 0 \\ -0 \\ \hline \end{array}$

4. $\begin{array}{r} 5 \\ -5 \\ \hline \end{array}$ $\begin{array}{r} 1 \\ -0 \\ \hline \end{array}$ $\begin{array}{r} 4 \\ -0 \\ \hline \end{array}$ $\begin{array}{r} 3 \\ -3 \\ \hline \end{array}$ $\begin{array}{r} 5 \\ -3 \\ \hline \end{array}$ $\begin{array}{r} 2 \\ -0 \\ \hline \end{array}$

THINK MATH

Write + or − in each .

$\begin{array}{r} 5 \\ \bigcirc\ 2 \\ \hline 3 \end{array}$ $\begin{array}{r} 2 \\ \bigcirc\ 2 \\ \hline 4 \end{array}$ $\begin{array}{r} 4 \\ \bigcirc\ 1 \\ \hline 3 \end{array}$ $\begin{array}{r} 3 \\ \bigcirc\ 2 \\ \hline 5 \end{array}$ $\begin{array}{r} 1 \\ \bigcirc\ 2 \\ \hline 3 \end{array}$ $\begin{array}{r} 5 \\ \bigcirc\ 3 \\ \hline 2 \end{array}$

Practice the facts

Add or subtract.

1.

$$\begin{array}{r} 4 \\ +1 \\ \hline \end{array} \qquad \begin{array}{r} 3 \\ +2 \\ \hline \end{array} \qquad \begin{array}{r} 0 \\ +0 \\ \hline \end{array} \qquad \begin{array}{r} 1 \\ +3 \\ \hline \end{array} \qquad \begin{array}{r} 2 \\ +1 \\ \hline \end{array}$$

2.

$$\begin{array}{r} 3 \\ -3 \\ \hline \end{array} \qquad \begin{array}{r} 5 \\ -1 \\ \hline \end{array} \qquad \begin{array}{r} 2 \\ -0 \\ \hline \end{array} \qquad \begin{array}{r} 1 \\ -1 \\ \hline \end{array} \qquad \begin{array}{r} 2 \\ -1 \\ \hline \end{array} \qquad \begin{array}{r} 4 \\ -2 \\ \hline \end{array}$$

3.

$$\begin{array}{r} 1 \\ +1 \\ \hline \end{array} \qquad \begin{array}{r} 2 \\ +2 \\ \hline \end{array} \qquad \begin{array}{r} 1 \\ +2 \\ \hline \end{array} \qquad \begin{array}{r} 4 \\ +0 \\ \hline \end{array} \qquad \begin{array}{r} 2 \\ +3 \\ \hline \end{array} \qquad \begin{array}{r} 2 \\ +1 \\ \hline \end{array}$$

4.

$$\begin{array}{r} 3 \\ -2 \\ \hline \end{array} \qquad \begin{array}{r} 2 \\ -1 \\ \hline \end{array} \qquad \begin{array}{r} 4 \\ -3 \\ \hline \end{array} \qquad \begin{array}{r} 5 \\ -2 \\ \hline \end{array} \qquad \begin{array}{r} 4 \\ -4 \\ \hline \end{array} \qquad \begin{array}{r} 5 \\ -1 \\ \hline \end{array}$$

5.

$$\begin{array}{r} 4 \\ +1 \\ \hline \end{array} \qquad \begin{array}{r} 3 \\ +2 \\ \hline \end{array} \qquad \begin{array}{r} 1 \\ +3 \\ \hline \end{array} \qquad \begin{array}{r} 1 \\ +1 \\ \hline \end{array} \qquad \begin{array}{r} 1 \\ +3 \\ \hline \end{array} \qquad \begin{array}{r} 3 \\ +0 \\ \hline \end{array}$$

6.

$$\begin{array}{r} 3 \\ -2 \\ \hline \end{array} \qquad \begin{array}{r} 3 \\ -0 \\ \hline \end{array} \qquad \begin{array}{r} 2 \\ -2 \\ \hline \end{array} \qquad \begin{array}{r} 5 \\ -3 \\ \hline \end{array} \qquad \begin{array}{r} 2 \\ +1 \\ \hline \end{array} \qquad \begin{array}{r} 5 \\ +0 \\ \hline \end{array}$$

Add or subtract.

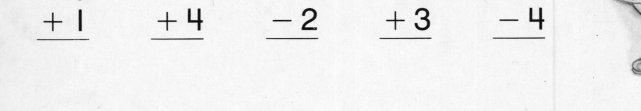

1.

$$\begin{array}{r} 1 \\ +\ 1 \\ \hline \end{array}$$
$$\begin{array}{r} 1 \\ +\ 4 \\ \hline \end{array}$$
$$\begin{array}{r} 5 \\ -\ 2 \\ \hline \end{array}$$
$$\begin{array}{r} 2 \\ +\ 3 \\ \hline \end{array}$$
$$\begin{array}{r} 4 \\ -\ 4 \\ \hline \end{array}$$

2.

$$\begin{array}{r} 5 \\ +\ 0 \\ \hline \end{array}$$
$$\begin{array}{r} 3 \\ -\ 2 \\ \hline \end{array}$$
$$\begin{array}{r} 4 \\ -\ 4 \\ \hline \end{array}$$
$$\begin{array}{r} 3 \\ -\ 0 \\ \hline \end{array}$$
$$\begin{array}{r} 5 \\ -\ 4 \\ \hline \end{array}$$
$$\begin{array}{r} 3 \\ +\ 1 \\ \hline \end{array}$$

3.

$$\begin{array}{r} 2 \\ +\ 1 \\ \hline \end{array}$$
$$\begin{array}{r} 4 \\ -\ 3 \\ \hline \end{array}$$
$$\begin{array}{r} 5 \\ -\ 5 \\ \hline \end{array}$$
$$\begin{array}{r} 1 \\ +\ 2 \\ \hline \end{array}$$
$$\begin{array}{r} 4 \\ +\ 1 \\ \hline \end{array}$$
$$\begin{array}{r} 3 \\ -\ 1 \\ \hline \end{array}$$

4.

$$\begin{array}{r} 1 \\ +\ 3 \\ \hline \end{array}$$
$$\begin{array}{r} 3 \\ +\ 2 \\ \hline \end{array}$$
$$\begin{array}{r} 4 \\ -\ 1 \\ \hline \end{array}$$
$$\begin{array}{r} 2 \\ +\ 2 \\ \hline \end{array}$$
$$\begin{array}{r} 4 \\ -\ 2 \\ \hline \end{array}$$
$$\begin{array}{r} 5 \\ -\ 1 \\ \hline \end{array}$$

SKILLKEEPER

Write the numbers.

1, _2_, ___, _4_   8, _9_, ___, ___

5, ___, _7_, ___   6, ___, ___, _9_

Practice the facts

Name _____

Tell a story.
Answer the question.

1.

How many are left? _____

2.

How many are left? _____

3.

How many are left? _____

4.

How many are left? _____

Problem solving—tell a story

Tell a story. Ring the correct number sentence.

1.

$\boxed{2 + 3 = 5}$
$5 - 3 = 2$

2.

$1 + 3 = 4$
$4 - 3 = 1$

3.

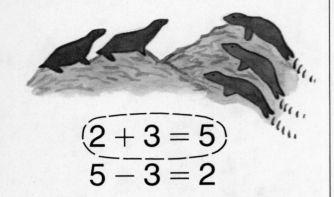

$5 - 1 = 4$
$4 + 1 = 5$

4.

$2 + 1 = 3$
$3 - 1 = 2$

5.

$1 + 3 = 4$
$4 - 3 = 1$

6.

$4 - 2 = 2$
$2 + 2 = 4$

Problem solving—choose the correct operation

CHAPTER REVIEW/TEST

Subtract.

1.

$4 - 2 = \underline{}$

2.

$3 - 1 = \underline{}$

3.

$5 - 3 = \underline{}$

4.

$4 - 3 = \underline{}$

5.

$3 - 0 = \underline{}$

6.

$$\begin{array}{r} 3¢ \\ -\ 1¢ \\ \hline ¢ \end{array}$$

Subtract.

7.
$$\begin{array}{r} 5 \\ -2 \\ \hline \end{array} \qquad \begin{array}{r} 3 \\ -2 \\ \hline \end{array} \qquad \begin{array}{r} 4 \\ -3 \\ \hline \end{array} \qquad \begin{array}{r} 5 \\ -4 \\ \hline \end{array} \qquad \begin{array}{r} 3 \\ -1 \\ \hline \end{array} \qquad \begin{array}{r} 4 \\ -1 \\ \hline \end{array}$$

8.
$$\begin{array}{r} 2 \\ -1 \\ \hline \end{array} \qquad \begin{array}{r} 4 \\ -2 \\ \hline \end{array} \qquad \begin{array}{r} 5 \\ -3 \\ \hline \end{array} \qquad \begin{array}{r} 3 \\ -3 \\ \hline \end{array} \qquad \begin{array}{r} 2 \\ -0 \\ \hline \end{array} \qquad \begin{array}{r} 5 \\ -1 \\ \hline \end{array}$$

9. Ring the correct number sentence.

$3 + 2 = 5$

$5 - 2 = 3$

CUMULATIVE REVIEW

How many are there?

1.

- ○ 4
- ○ 3
- ○ 5

2.

- ○ 9
- ○ 10
- ○ 12

Pick the missing number.

3.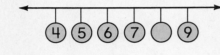

- ○ 8
- ○ 3
- ○ 2

4.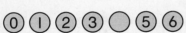

- ○ 8
- ○ 7
- ○ 4

Add.

5.

$$2 + 1 = \underline{}$$

- ○ 6
- ○ 3
- ○ 4

6.

$$3 + 2 = \underline{}$$

- ○ 4
- ○ 6
- ○ 5

7.
$$\begin{array}{r} 4 \\ + 1 \\ \hline \end{array}$$

- ○ 5
- ○ 6
- ○ 7

8.
$$\begin{array}{r} 2¢ \\ + 2¢ \\ \hline \end{array}$$

- ○ 9¢
- ○ 4¢
- ○ 5¢

9. Choose the correct number sentence.

- ○ 3 + 1 = 4
- ○ 0 + 4 = 4

ANOTHER LOOK

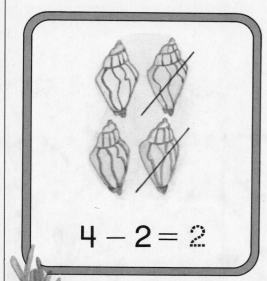

$$4 - 2 = 2$$

Cross out. Then subtract.

1. $\begin{array}{r} 5 \\ -1 \\ \hline \end{array}$

2. $\begin{array}{r} 3 \\ -2 \\ \hline \end{array}$

3. $\begin{array}{r} 4 \\ -3 \\ \hline \end{array}$

4. $\begin{array}{r} 5 \\ -2 \\ \hline \end{array}$

Draw your own. Cross out. Subtract.

5. $\begin{array}{r} 4 \\ -2 \\ \hline \end{array}$

6. $\begin{array}{r} 3 \\ -1 \\ \hline \end{array}$

7. $\begin{array}{r} 5 \\ -3 \\ \hline \end{array}$

8. $\begin{array}{r} 3 \\ -3 \\ \hline \end{array}$

$$\begin{array}{r} 5 \\ -4 \\ \hline \end{array}$$

ENRICHMENT

Follow the path.

4   − 1   3   + 2   5   − 4   1   + 2   3   − 1   2
End

5   − 2   3   + 1   − 4   + 3   + 2   5
End

2   + 2   − 3   + 4   − 3   + 2   4
End

Enrichment—addition and subtraction

COUNTING ON TO ADD

 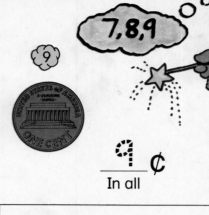 

7, 8, 9

9 ¢
In all

How much money is there?
Count on.

1.

7 ¢

2.

10 ¢

3.

_____ ¢

4.

_____ ¢

5.

_____ ¢

6.

_____ ¢

Counting on

How much money is there?

1.

8 ¢

2.

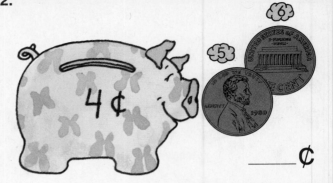

____ ¢

3.

____ ¢

4.

____ ¢

5.

____ ¢

6.

____ ¢

SKILLKEEPER

Subtract.

$$\begin{array}{r} 4 \\ -1 \\ \hline \end{array} \qquad \begin{array}{r} 2 \\ -1 \\ \hline \end{array} \qquad \begin{array}{r} 5 \\ -1 \\ \hline \end{array} \qquad \begin{array}{r} 4 \\ -2 \\ \hline \end{array} \qquad \begin{array}{r} 3 \\ -0 \\ \hline \end{array} \qquad \begin{array}{r} 5 \\ -2 \\ \hline \end{array}$$

Counting on

Name _____

$6 + 1 = \underline{7}$

Count on to add.

1.

$5 + 1 = \underline{6}$

2.

$7 + 1 = \underline{\quad}$

3.

$8 + 1 = \underline{\quad}$

4.

$4 + 1 = \underline{\quad}$

5.

$9 + 1 = \underline{\quad}$

6.

$3 + 1 = \underline{\quad}$

Add. Start with the greater number.

1.
$$6 \quad \boxed{6,7} \quad 1 \quad \boxed{6,7} \quad 7 \quad \boxed{7,8} \quad 1 \quad \boxed{7,8}$$
$$\frac{+1}{\quad} \qquad \frac{+6}{\quad} \qquad \frac{+1}{\quad} \qquad \frac{+7}{\quad}$$

2.
$$\frac{9}{+1} \qquad \frac{1}{+8} \qquad \frac{6}{+1} \qquad \frac{1}{+4} \qquad \frac{1}{+7} \qquad \frac{9}{+1}$$

3.
$$\frac{1}{+6} \qquad \frac{8}{+1} \qquad \frac{4}{+1} \qquad \frac{1}{+9} \qquad \frac{7}{+1} \qquad \frac{1}{+8}$$

4.
$$\frac{5}{+1} \qquad \frac{6}{+1} \qquad \frac{1}{+7} \qquad \frac{1}{+5} \qquad \frac{9}{+1} \qquad \frac{8}{+1}$$

THINK MATH

Make your own.

$$\frac{+\rule{1cm}{0.4pt}}{9} \qquad \frac{+\rule{1cm}{0.4pt}}{11} \qquad \frac{+\rule{1cm}{0.4pt}}{8} \qquad \frac{+\rule{1cm}{0.4pt}}{12} \qquad \frac{+\rule{1cm}{0.4pt}}{7} \qquad \frac{+\rule{1cm}{0.4pt}}{10}$$

Counting on to add 1

Name _____

$7 + 2 = \underline{9¢}$

Count on to add.

1.

$6 + 2 = \underline{8¢}$

2.

$9 + 2 = \underline{}¢$

3.

$5 + 2 = \underline{}¢$

4.

$4 + 2 = \underline{}¢$

5.

$8 + 2 = \underline{}¢$

6.

$7 + 2 = \underline{}¢$

Add. Start with the greater number.

1.

$$8 \quad \boxed{8, 9, 10} \qquad 2 \quad \boxed{7, 8, 9} \qquad 6 \quad \boxed{6, 7, 8} \qquad 2 \quad \boxed{9, 10, 11}$$
$$+2 \qquad\qquad +7 \qquad\qquad +2 \qquad\qquad +9$$

2.

$$\begin{array}{cccccc} 2 & 6 & 4 & 2 & 8 & 2 \\ +7 & +2 & +2 & +9 & +2 & +5 \\ \hline \end{array}$$

3.

$$\begin{array}{cccccc} 1 & 5 & 2 & 4 & 1 & 8 \\ +6 & +2 & +7 & +1 & +7 & +2 \\ \hline \end{array}$$

4.

$$\begin{array}{cccccc} 2 & 9 & 1 & 6 & 2 & 8 \\ +4 & +1 & +5 & +2 & +9 & +1 \\ \hline \end{array}$$

SKILLKEEPER

Count back.

10, _9_, _8_   8, _7_, ___

4, ___, _2_   9, ___, _7_

Practice the facts

Name _____

Add.

1. 9   7   5
       +1   +2   +2

2. 2   2   7   2
       +9   +3   +1   + 5
                         ———
                          7

3. 5   3   1   0
       +2   +1   +8   +4

4. 1   6   3   9   8   2
       +3   +2   +2   +2   +2   +2

5. 1   0   6   8   4   2
       +9   +2   +1   +1   +1   +7

6. 2   2   1   2   3   1
       +5   +8   +4   +6   +0   +6

Practice the facts

Add and color.

5 Blue
6 Purple
7 Yellow
8 Red
9 Green
10 Orange

$5 + 2 =$ ___

$1 + 6 =$ ___

$7 + 1 =$ ___

$2 + 6 =$ ___

$\begin{array}{r} 4 \\ +2 \\ \hline \end{array}$

$\begin{array}{r} 2 \\ +8 \\ \hline \end{array}$

$\begin{array}{r} 1 \\ +5 \\ \hline \end{array}$

$\begin{array}{r} 7 \\ +2 \\ \hline \end{array}$

$\begin{array}{r} 3 \\ +2 \\ \hline \end{array}$

$\begin{array}{r} 1 \\ +4 \\ \hline \end{array}$

$\begin{array}{r} 8 \\ +1 \\ \hline \end{array}$

$1 + 9 =$ ___

$8 + 2 =$ ___

Practice the facts

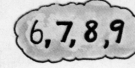
6, 7, 8, 9

6 peaches

$6 + 3 = \underline{9}$

Count on to add.

1.

5 peaches

5, 6, 7, 8

$5 + 3 = \underline{8}$

2.

4 peaches

4, 5, 6, 7

$4 + 3 = \underline{}$

3.

7 peaches

$7 + 3 = \underline{}$

4.

8 peaches

$8 + 3 = \underline{}$

5.

9 peaches

$9 + 3 = \underline{}$

6.

3 peaches

$3 + 3 = \underline{}$

Add.

1. $\begin{array}{r} 7 \\ +3 \\ \hline \end{array}$ (7,8,9,10) $\begin{array}{r} 3 \\ +8 \\ \hline \end{array}$ (8,9,10,11) $\begin{array}{r} 3 \\ +5 \\ \hline \end{array}$ (5,6,7,8) $\begin{array}{r} 9 \\ +3 \\ \hline \end{array}$ (9,10,11,12)

2. $\begin{array}{r} 3 \\ +5 \\ \hline \end{array}$ $\begin{array}{r} 3 \\ +3 \\ \hline \end{array}$ $\begin{array}{r} 3 \\ +8 \\ \hline \end{array}$ $\begin{array}{r} 3 \\ +6 \\ \hline \end{array}$ $\begin{array}{r} 4 \\ +3 \\ \hline \end{array}$ $\begin{array}{r} 7 \\ +3 \\ \hline \end{array}$

3. $\begin{array}{r} 2 \\ +7 \\ \hline \end{array}$ $\begin{array}{r} 6 \\ +1 \\ \hline \end{array}$ $\begin{array}{r} 3 \\ +9 \\ \hline \end{array}$ $\begin{array}{r} 1 \\ +9 \\ \hline \end{array}$ $\begin{array}{r} 8 \\ +2 \\ \hline \end{array}$ $\begin{array}{r} 3 \\ +7 \\ \hline \end{array}$

4. $\begin{array}{r} 2 \\ +9 \\ \hline \end{array}$ $\begin{array}{r} 6 \\ +3 \\ \hline \end{array}$ $\begin{array}{r} 1 \\ +8 \\ \hline \end{array}$ $\begin{array}{r} 3 \\ +8 \\ \hline \end{array}$ $\begin{array}{r} 7 \\ +1 \\ \hline \end{array}$ $\begin{array}{r} 2 \\ +6 \\ \hline \end{array}$

THINK MATH

7 in all. How many are hiding?

_____ more

Practice the facts

Add.

1.
$$\begin{array}{r} 2 \\ +7 \\ \hline \end{array}$$
$$\begin{array}{r} 9 \\ +1 \\ \hline \end{array}$$
$$\begin{array}{r} 4 \\ +2 \\ \hline \end{array}$$
$$\begin{array}{r} 8 \\ +3 \\ \hline \end{array}$$
$$\begin{array}{r} 3 \\ +9 \\ \hline \end{array}$$
$$\begin{array}{r} 6 \\ +3 \\ \hline \end{array}$$

2.
$$\begin{array}{r} 5 \\ +2 \\ \hline \end{array}$$
$$\begin{array}{r} 2 \\ +3 \\ \hline \end{array}$$
$$\begin{array}{r} 2 \\ +9 \\ \hline \end{array}$$
$$\begin{array}{r} 3 \\ +7 \\ \hline \end{array}$$
$$\begin{array}{r} 2 \\ +8 \\ \hline \end{array}$$
$$\begin{array}{r} 3 \\ +5 \\ \hline \end{array}$$

3.
$$\begin{array}{r} 2 \\ +6 \\ \hline \end{array}$$
$$\begin{array}{r} 9 \\ +3 \\ \hline \end{array}$$
$$\begin{array}{r} 7 \\ +3 \\ \hline \end{array}$$
$$\begin{array}{r} 1 \\ +8 \\ \hline \end{array}$$
$$\begin{array}{r} 3 \\ +4 \\ \hline \end{array}$$
$$\begin{array}{r} 3 \\ +3 \\ \hline \end{array}$$

4.
$$\begin{array}{r} 8 \\ +2 \\ \hline \end{array}$$
$$\begin{array}{r} 5 \\ +1 \\ \hline \end{array}$$
$$\begin{array}{r} 9 \\ +2 \\ \hline \end{array}$$
$$\begin{array}{r} 7 \\ +1 \\ \hline \end{array}$$
$$\begin{array}{r} 3 \\ +8 \\ \hline \end{array}$$
$$\begin{array}{r} 6 \\ +1 \\ \hline \end{array}$$

Practice the facts

Finish each table.

1.

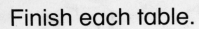

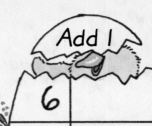

Add 2

Add 2	
7	9
5	7
8	

Add 1

Add 1	
6	
5	
8	

5 + 2

Add 2	
4	6
5	7

2.

Add 3	
6	
9	
8	

Add 0	
9	
6	
8	

Add 2	
6	
9	
4	

3.

Add 3	
4	
2	
7	

Add 1	
7	
9	
4	

Add 3	
8	
3	
5	

SKILLKEEPER

Add or subtract.

$$\begin{array}{r} 4 \\ +1 \\ \hline \end{array} \qquad \begin{array}{r} 3 \\ -2 \\ \hline \end{array} \qquad \begin{array}{r} 1 \\ +3 \\ \hline \end{array} \qquad \begin{array}{r} 5 \\ -1 \\ \hline \end{array} \qquad \begin{array}{r} 0 \\ +4 \\ \hline \end{array} \qquad \begin{array}{r} 2 \\ -2 \\ \hline \end{array}$$

Practice the facts

Name _____

Match. Add. Tell a story.

1.

$7 + 1 = \underline{}$

2.

$7 + 2 = \underline{}$

3.

$6 + 2 = \underline{}$

4.

$6 + 3 = \underline{}$

5.

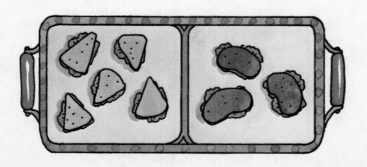

$5 + 3 = \underline{}$

Problem solving—tell a story

_____

_____

_____

_____

_____

Jan has a .

Jim has a  .

Sue has  .

Draw a ring
around Lyn!

Lyn gave Ed a .

Problem solving strategy—use logical reasoning

Name _____

CHAPTER REVIEW/TEST

Add.

1.

$$8 + 2 = \underline{\quad} ¢$$

2.

$$9 + 3 = \underline{\quad}$$

Add.

3.
$$\begin{array}{r} 2 \\ +7 \\ \hline \end{array} \quad \begin{array}{r} 6 \\ +1 \\ \hline \end{array} \quad \begin{array}{r} 3 \\ +5 \\ \hline \end{array} \quad \begin{array}{r} 5 \\ +2 \\ \hline \end{array} \quad \begin{array}{r} 1 \\ +9 \\ \hline \end{array} \quad \begin{array}{r} 9 \\ +3 \\ \hline \end{array}$$

4.
$$\begin{array}{r} 1 \\ +4 \\ \hline \end{array} \quad \begin{array}{r} 9 \\ +2 \\ \hline \end{array} \quad \begin{array}{r} 3 \\ +7 \\ \hline \end{array} \quad \begin{array}{r} 2 \\ +4 \\ \hline \end{array} \quad \begin{array}{r} 4 \\ +3 \\ \hline \end{array} \quad \begin{array}{r} 7 \\ +1 \\ \hline \end{array}$$

5.
$$\begin{array}{r} 2 \\ +6 \\ \hline \end{array} \quad \begin{array}{r} 8 \\ +3 \\ \hline \end{array} \quad \begin{array}{r} 1 \\ +8 \\ \hline \end{array} \quad \begin{array}{r} 5 \\ +1 \\ \hline \end{array} \quad \begin{array}{r} 8 \\ +2 \\ \hline \end{array} \quad \begin{array}{r} 3 \\ +6 \\ \hline \end{array}$$

6. Match. Add.

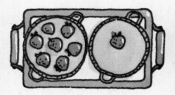  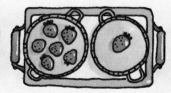 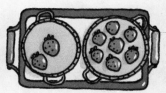

$$6+1=\underline{\quad} \qquad 7+1=\underline{\quad} \qquad 7+2=\underline{\quad} \qquad 5+3=\underline{\quad}$$

CUMULATIVE REVIEW

Add.

1.
$2 + 3 =$ ___
- ○ 3
- ○ 2
- ○ 5

2.
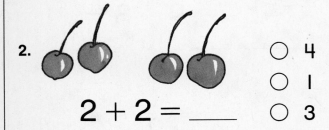
$2 + 2 =$ ___
- ○ 4
- ○ 1
- ○ 3

3.
$$\begin{array}{r} 3 \\ + 1 \\ \hline \end{array}$$
- ○ 4
- ○ 5
- ○ 3

4.
$$\begin{array}{r} 1¢ \\ + 2¢ \\ \hline \end{array}$$
- ○ 2¢
- ○ 0¢
- ○ 3¢

Subtract.

5.
$3 - 1 =$ ___
- ○ 5
- ○ 2
- ○ 0

6.

$4 - 3 =$ ___
- ○ 1
- ○ 2
- ○ 3

7.
$$\begin{array}{r} 3 \\ - 0 \\ \hline \end{array}$$
- ○ 3
- ○ 2
- ○ 0

8.
$$\begin{array}{r} 5 \\ - 4 \\ \hline \end{array}$$
- ○ 3
- ○ 1
- ○ 2

9. Choose the correct number sentence.

- ○ $2 + 1 = 3$
- ○ $0 + 3 = 3$

ANOTHER LOOK

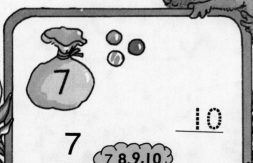

Add.

1. $\begin{array}{r} 7 \\ +\ 1 \\ \hline \end{array}$ 7,8 $\begin{array}{r} 1 \\ +\ 6 \\ \hline \end{array}$ 6,7 $\begin{array}{r} 9 \\ +\ 1 \\ \hline \end{array}$ 9,10

2. $\begin{array}{r} 1 \\ +\ 8 \\ \hline \end{array}$ $\begin{array}{r} 1 \\ +\ 5 \\ \hline \end{array}$ $\begin{array}{r} 3 \\ +\ 1 \\ \hline \end{array}$

3. $\begin{array}{r} 5 \\ +\ 2 \\ \hline \end{array}$ 5,6,7 $\begin{array}{r} 2 \\ +\ 8 \\ \hline \end{array}$ 8,9,10 $\begin{array}{r} 6 \\ +\ 2 \\ \hline \end{array}$ 6,7,8

4. $\begin{array}{r} 2 \\ +\ 3 \\ \hline \end{array}$ $\begin{array}{r} 4 \\ +\ 2 \\ \hline \end{array}$ $\begin{array}{r} 2 \\ +\ 7 \\ \hline \end{array}$

5. $\begin{array}{r} 3 \\ +\ 6 \\ \hline \end{array}$ 6,7,8,9 $\begin{array}{r} 9 \\ +\ 3 \\ \hline \end{array}$ 9,10,11,12

6. $\begin{array}{r} 7 \\ +\ 3 \\ \hline \end{array}$ $\begin{array}{r} 3 \\ +\ 4 \\ \hline \end{array}$ $\begin{array}{r} 5 \\ +\ 3 \\ \hline \end{array}$

Name _____

I.

| 5 birds in all. |

How many are hiding? _____

2.

| 4 cats in all. |

How many are hiding? _____

3.

| 7 fish in all. |

How many are hiding? _____

4.

| 6 dogs in all. |

How many are hiding? _____

Enrichment—missing addends

COUNTING BACK TO SUBTRACT

8¢   8, 7, 6

___6___ ¢

1. How much money is left? Count back.

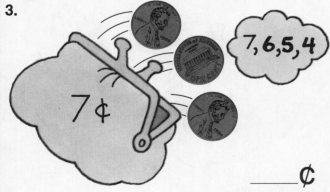

7¢   7, 6

___6___ ¢

2.

9¢   9, 8, 7

_____ ¢

3.

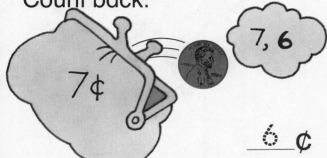

7¢   7, 6, 5, 4

_____ ¢

4.

8¢   8, 7

_____ ¢

5.

10¢   10, 9, 8

_____ ¢

6.

12¢   12, 11, 10, 9

_____ ¢

Counting back

How much money is left?

1.

_____ ¢

2.

_____ ¢

3.

_____ ¢

4.

_____ ¢

5.

_____ ¢

6.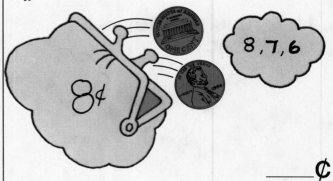

_____ ¢

SKILLKEEPER

Add.

$$\begin{array}{r} 5 \\ +1 \\ \hline \end{array} \qquad \begin{array}{r} 8 \\ +1 \\ \hline \end{array} \qquad \begin{array}{r} 7 \\ +2 \\ \hline \end{array} \qquad \begin{array}{r} 9 \\ +2 \\ \hline \end{array} \qquad \begin{array}{r} 6 \\ +3 \\ \hline \end{array} \qquad \begin{array}{r} 4 \\ +3 \\ \hline \end{array}$$

Counting back

 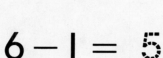 

$6 - 1 = \underline{5}$

Count back to subtract.

1.

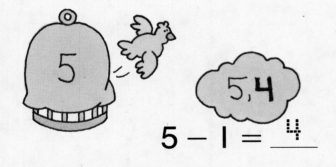

$5 - 1 = \underline{4}$

2.

$7 - 1 = \underline{}$

3.

$8 - 1 = \underline{}$

4.

$4 - 1 = \underline{}$

5.

$10 - 1 = \underline{}$

6.

$9 - 1 = \underline{}$

Subtract.

1.
$$8 \quad \text{(8, 7)}$$
$$-1$$

$$6 \quad \text{(6, 5)}$$
$$-1$$

$$9 \quad \text{(9, 8)}$$
$$-1$$

$$10 \quad \text{(10, 9)}$$
$$-1$$

$$7 \quad \text{(7, 6)}$$
$$-1$$

2.
$$9 \qquad 10 \qquad 4 \qquad 6 \qquad 8 \qquad 7$$
$$-1 \qquad -1 \qquad -1 \qquad -1 \qquad -1 \qquad -1$$

3.
$$8 \qquad 9 \qquad 5 \qquad 6 \qquad 10 \qquad 7$$
$$-1 \qquad -1 \qquad -1 \qquad -1 \qquad -1 \qquad -1$$

4.
$$8 \qquad 4 \qquad 9 \qquad 5 \qquad 10 \qquad 3$$
$$-1 \qquad -1 \qquad -1 \qquad -1 \qquad -1 \qquad -1$$

THINK MATH

Continue the patterns.

| 2 | 3 | 4 | 2 | 3 | 4 | 2 | | | |

| A | B | C | A | B | C | A | | | |

| 1 | A | 2 | B | 3 | C | 4 | | | |

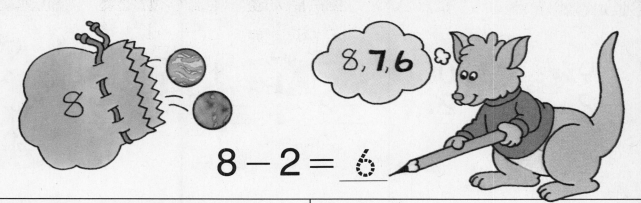

$$8 - 2 = \underline{6}$$

Count back to subtract.

1.

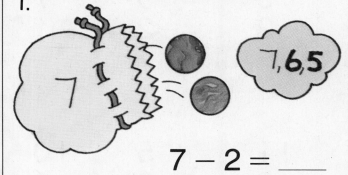

$$7 - 2 = \underline{}$$

2.

$$10 - 2 = \underline{}$$

3.

$$5 - 2 = \underline{}$$

4.

$$9 - 2 = \underline{}$$

5.

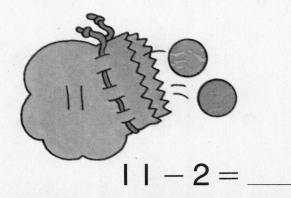

$$11 - 2 = \underline{}$$

6.

$$6 - 2 = \underline{}$$

Subtract.

8,7,6

1.
$$\begin{array}{r} 9 \\ -2 \\ \hline \end{array}$$ 9, 8, 7
$$\begin{array}{r} 10 \\ -2 \\ \hline \end{array}$$ 10, 9, 8
$$\begin{array}{r} 7 \\ -2 \\ \hline \end{array}$$ 7, 6, 5
$$\begin{array}{r} 11 \\ -2 \\ \hline \end{array}$$ 11, 10, 9
$$\begin{array}{r} 8 \\ -2 \\ \hline \end{array}$$

2.
$$\begin{array}{r} 8 \\ -2 \\ \hline \end{array}$$
$$\begin{array}{r} 11 \\ -2 \\ \hline \end{array}$$
$$\begin{array}{r} 9 \\ -1 \\ \hline \end{array}$$
$$\begin{array}{r} 10 \\ -2 \\ \hline \end{array}$$
$$\begin{array}{r} 5 \\ -2 \\ \hline \end{array}$$
$$\begin{array}{r} 7 \\ -1 \\ \hline \end{array}$$

3.
$$\begin{array}{r} 9 \\ -2 \\ \hline \end{array}$$
$$\begin{array}{r} 2 \\ -2 \\ \hline \end{array}$$
$$\begin{array}{r} 6 \\ -2 \\ \hline \end{array}$$
$$\begin{array}{r} 11 \\ -2 \\ \hline \end{array}$$
$$\begin{array}{r} 5 \\ -0 \\ \hline \end{array}$$
$$\begin{array}{r} 10 \\ -1 \\ \hline \end{array}$$

4.
$$\begin{array}{r} 6 \\ -2 \\ \hline \end{array}$$
$$\begin{array}{r} 7 \\ -1 \\ \hline \end{array}$$
$$\begin{array}{r} 11 \\ -2 \\ \hline \end{array}$$
$$\begin{array}{r} 1 \\ -1 \\ \hline \end{array}$$
$$\begin{array}{r} 10 \\ -2 \\ \hline \end{array}$$
$$\begin{array}{r} 9 \\ -1 \\ \hline \end{array}$$

SKILLKEEPER

Add.

$$\begin{array}{r} 1 \\ +9 \\ \hline \end{array}$$
$$\begin{array}{r} 2 \\ +8 \\ \hline \end{array}$$
$$\begin{array}{r} 7 \\ +3 \\ \hline \end{array}$$
$$\begin{array}{r} 9 \\ +2 \\ \hline \end{array}$$
$$\begin{array}{r} 6 \\ +1 \\ \hline \end{array}$$
$$\begin{array}{r} 3 \\ +4 \\ \hline \end{array}$$

Practice the facts

Name _____

Subtract.

1.
$$9 - 1$$ $$11 - 2$$ $$8 - 2$$

2.
$$7 - 1$$ $$10 - 2$$ $$8 - 1$$

On the chalkboard:
$$8 - 2 \over 6$$ $$9 - 1 \over 8$$ $$6 - 2 \over 4$$ $$7 - 1 \over 6$$

3.
$$2 - 2$$ $$5 - 1$$ $$7 - 1$$

4.
$$6 - 2$$ $$1 - 1$$ $$10 - 2$$ $$3 - 2$$ $$10 - 1$$ $$4 - 2$$

5.
$$4 - 1$$ $$9 - 2$$ $$9 - 1$$ $$3 - 1$$ $$11 - 2$$ $$2 - 1$$

6.
$$7 - 2$$ $$8 - 1$$ $$9 - 2$$ $$10 - 1$$ $$6 - 1$$ $$5 - 2$$

Practice the facts

Some birds are in the wrong nests.
Mark them.

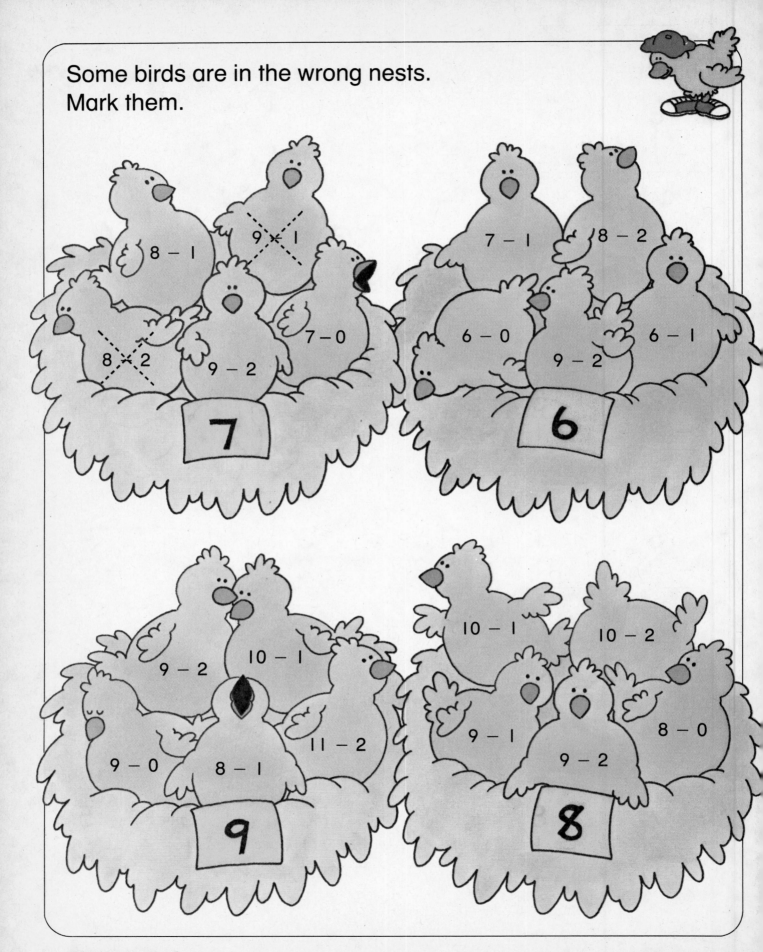

8 − 1
9 × 1
7 − 0
8 × 2
9 − 2

7

7 − 1
8 − 2
6 − 0
9 − 2
6 − 1

6

9 − 2
10 − 1
9 − 0
8 − 1
11 − 2

9

10 − 1
10 − 2
9 − 1
8 − 0
9 − 2

8

Practice the facts

Name _____

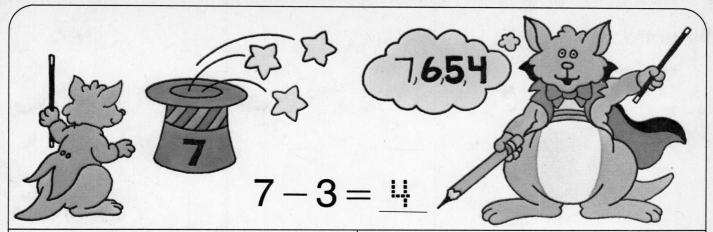

$7 - 3 = \underline{4}$

Count back to subtract.

1.

9, 8, 7, 6

$9 - 3 = \underline{6}$

2.

6, 5, 4, 3

$6 - 3 = \underline{\hphantom{0}}$

3.

11, 10, 9, 8

$11 - 3 = \underline{\hphantom{0}}$

4.

8, 7, 6, 5

$8 - 3 = \underline{\hphantom{0}}$

5.

12, 11, 10, 9

$12 - 3 = \underline{\hphantom{0}}$

6.

10, 9, 8, 7

$10 - 3 = \underline{\hphantom{0}}$

Counting back to subtract 3

Subtract.

7,6,5,4

1.
$$8 \quad 8,7,6,5 \quad 10 \quad 10,9,8,7 \quad 12 \quad 12,11,10,9 \quad 9 \quad 9,8,7,6 \quad 7$$
$$-3 \qquad\qquad -3 \qquad\qquad -3 \qquad\qquad -3 \qquad\qquad -3$$

2.
$$6 \qquad 12 \qquad 8 \qquad 11 \qquad 9 \qquad 10$$
$$-3 \qquad -3 \qquad -2 \qquad -3 \qquad -2 \qquad -3$$

3.
$$7 \qquad 11 \qquad 6 \qquad 9 \qquad 12 \qquad 8$$
$$-1 \qquad -2 \qquad -1 \qquad -3 \qquad -3 \qquad -3$$

4.
$$7 \qquad 10 \qquad 8 \qquad 12 \qquad 9 \qquad 11$$
$$-2 \qquad -3 \qquad -1 \qquad -3 \qquad -3 \qquad -3$$

THINK MATH

Ted lost 3 of his
pencils. How many
does he have left?

8 pencils

_____ pencils

Practice the facts

Subtract.

1. $\begin{array}{r} 8 \\ -1 \\ \hline \end{array}$ $\begin{array}{r} 3 \\ -1 \\ \hline \end{array}$ $\begin{array}{r} 8 \\ -3 \\ \hline \end{array}$ $\begin{array}{r} 9 \\ -1 \\ \hline \end{array}$ $\begin{array}{r} 11 \\ -2 \\ \hline \end{array}$ $\begin{array}{r} 6 \\ -2 \\ \hline \end{array}$

2. $\begin{array}{r} 9 \\ -2 \\ \hline \end{array}$ $\begin{array}{r} 7 \\ -1 \\ \hline \end{array}$ $\begin{array}{r} 9 \\ -3 \\ \hline \end{array}$ $\begin{array}{r} 3 \\ -3 \\ \hline \end{array}$ $\begin{array}{r} 7 \\ -2 \\ \hline \end{array}$ $\begin{array}{r} 11 \\ -3 \\ \hline \end{array}$

3. $\begin{array}{r} 7 \\ -3 \\ \hline \end{array}$ $\begin{array}{r} 5 \\ -2 \\ \hline \end{array}$ $\begin{array}{r} 3 \\ -3 \\ \hline \end{array}$ $\begin{array}{r} 11 \\ -2 \\ \hline \end{array}$ $\begin{array}{r} 6 \\ -3 \\ \hline \end{array}$ $\begin{array}{r} 5 \\ -1 \\ \hline \end{array}$

4. $\begin{array}{r} 6 \\ -1 \\ \hline \end{array}$ $\begin{array}{r} 8 \\ -0 \\ \hline \end{array}$ $\begin{array}{r} 6 \\ -2 \\ \hline \end{array}$ $\begin{array}{r} 5 \\ -3 \\ \hline \end{array}$ $\begin{array}{r} 10 \\ -1 \\ \hline \end{array}$ $\begin{array}{r} 4 \\ -2 \\ \hline \end{array}$

5. $\begin{array}{r} 10 \\ -2 \\ \hline \end{array}$ $\begin{array}{r} 10 \\ -3 \\ \hline \end{array}$ $\begin{array}{r} 0 \\ -0 \\ \hline \end{array}$ $\begin{array}{r} 8 \\ -2 \\ \hline \end{array}$ $\begin{array}{r} 12 \\ -3 \\ \hline \end{array}$ $\begin{array}{r} 4 \\ -1 \\ \hline \end{array}$

Practice the facts

Finish each table.

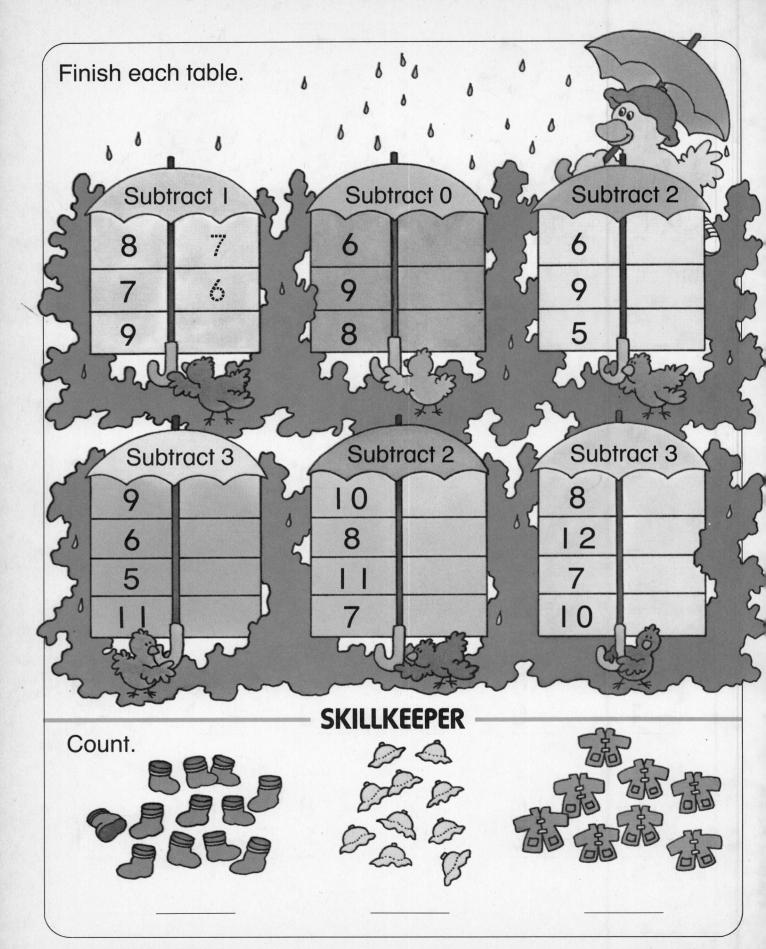

Subtract 1

8	7
7	6
9	

Subtract 0

6	
9	
8	

Subtract 2

6	
9	
5	

Subtract 3

9	
6	
5	
11	

Subtract 2

10	
8	
11	
7	

Subtract 3

8	
12	
7	
10	

SKILLKEEPER

Count.

_____   _____   _____

Practice the facts

Add or subtract.

1.

$$\begin{array}{r} 9 \\ -1 \\ \hline \end{array}$$
$$\begin{array}{r} 7 \\ +2 \\ \hline \end{array}$$

$$\begin{array}{r} 7 \\ +3 \\ \hline 10 \end{array}$$
$$\begin{array}{r} 10 \\ -3 \\ \hline 7 \end{array}$$

2.

$$\begin{array}{r} 8 \\ +1 \\ \hline \end{array}$$
$$\begin{array}{r} 10 \\ -2 \\ \hline \end{array}$$

3.

$$\begin{array}{r} 7 \\ -2 \\ \hline \end{array}$$
$$\begin{array}{r} 6 \\ +3 \\ \hline \end{array}$$

4.

$$\begin{array}{r} 11 \\ -3 \\ \hline \end{array}$$
$$\begin{array}{r} 6 \\ +0 \\ \hline \end{array}$$
$$\begin{array}{r} 6 \\ +2 \\ \hline \end{array}$$
$$\begin{array}{r} 10 \\ -1 \\ \hline \end{array}$$
$$\begin{array}{r} 9 \\ +1 \\ \hline \end{array}$$
$$\begin{array}{r} 8 \\ -2 \\ \hline \end{array}$$

5.

$$\begin{array}{r} 7 \\ +1 \\ \hline \end{array}$$
$$\begin{array}{r} 9 \\ -3 \\ \hline \end{array}$$
$$\begin{array}{r} 9 \\ +3 \\ \hline \end{array}$$
$$\begin{array}{r} 11 \\ -2 \\ \hline \end{array}$$
$$\begin{array}{r} 8 \\ -8 \\ \hline \end{array}$$
$$\begin{array}{r} 5 \\ +2 \\ \hline \end{array}$$

6.

$$\begin{array}{r} 8 \\ -3 \\ \hline \end{array}$$
$$\begin{array}{r} 7 \\ +3 \\ \hline \end{array}$$
$$\begin{array}{r} 9 \\ -2 \\ \hline \end{array}$$
$$\begin{array}{r} 9 \\ +2 \\ \hline \end{array}$$
$$\begin{array}{r} 12 \\ -3 \\ \hline \end{array}$$
$$\begin{array}{r} 5 \\ +3 \\ \hline \end{array}$$

Practice the facts

Add or subtract.
Color.

5 orange
6 green
7 yellow
8 purple
9 red

$\begin{array}{r} 1 \\ +8 \\ \hline \end{array}$

$\begin{array}{r} 8 \\ -2 \\ \hline \end{array}$

$\begin{array}{r} 2 \\ +6 \\ \hline \end{array}$

$\begin{array}{r} 2 \\ +3 \\ \hline \end{array}$

$\begin{array}{r} 11 \\ -3 \\ \hline \end{array}$

$\begin{array}{r} 4 \\ +3 \\ \hline \end{array}$

$\begin{array}{r} 8 \\ -1 \\ \hline \end{array}$

$\begin{array}{r} 5 \\ +3 \\ \hline \end{array}$

$\begin{array}{r} 9 \\ -3 \\ \hline \end{array}$

$\begin{array}{r} 9 \\ -2 \\ \hline \end{array}$

$\begin{array}{r} 12 \\ -3 \\ \hline \end{array}$

$\begin{array}{r} 2 \\ +5 \\ \hline \end{array}$

$\begin{array}{r} 7 \\ +1 \\ \hline \end{array}$

$\begin{array}{r} 9 \\ -1 \\ \hline \end{array}$

$\begin{array}{r} 11 \\ -2 \\ \hline \end{array}$

$\begin{array}{r} 3 \\ +3 \\ \hline \end{array}$

$\begin{array}{r} 6 \\ +3 \\ \hline \end{array}$

$\begin{array}{r} 5 \\ +3 \\ \hline \end{array}$

$\begin{array}{r} 10 \\ -3 \\ \hline \end{array}$

$\begin{array}{r} 7 \\ +2 \\ \hline \end{array}$

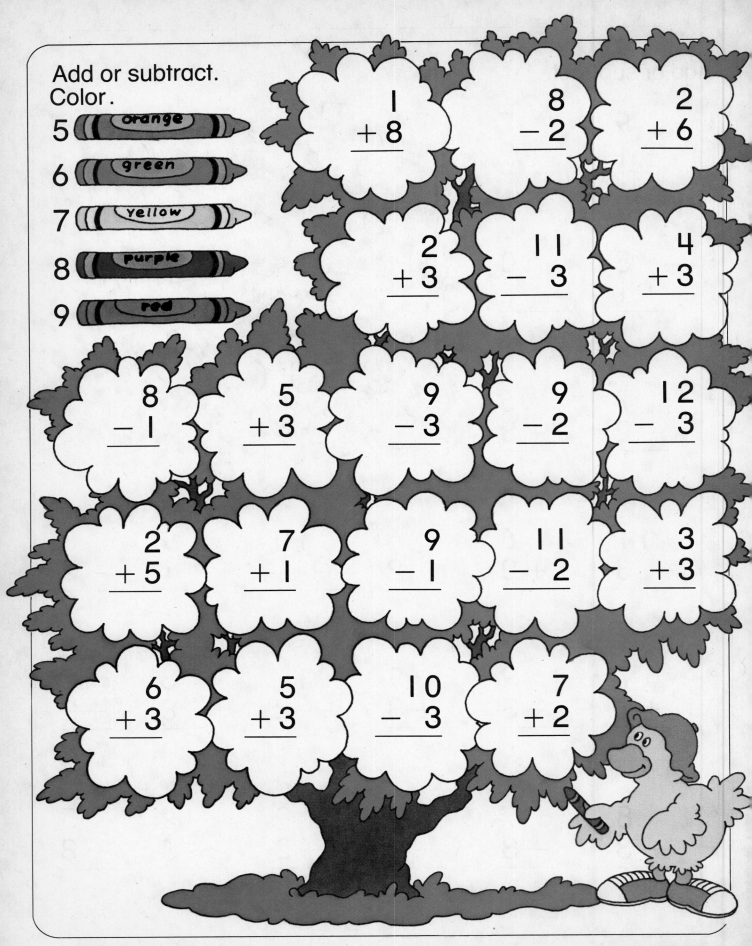

Practice the facts

QUESTION
DATA
PLAN
ANSWER
CHECK

Name ______________________________

Fill in the blank. Answer the question. Tell a story.

1.

7 in all

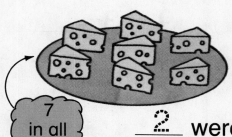

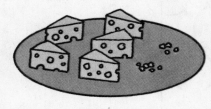

__2__ were eaten. How many are left? ____ pieces

2.

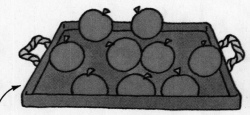

9 in all

____ were eaten. How many are left? ____ apples

3.

8 in all

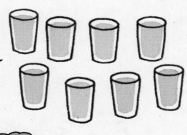

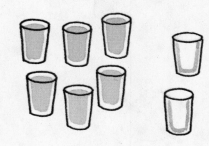

Sam drank ____. How many are left? ____drinks

4.

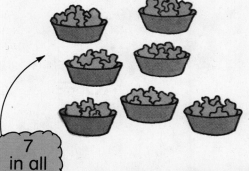

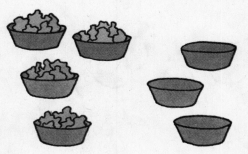

7 in all

____ were eaten. How many are left? ____ salads

Tell a story. Match. Subtract.

1.

$9 - 3 = \underline{\hspace{1cm}}$

2.

$8 - 2 = \underline{\hspace{1cm}}$

3.

$7 - 2 = \underline{\hspace{1cm}}$

4.
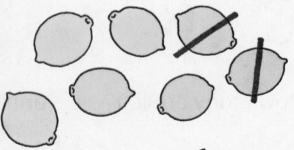

$8 - 3 = \underline{\hspace{1cm}}$

5.

$7 - 3 = \underline{\hspace{1cm}}$

Problem solving—tell a story

CHAPTER REVIEW/TEST

1.

$$2 - 1 = \underline{\quad}$$

2.

$$9 - 2 = \underline{\quad}$$

Subtract.

3.
$$\begin{array}{r} 10 \\ -\ 2 \\ \hline \end{array} \qquad \begin{array}{r} 9 \\ -1 \\ \hline \end{array} \qquad \begin{array}{r} 7 \\ -1 \\ \hline \end{array} \qquad \begin{array}{r} 2 \\ -1 \\ \hline \end{array} \qquad \begin{array}{r} 10 \\ -\ 1 \\ \hline \end{array} \qquad \begin{array}{r} 8 \\ -1 \\ \hline \end{array}$$

4.
$$\begin{array}{r} 6 \\ -1 \\ \hline \end{array} \qquad \begin{array}{r} 4 \\ -1 \\ \hline \end{array} \qquad \begin{array}{r} 5 \\ -1 \\ \hline \end{array} \qquad \begin{array}{r} 7 \\ -3 \\ \hline \end{array} \qquad \begin{array}{r} 6 \\ -2 \\ \hline \end{array} \qquad \begin{array}{r} 9 \\ -3 \\ \hline \end{array}$$

5.
$$\begin{array}{r} 11 \\ -\ 3 \\ \hline \end{array} \qquad \begin{array}{r} 8 \\ -2 \\ \hline \end{array} \qquad \begin{array}{r} 5 \\ -2 \\ \hline \end{array} \qquad \begin{array}{r} 10 \\ -\ 3 \\ \hline \end{array} \qquad \begin{array}{r} 12 \\ -\ 3 \\ \hline \end{array} \qquad \begin{array}{r} 3 \\ -2 \\ \hline \end{array}$$

Ring the correct card. Subtract.

6.

$9 - 2 =$	$8 - 2 =$

7.

$8 - 3 =$	$8 - 2 =$

CUMULATIVE REVIEW

Subtract.

1.

$3 - 1 = \_\_\_$

- ○ 3
- ○ 2
- ○ 1

2.

$4 - 3 = \_\_\_$

- ○ 5
- ○ 2
- ○ 1

3.

$\begin{array}{r} 5 \\ -3 \\ \hline \end{array}$

- ○ 2
- ○ 0
- ○ 4

4.

$\begin{array}{r} 5 \\ -1 \\ \hline \end{array}$

- ○ 4
- ○ 0
- ○ 2

Add.

5.

$3 + 1 = \_\_\_$

- ○ 0
- ○ 6
- ○ 4

6.

$8 + 2 = \_\_\_$

- ○ 6
- ○ 10
- ○ 9

7.

$\begin{array}{r} 4 \\ +3 \\ \hline \end{array}$

- ○ 7
- ○ 8
- ○ 1

8.

$\begin{array}{r} 8 \\ +3 \\ \hline \end{array}$

- ○ 5
- ○ 11
- ○ 9

9. Choose the correct number sentence.

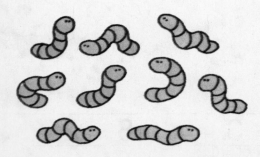

- ○ $8 + 2 = 10$
- ○ $7 + 1 = 8$
- ○ $9 + 3 = 12$

ANOTHER LOOK

9
−1
8

9
9, **8**

8
−2
6

8, **7, 6**

10
−3
7

10, **9, 8, 7**

Subtract. Count back.

1. 6 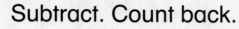 6, 5   8   8, 7   10   10, 9
−1   −1   −1

2. 10   9   4
−1   −1   −1

3. 7   7, 6, 5   9   9, 8, 7   8   8, 7, 6
−2   −2   −2

4. 10   6   7
−2   −2   −2

5. 9   9, 8, 7, 6   11   11, 10, 9, 8
−3   −3

6. 8   12   10
−3   −3   −3

ENRICHMENT

Ring the mystery number.
It is in the picture only one time.

PLACE VALUE AND COUNTING

1. Color ten  Red . How many are there?

__1__ ten __2__ ones

2. Color ten Yellow . How many are there?

____ ten ____ ones

3. Color ten Blue . How many are there?

____ ten ____ ones

Tens and ones to 19

Ring ten. How many are there?

1.

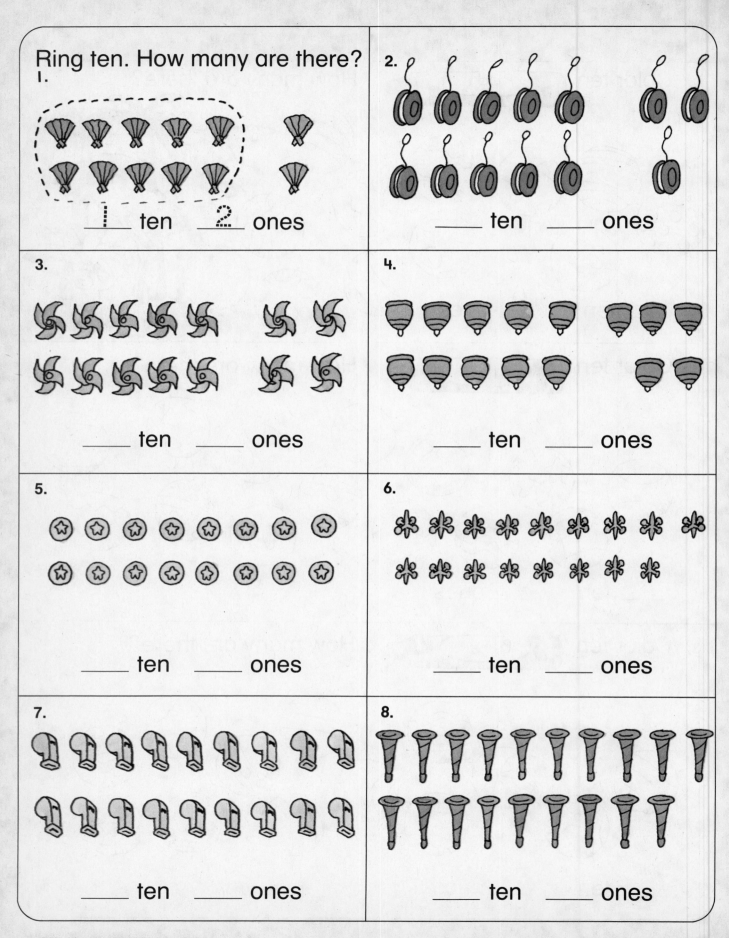

_1_ ten   _2_ ones

2.

_____ ten   _____ ones

3.

_____ ten   _____ ones

4.

_____ ten   _____ ones

5.

_____ ten   _____ ones

6.

_____ ten   _____ ones

7.

_____ ten   _____ ones

8.

_____ ten   _____ ones

Tens and ones to 19

Name _____

___1___ ten ___0___ ones ___10___
ten

___1___ ten ___1___ one ___11___
eleven

How many are there?

1. ___ ten ___ ones ___
twelve

2. ___ ten ___ ones ___
thirteen

3. ___ ten ___ ones ___
fourteen

4. ___ ten ___ ones ___
fifteen

5. ___ ten ___ ones ___
sixteen

6. ___ ten ___ ones ___
seventeen

7. ___ ten ___ ones ___
eighteen

8. ___ ten ___ ones ___
nineteen

Reading and writing numbers to 19

(one hundred fifteen) **115**

How many are there?

1.

___1___ ten ___5___ ones ___15___

2.

_____ ten _____ ones _____

3.

_____ ten _____ ones _____

4.

_____ ten _____ one _____

5.

_____ ten _____ ones _____

6.

_____ ten _____ ones _____

7.

_____ ten _____ ones _____

8.

_____ ten _____ ones _____

SKILLKEEPER

Subtract.

$$9 - 2 \qquad 7 - 1 \qquad 8 - 3 \qquad 11 - 3 \qquad 7 - 2 \qquad 11 - 2$$

Reading and writing numbers to 19

Name _____

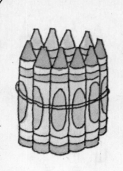  

__2__ tens __4__ ones

How many are there?

1.

__3__ tens __2__ ones

2.

_____ tens _____ ones

3.

_____ tens _____ ones

4.

_____ tens _____ ones

5.

_____ tens _____ ones

6.

_____ tens _____ ones

Tens and ones less than 40

How many are there?

1.

_____ tens _____ one

2.

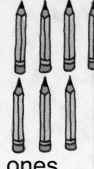

_____ tens _____ ones

3.

_____ tens _____ ones

4.

_____ tens _____ ones

5.

_____ tens _____ ones

6.

_____ tens _____ ones

SKILLKEEPER

Add.

$$\begin{array}{r} 8 \\ +2 \\ \hline \end{array} \qquad \begin{array}{r} 6 \\ +3 \\ \hline \end{array} \qquad \begin{array}{r} 3 \\ +9 \\ \hline \end{array} \qquad \begin{array}{r} 7 \\ +2 \\ \hline \end{array} \qquad \begin{array}{r} 9 \\ +1 \\ \hline \end{array} \qquad \begin{array}{r} 3 \\ +8 \\ \hline \end{array}$$

Name _____

__2__ tens __0__ ones

__20__

twenty

__3__ tens __0__ ones

__30__

thirty

How many are there?

1.

__2__ tens __3__ ones

__23__

2.

____ tens ____ ones

_____

3.

____ tens ____ ones

_____

4.

____ tens ____ ones

_____

5.

____ tens ____ one

_____

6.

____ tens ____ one

_____

Reading and writing numbers less than 40

How many are there?

1. _____ tens _____ ones _____

2. _____ tens _____ ones _____

3. _____ tens _____ ones _____

4. _____ tens _____ ones _____

5. _____ tens _____ ones _____

6. _____ tens _____ one _____

7. _____ tens _____ ones _____

8. _____ tens _____ ones _____

THINK MATH

Ring Joe's balloon.
It is red.
It has a happy face.

Reading and writing numbers less than 40

24

Color.

1. 21			
2. 15			
3. 34			
4. 26			
5. 19			
6. 37			

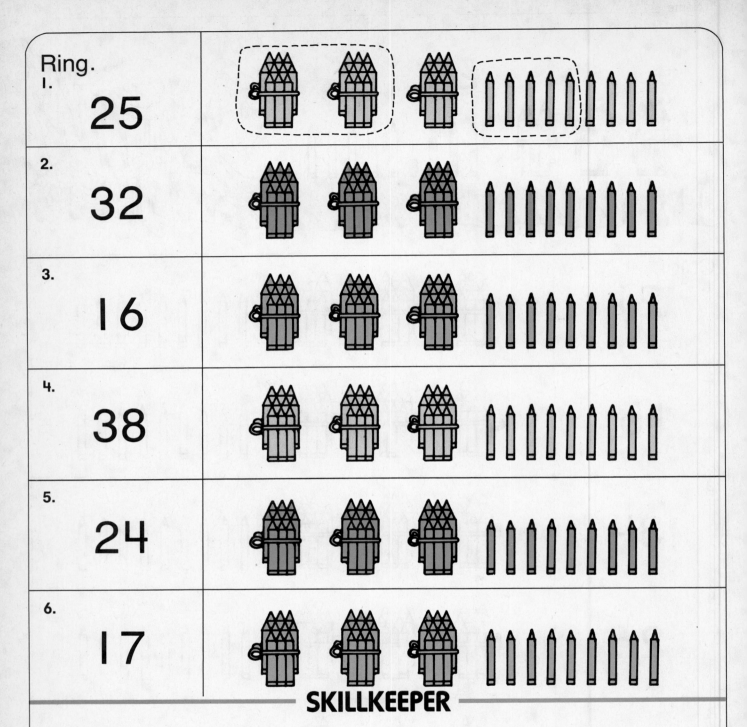

Ring. 1. **25**	
2. **32**	
3. **16**	
4. **38**	
5. **24**	
6. **17**	

SKILLKEEPER

Add or subtract.

$$\begin{array}{r} 3 \\ +7 \\ \hline \end{array} \qquad \begin{array}{r} 11 \\ -3 \\ \hline \end{array} \qquad \begin{array}{r} 1 \\ +8 \\ \hline \end{array} \qquad \begin{array}{r} 10 \\ -1 \\ \hline \end{array} \qquad \begin{array}{r} 2 \\ +8 \\ \hline \end{array} \qquad \begin{array}{r} 11 \\ -2 \\ \hline \end{array}$$

Modeling numbers less than 40

Name _____

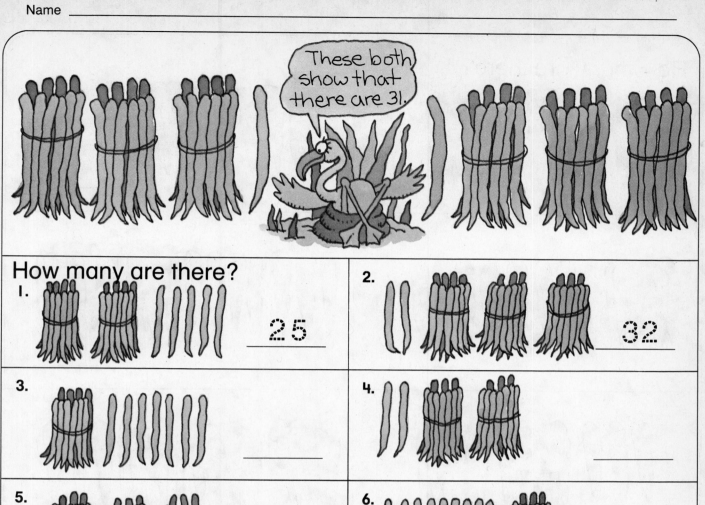

These both show that there are 31.

How many are there?

1. 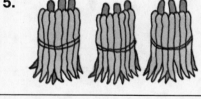 25

2. 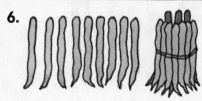 32

3. 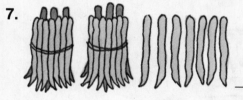 _____

4. 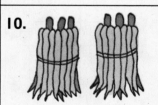 _____

5. _____

6. _____

7. _____

8. _____

9. 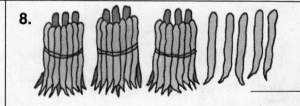 _____

10. _____

11.  _____

12. 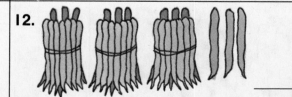 _____

Understanding place value models

How many are there?

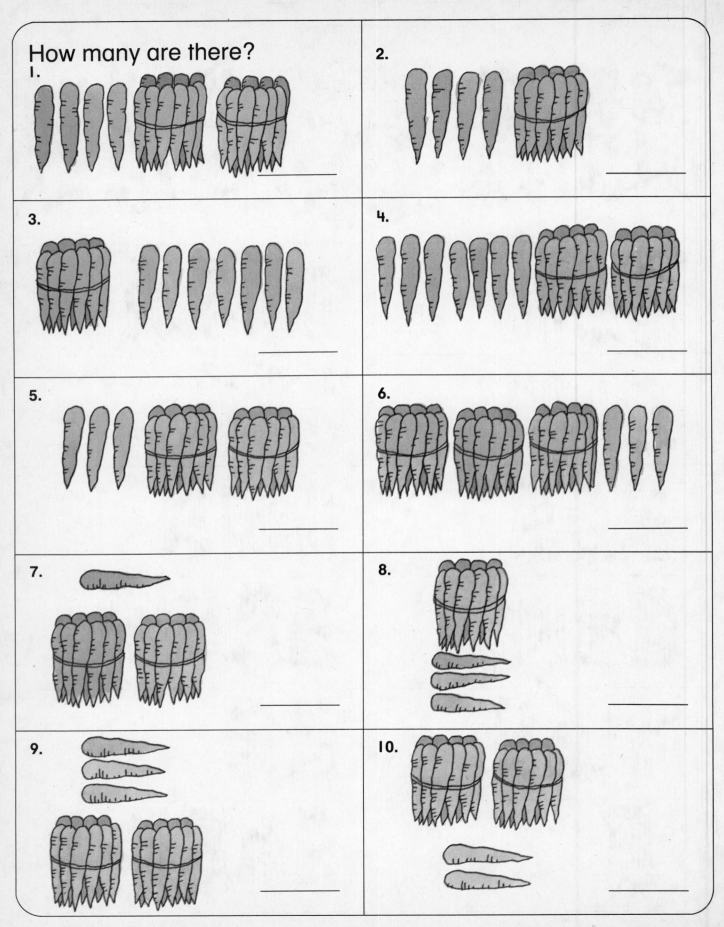

1.

2.

3.

4.

5.

6.

7.

8.

9.

10.

Understanding place value models

Name _____

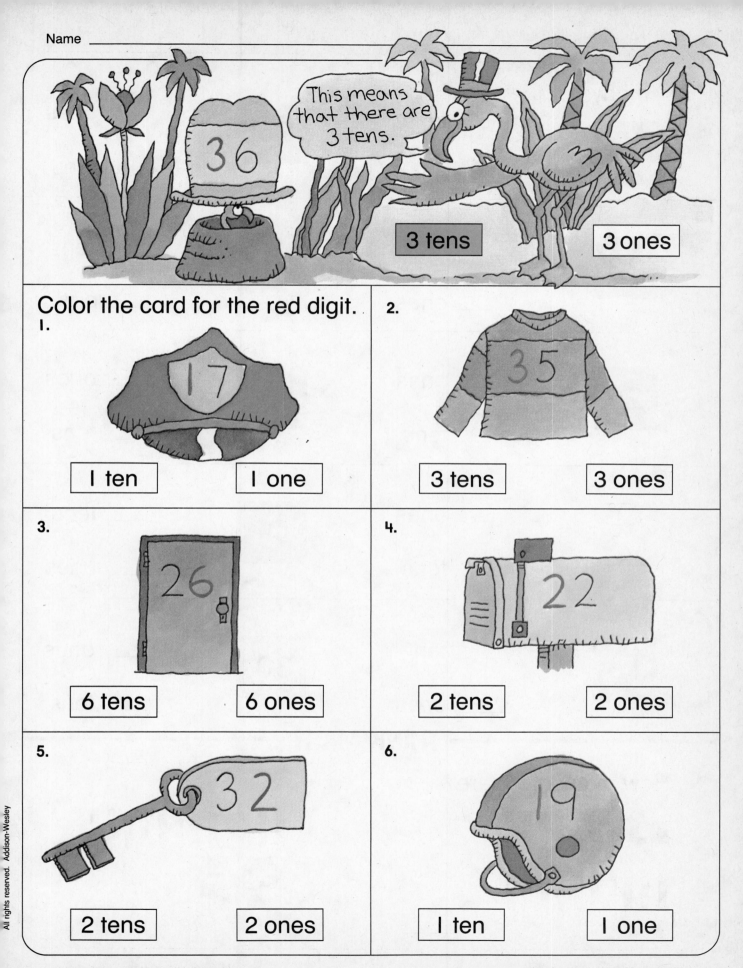

This means that there are 3 tens.

3 tens   3 ones

Color the card for the red digit.

1.

1 ten   1 one

2.

3 tens   3 ones

3.

6 tens   6 ones

4.

2 tens   2 ones

5.

2 tens   2 ones

6.

1 ten   1 one

Understanding place value without models

How many are there?

1.
| 36 |

___3___ tens

___6___ ones

2.
| 25 |

___5___ ones

___2___ tens

3.
| 28 |

_____ tens

_____ ones

4.
| 31 |

_____ tens

_____ one

5.
| 20 |

_____ ones

_____ tens

6.
| 37 |

_____ ones

_____ tens

7.
| 29 |

_____ ones

_____ tens

8.
| 34 |

_____ tens

_____ ones

9.
| 16 |

_____ ten

_____ ones

10.
| 30 |

_____ ones

_____ tens

THINK MATH

How many are there?

_____

_____

Understanding place value

How many are there?

1. 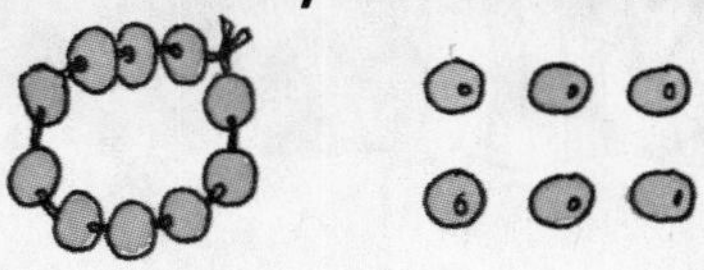 16

2. 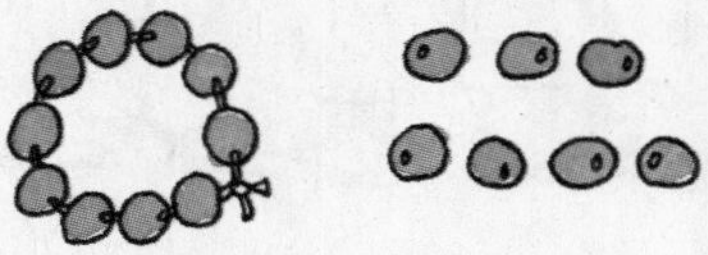 17

3. _____

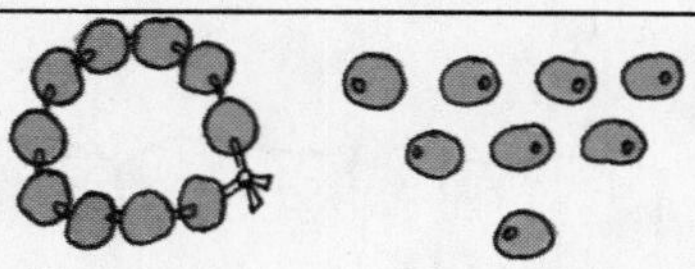

4. _____

5. _____

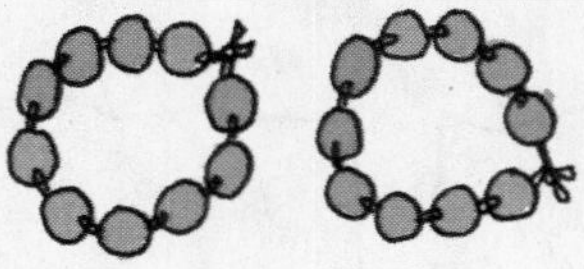

6. _____

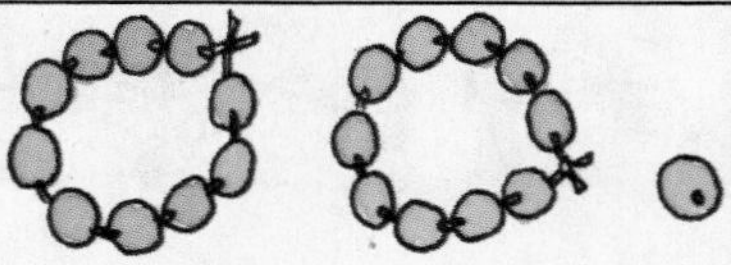

7. _____

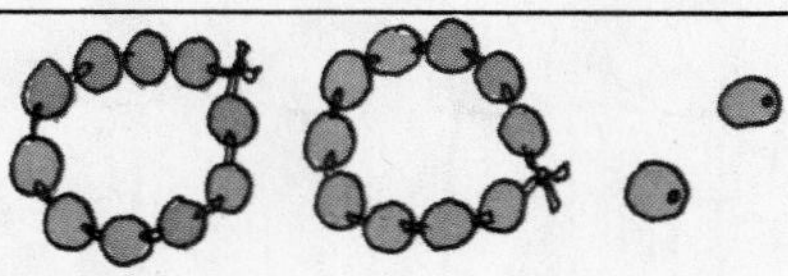

8. _____

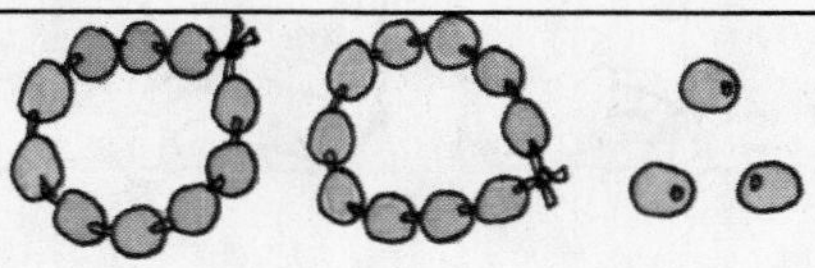

9. _____

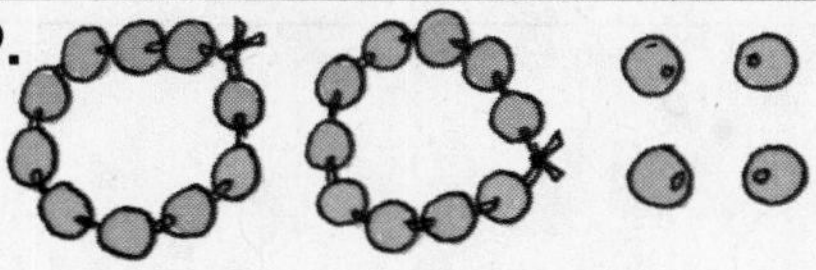

10. _____

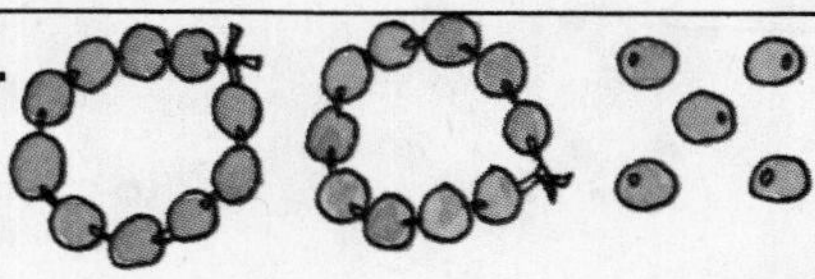

11. _____

12. _____

13. _____

14. _____

15. _____

16. _____

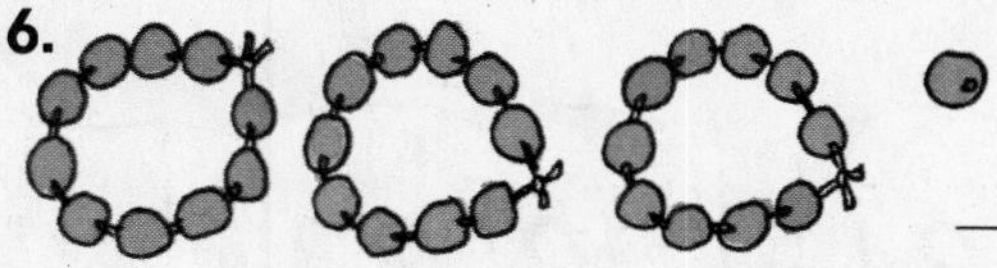

17. _____

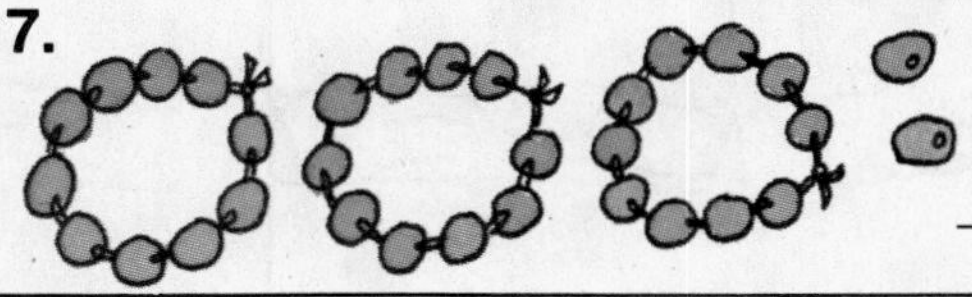

18. _____

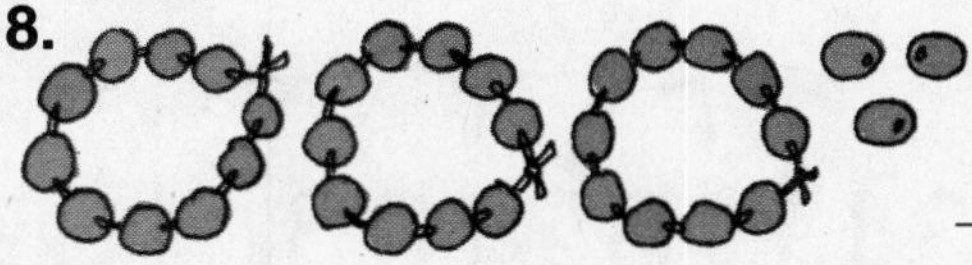

19. _____

20. _____

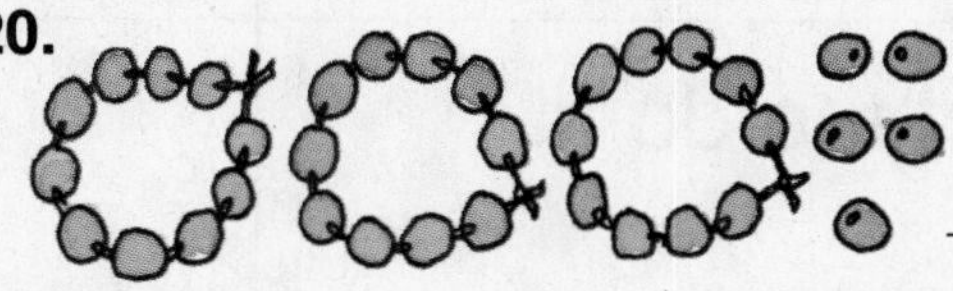

21. _____

22. _____

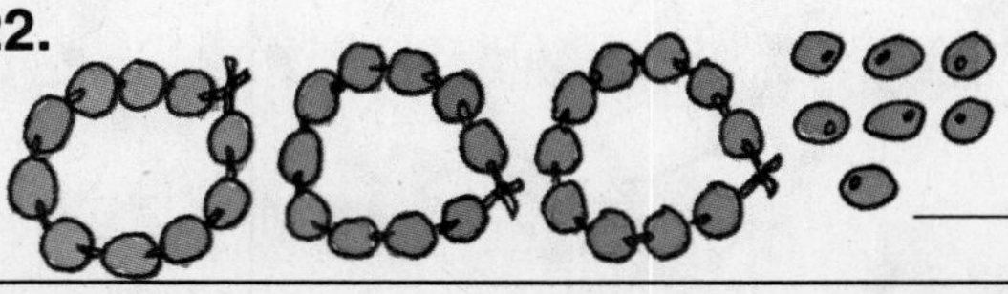

Counting and order

(one hundred twenty-seven) **127**

Finish each row.

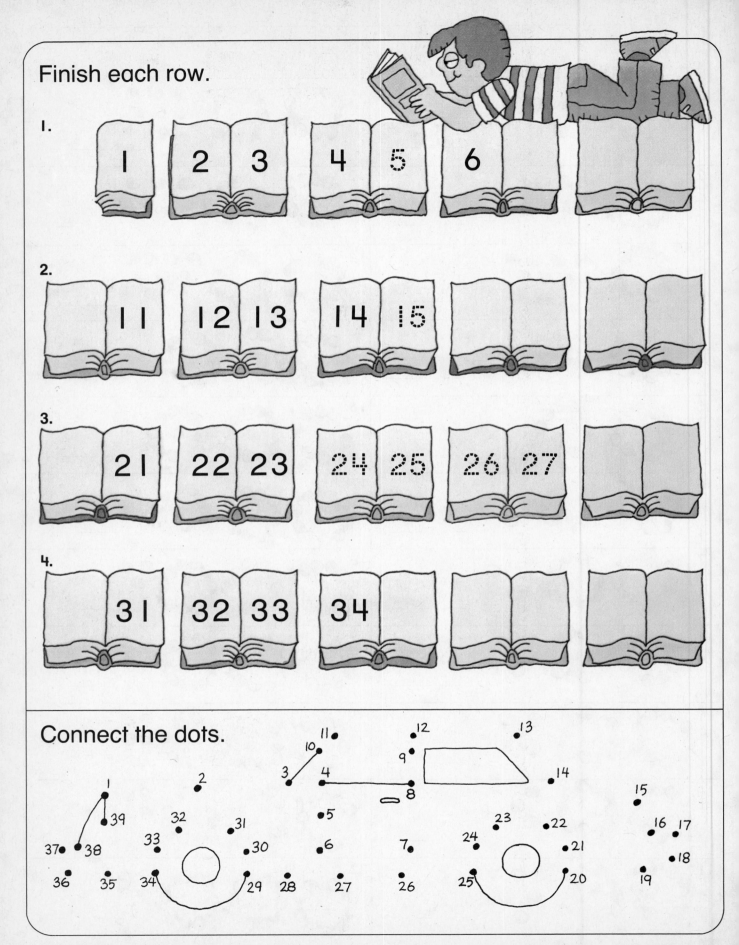

1.

1 2 3 4 5 6

2.

11 12 13 14 15

3.

21 22 23 24 25 26 27

4.

31 32 33 34

Connect the dots.

Counting and order through 39

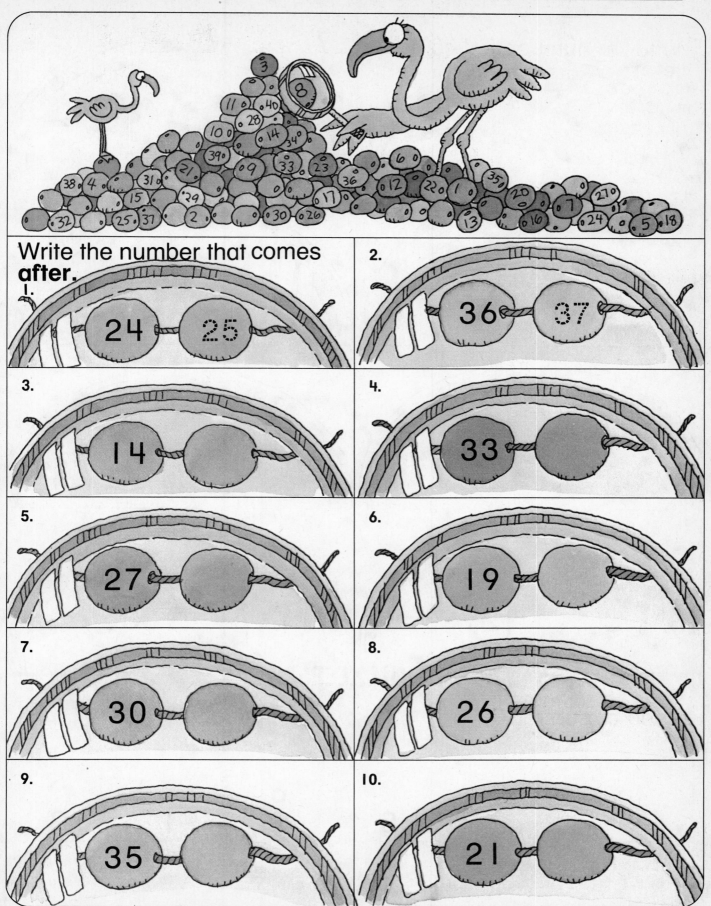

Write the number that comes after.

1. 24 | 25

2. 36 | 37

3. 14 |

4. 33 |

5. 27 |

6. 19 |

7. 30 |

8. 26 |

9. 35 |

10. 21 |

Write the number that comes **before.**

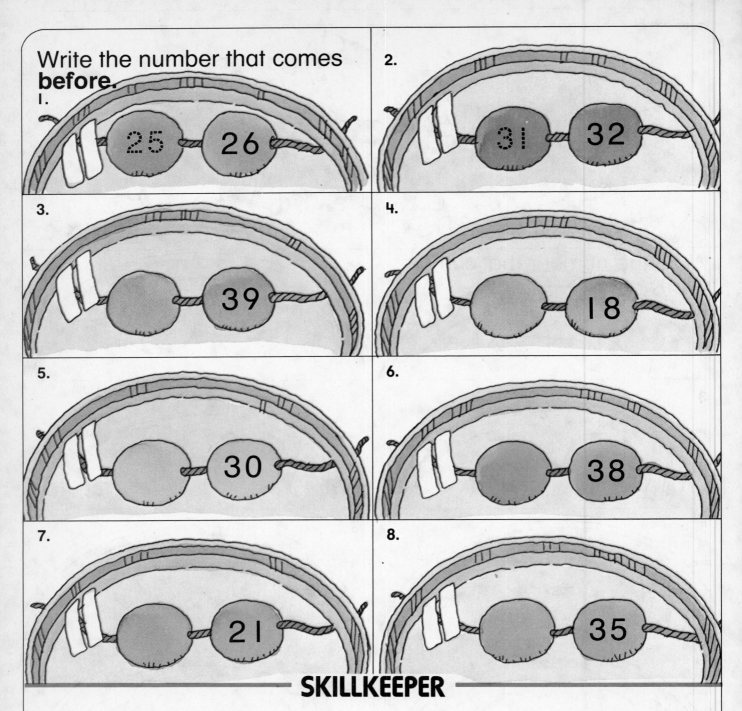

1. 25 26
2. 31 32
3. ___ 39
4. ___ 18
5. ___ 30
6. ___ 38
7. ___ 21
8. ___ 35

SKILLKEEPER

Add or subtract.

$$\begin{array}{r} 6 \\ +3 \\ \hline \end{array} \qquad \begin{array}{r} 10 \\ -\ 2 \\ \hline \end{array} \qquad \begin{array}{r} 2 \\ +8 \\ \hline \end{array} \qquad \begin{array}{r} 6 \\ -2 \\ \hline \end{array} \qquad \begin{array}{r} 7 \\ +1 \\ \hline \end{array} \qquad \begin{array}{r} 9 \\ -3 \\ \hline \end{array}$$

Counting—number before

Name _____

Count the tens.
Write the number.

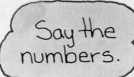
Say the
numbers.

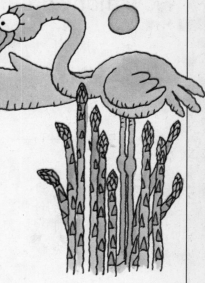

1. 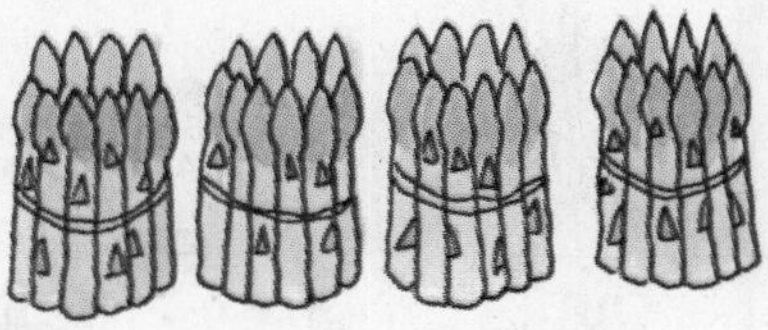  _4_ tens _40_
forty

2. 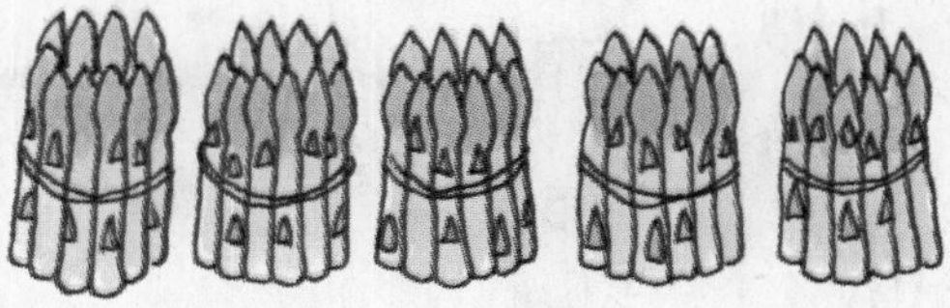 _____ tens _____
fifty

3. 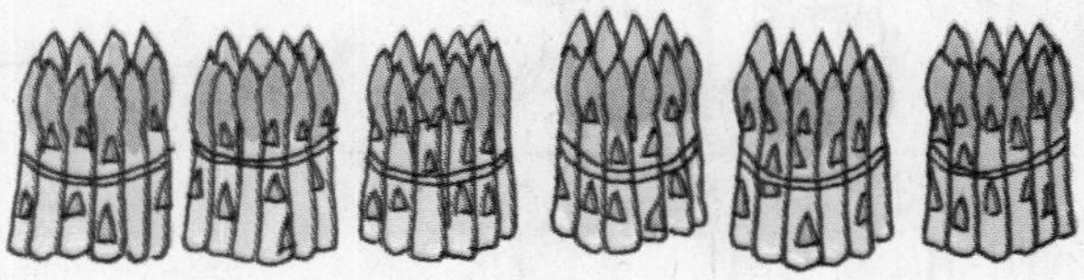 _____ tens _____
sixty

4. 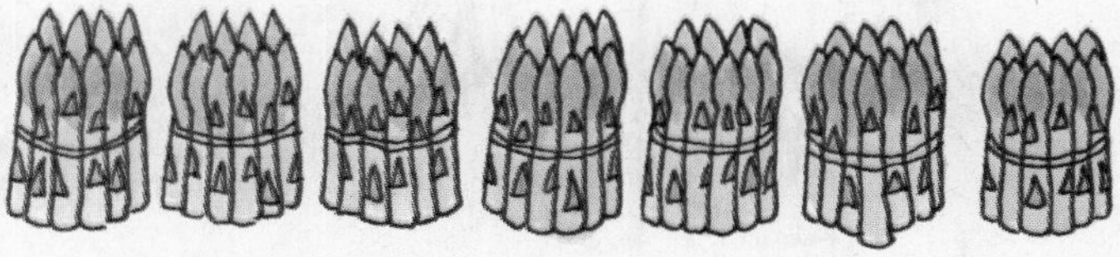 _____ tens _____
seventy

5. 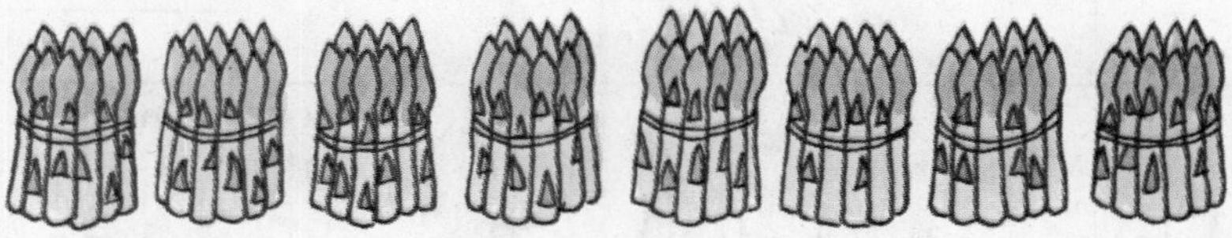 _____ tens _____
eighty

6.  _____ tens _____
ninety

Write the missing numbers.

7. 10 20 30 40 ___ ___ 70 80 ___

8. 10 20 ___ ___ ___ 60 70 ___

9. 10 ___ ___ ___ 50 ___ ___ 80 90

Decade names

How many are there?

1. 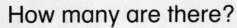
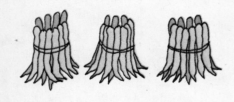 _50_

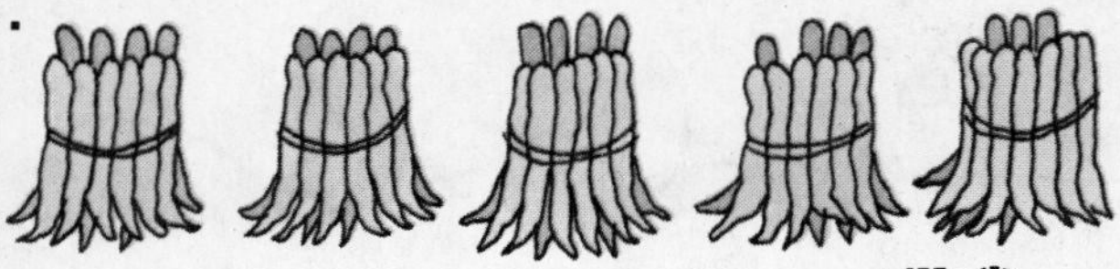

2. 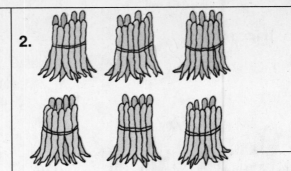 _____

3. 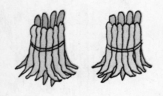 _____

4. 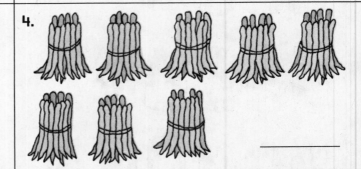 _____

5. 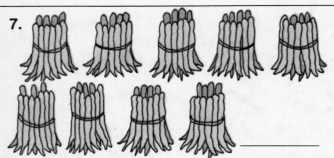 _____

6. 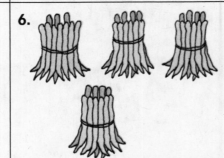 _____

7. 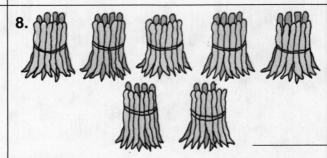 _____

8. _____

THINK MATH

How many ways can you make 5?

___4___ + ___1___ = 5   _____ + _____ = 5   _____ + _____ = 5

_____ + _____ = 5   _____ + _____ = 5   _____ + _____ = 5

Decade names

Name ______________________________

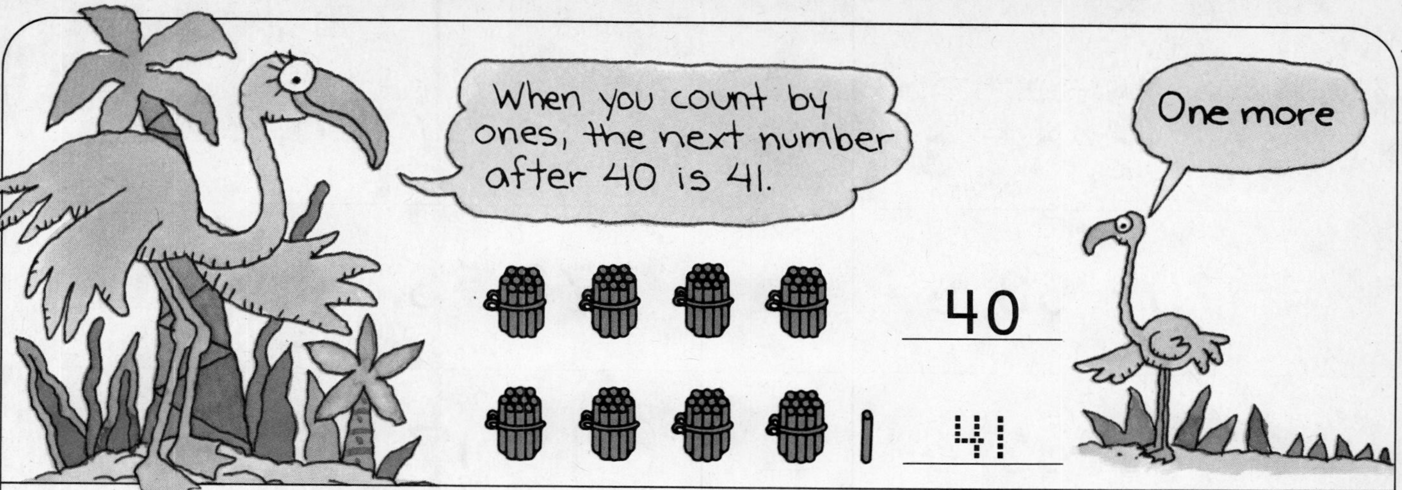

When you count by ones, the next number after 40 is 41.
One more
40
41

Draw one more. Write the number.

1.
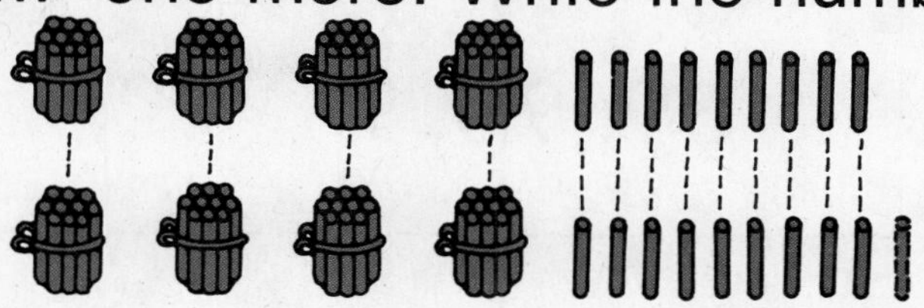

49

50

2.
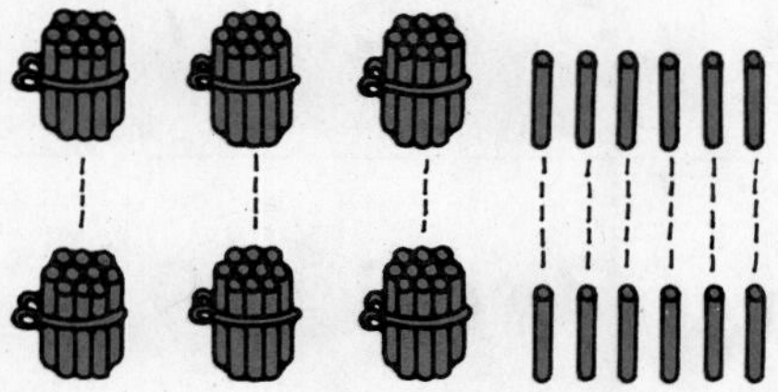

36

______

3.
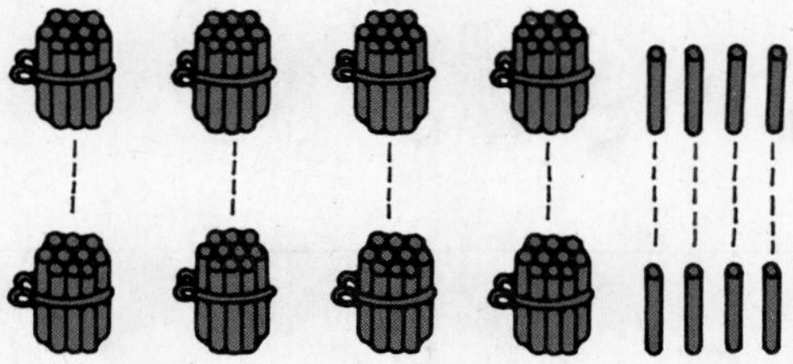

44

______

4.
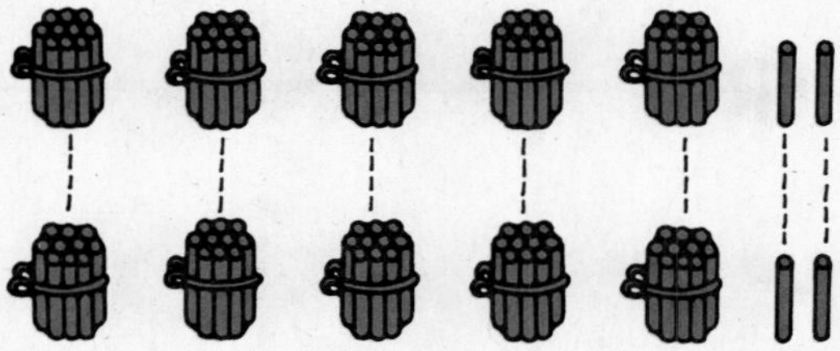

52

______

5.
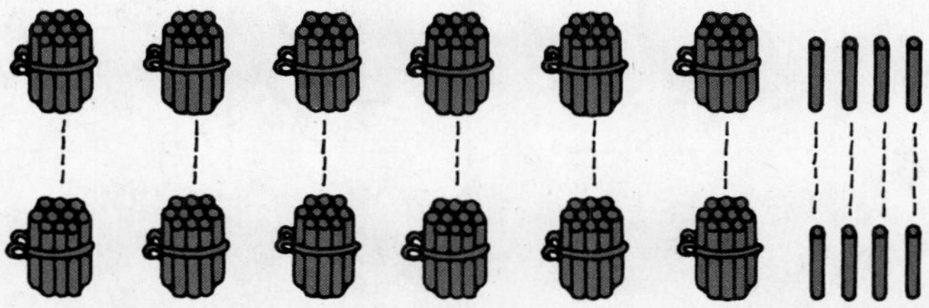

64

______

Write the number that is next.

1. 31, 32, 33, 34, ____

2. 26, 27, 28, 29, ____

3. 51, 52, 53, 54, ____

4. 72, 73, 74, 75, ____

5. 61, 62, 63, 64, ____

6. 16, 17, 18, 19, ____

7. 37, 38, 39, 40, ____

8. 89, 90, 91, 92, ____

9. 36, 37, 38, 39, ____

10. 74, 75, 76, 77, ____

11. 77, 78, 79, 80, ____

12. 66, 67, 68, 69, ____

13. 15, 16, 17, 18, ____

14. 79, 80, 81, 82, ____

15. 86, 87, 88, 89, ____

16. 43, 44, 45, 46, ____

SKILLKEEPER

Add or subtract.

$$8 + 3$$ $$11 - 2$$ $$2 + 7$$ $$10 - 3$$ $$9 - 2$$ $$3 + 8$$

Counting—one more

Name _____

Finish each row.

1. | 40 | 41 | 42 | 43 | 44 | 45 | 46 | | | |

2. | 50 | 51 | 52 | 53 | 54 | | | | | |

3. | 60 | 61 | 62 | 63 | | | | | | |

4. | 70 | 71 | 72 | | | | | | | |

5. | 80 | 81 | | | | | | | | |

6. | 90 | | | | | | | | | |

Counting and order through 99

(one hundred thirty-five) 135

Join the dots. Start at 55.

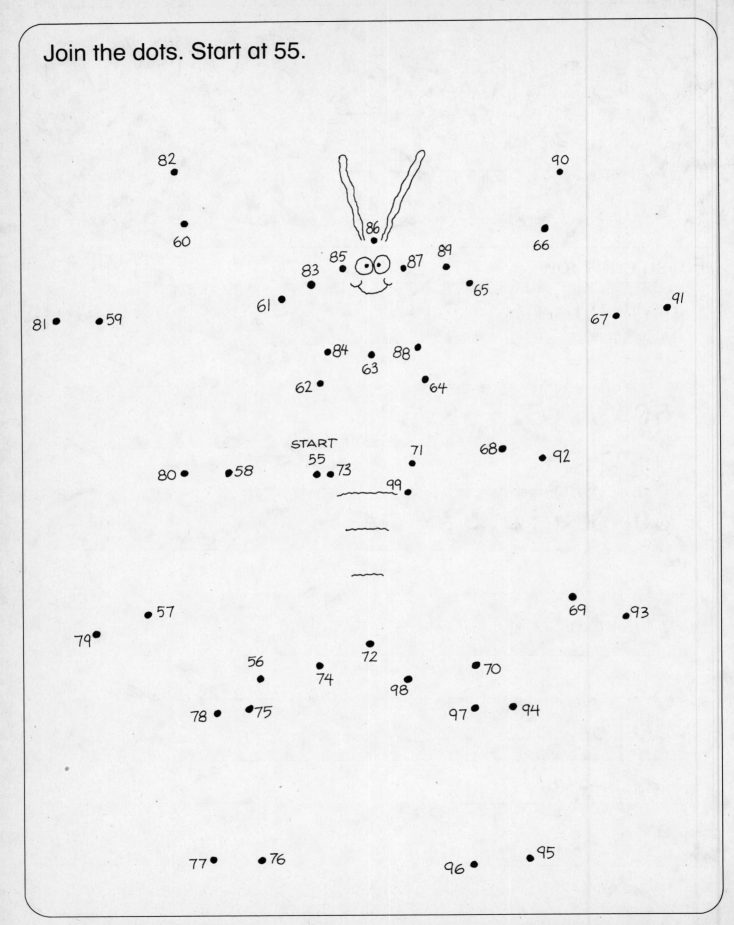

Counting and order through 99

Name _____

Ring the greater number.

1. 
34
24

2. 
26
29

3. 
17
22

4. 
32
28

5.	**6.**	**7.**	**8.**	**9.**	**10.**
24	56	35	67	28	90
27	46	53	71	31	88

Comparing numbers—greater and less

34

24

24 is less than 34.

Ring the number that is less.

1.
26

23

2.
32

22

3.
27

31

4.
40

34

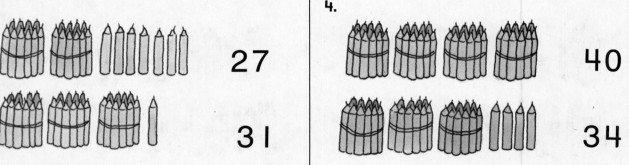

5.	6.	7.	8.	9.	10.
75	46	76	30	90	87
85	43	81	27	92	78

Comparing numbers—greater and less

Name _____

| first
1st | second
2nd | third
3rd | fourth
4th | fifth
5th | sixth
6th | seventh
7th | eighth
8th | ninth
9th | tenth
10th |

Color.

1.

second Green

fifth Blue

2.

first Red

fourth Yellow

3.

third Brown

tenth Black

4.

ninth Purple

fifth Orange

Ordinal numbers to tenth

Match.

1.

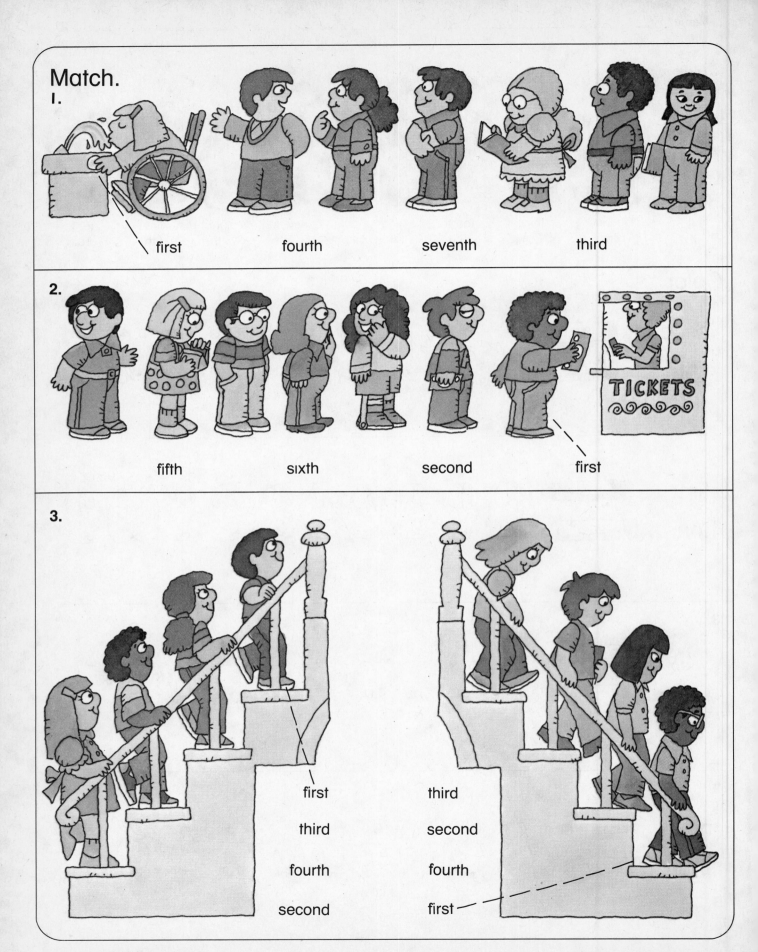

first   fourth   seventh   third

2.

fifth   sixth   second   first

3.

first   third

third   second

fourth   fourth

second   first

      Ordinal numbers to tenth

How many are there? Count by twos.

1.

legs

_____
In all

$\underline{2}$ $\underline{4}$ $\underline{6}$ $\underline{}$ $\underline{}$ $\underline{}$

2.

ears

_____
In all

_____ _____ _____ _____ _____ _____ _____

How many are there? Count by fives.

3.

fingers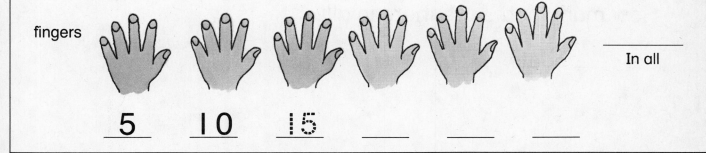

_____
In all

$\underline{5}$ $\underline{10}$ $\underline{15}$ $\underline{}$ $\underline{}$ $\underline{}$

4.

toes

_____
In all

_____ _____ _____ _____ _____ _____ _____

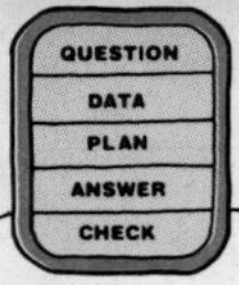

Finish the picture. Solve the problem.

1. 7 apples are on the table.
   4 apples are in the box.
   How many apples are there in all?

   _____ apples

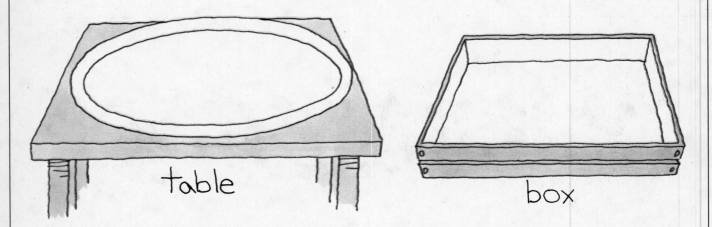

table

box

2. 4 boats are in the grass.
   4 boats are in the water.
   How many boats are there in all?

   _____ boats

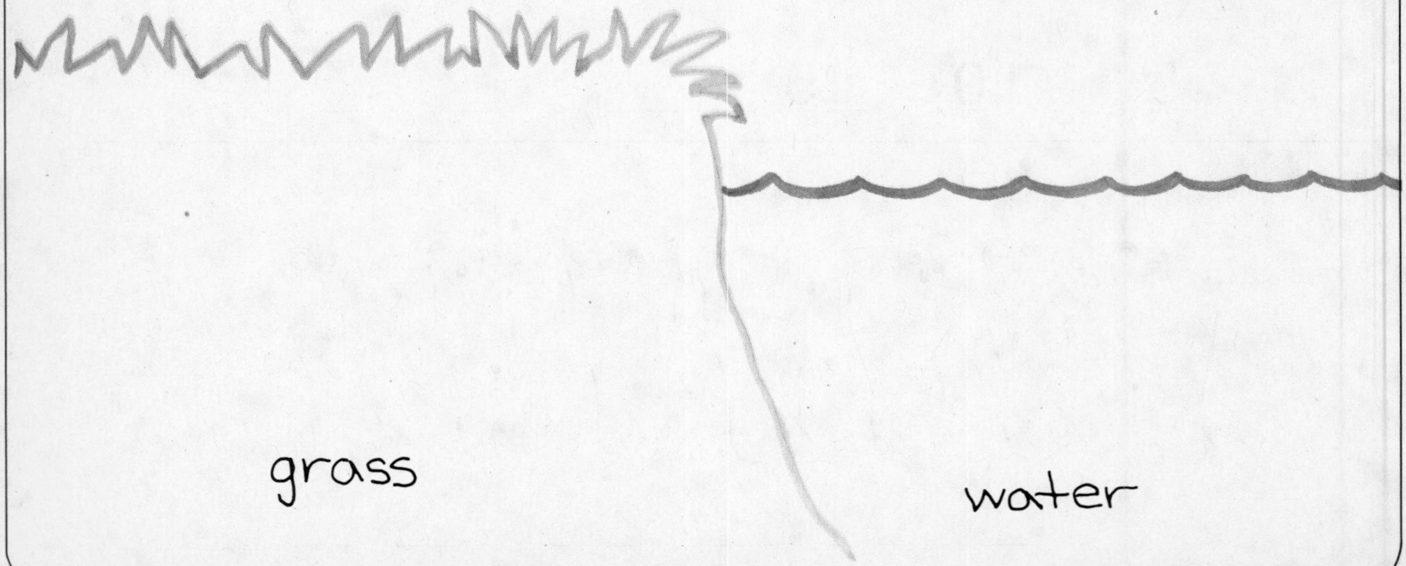

grass

water

Name _____

How many are there?

1. _____ ten
_____ ones

2. _____ tens
_____ ones

3. **38** _____ tens
_____ ones

4. **47** _____ ones
_____ tens

5. Finish each row.

| 23 | 24 | 25 | 26 | | | | | |

| 10 | 20 | 30 | 40 | | | | |

| 75 | 76 | 77 | 78 | | | | | |

6. Which number is greater?

27   36   38   57
24   56   42   75

7. Match.

second   first   third   fifth   fourth

8. Count by twos.

2 4 ___ ___ ___

9. Count by fives.

5 10 15 ___ ___

CUMULATIVE REVIEW

Add.

1. $7 + 1 =$ ___
   - ○ 8
   - ○ 9
   - ○ 6

2. $5 + 2 =$ ___
   - ○ 4
   - ○ 7
   - ○ 5

3. $\begin{array}{r} 1 \\ + 4 \\ \hline \end{array}$
   - ○ 3
   - ○ 5
   - ○ 7

4. $\begin{array}{r} 8 \\ + 2 \\ \hline \end{array}$
   - ○ 6
   - ○ 12
   - ○ 10

Subtract.

5. $6 - 1 =$ ___
   - ○ 4
   - ○ 5
   - ○ 7

6. $9 - 2 =$ ___
   - ○ 7
   - ○ 11
   - ○ 10

7. $\begin{array}{r} 12 \\ - 3 \\ \hline \end{array}$
   - ○ 11
   - ○ 12
   - ○ 9

8. $\begin{array}{r} 11 \\ - 2 \\ \hline \end{array}$
   - ○ 7
   - ○ 6
   - ○ 9

9. Choose the correct one.

   - ○ $9 + 2 =$ 11
   - ○ $8 + 1 =$ 9
   - ○ $11 + 1 =$ 12

Name _____

ANOTHER LOOK

__2__ tens __4__ ones

__24__

__1__ ten __7__ ones

__17__

11	12	13	14	15	16
35	36	37	38	39	40
67	68	69	70	71	72

How many are there?

1.

____ tens ____ ones

_____

2.

____ tens ____ ones

_____

3. Count.

25, 26, ____, ____, ____

50, 51, ____, ____, ____

65, 66, ____, ____, ____

88, 89, ____, ____, ____

ENRICHMENT

Which one does not belong?

1.

2.

3.

4.

5.

Enrichment—classification

Name _____

TIME AND MONEY

Write the numbers. Color the long hand 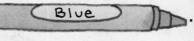.

Color the short hand 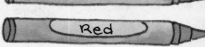.

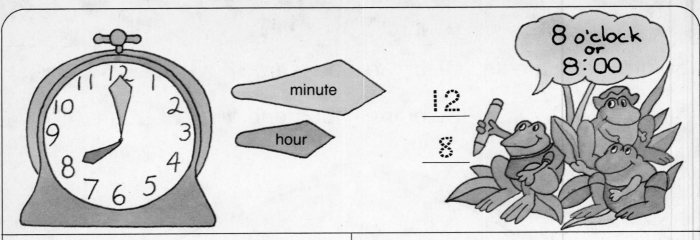

8 o'clock
or
8:00

12
8

Where are the hands?

1.

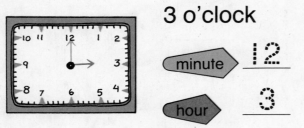

3 o'clock

minute   12

hour   3

2.

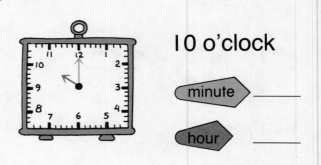

10 o'clock

minute   _____

hour   _____

3.

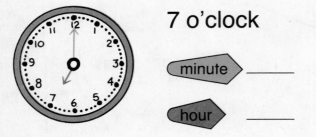

7 o'clock

minute   _____

hour   _____

4.

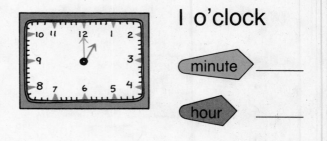

1 o'clock

minute   _____

hour   _____

5.

6 o'clock

minute   _____

hour   _____

6.

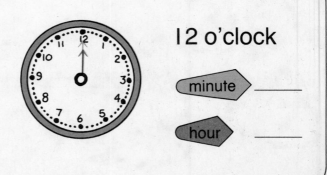

12 o'clock

minute   _____

hour   _____

Parts of the clock face

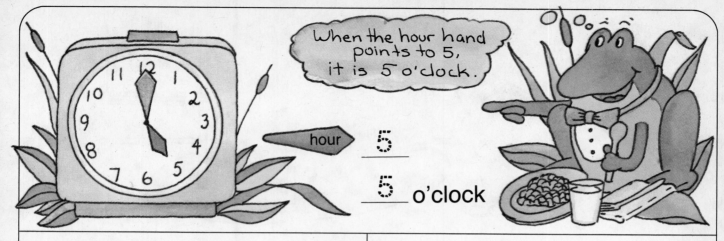

When the hour hand points to 5, it is 5 o'clock.

hour   _5_

_5_ o'clock

Where does the hour hand point?

1.

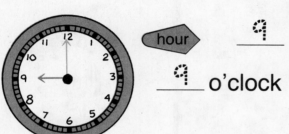

hour   _9_

_9_ o'clock

2.

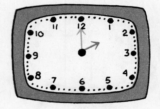

hour   ____

____ o'clock

3.

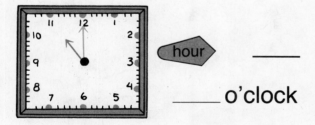

hour   ____

____ o'clock

4.

hour   ____

____ o'clock

5.

hour   ____

____ o'clock

6.

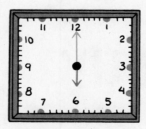

hour   ____

____ o'clock

7:00

Draw the hour hands on the clocks.

1.

8:00

2.

9:00

3.

10:00

4.

12:00

SKILLKEEPER

How many are there?

_____

_____

Drawing the hour hand

_____ o'clock

1:00

Write the time two ways.

1.

_____ o'clock

___ : ___

2.

_____ o'clock

___ : ___

3.

_____ o'clock

___ : ___

4.

_____ o'clock

___ : ___

5.

_____ o'clock

___ : ___

6.

_____ o'clock

___ : ___

Writing time to the hour

Match the clocks.

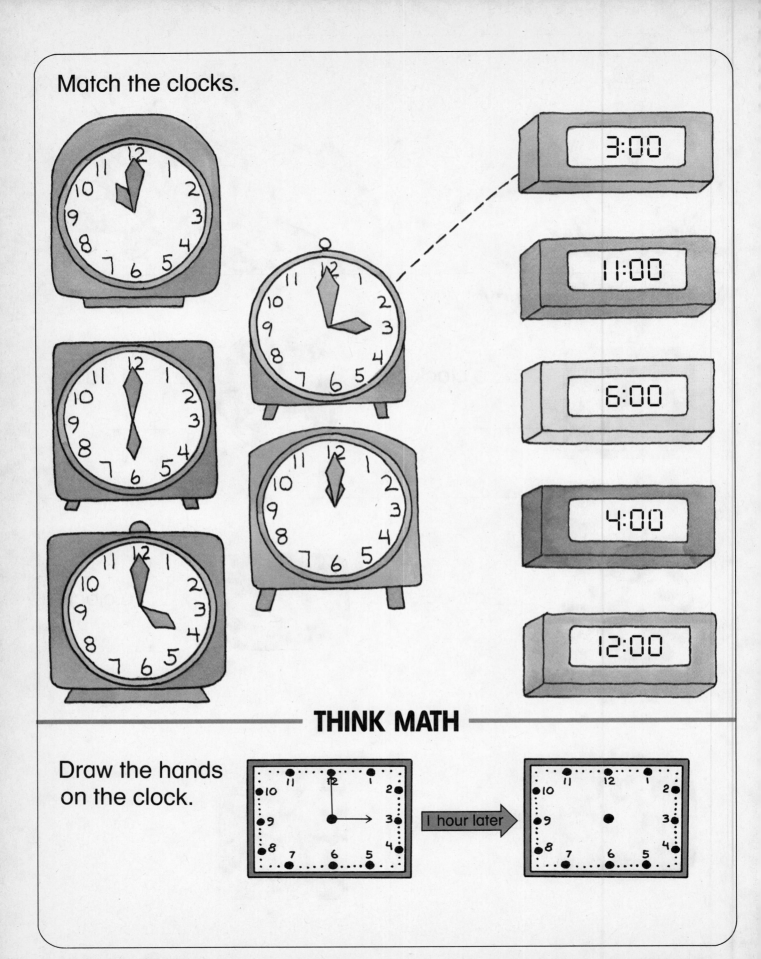

THINK MATH

Draw the hands on the clock.

1 hour later

Matching clock faces with digital clocks

__2__ o'clock   __30__ minutes after __2__ o'clock.

1.

_____ o'clock

_____ minutes after _____ o'clock

2.

_____ o'clock

_____ minutes after _____ o'clock

3.

_____ o'clock

_____ minutes after _____ o'clock

Reading time to the half hour

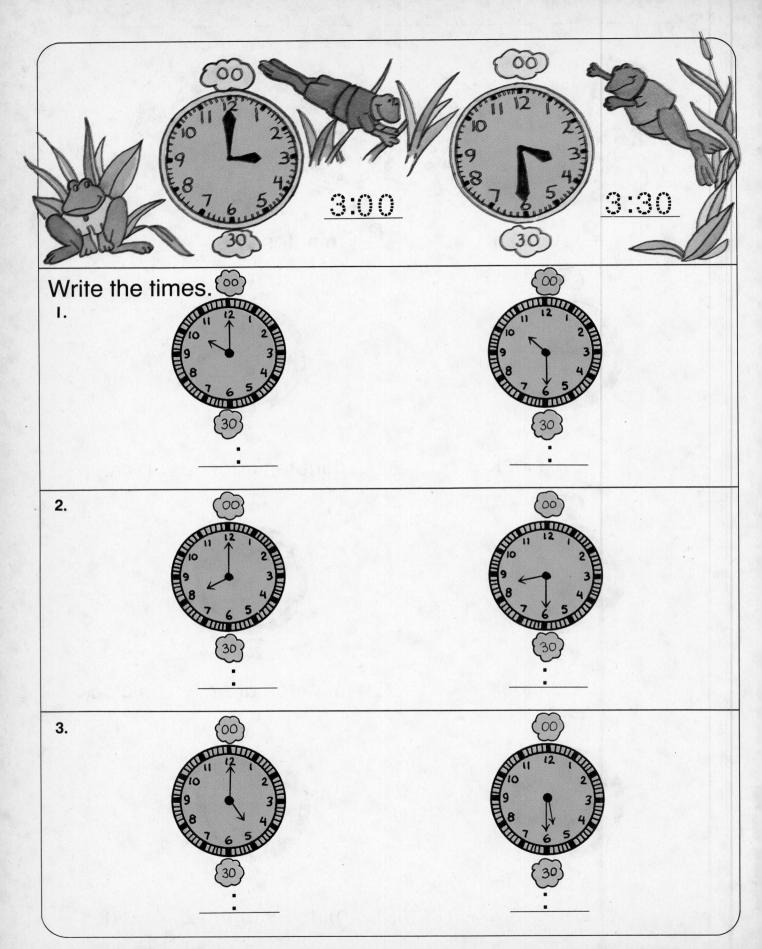

3:00

3:30

Write the times.

1.

_____

_____

2.

_____

_____

3.

_____

_____

Writing time to the half hour

Write the times.

1.

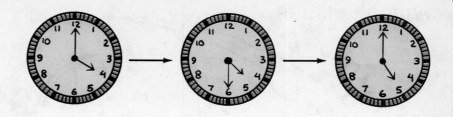

4:00   4:30   5:00

2.

___:___   ___:___   ___:___

3.

___:___   ___:___   ___:___

4.

___:___   ___:___   ___:___

Name _____

Hour and half-hour sequence

Write the times.

SKILLKEEPER

Add.

$$
\begin{array}{cc}
6 \\
+1 \\
\hline
\end{array}
\qquad
\begin{array}{cc}
9 \\
+0 \\
\hline
\end{array}
\qquad
\begin{array}{cc}
7 \\
+1 \\
\hline
\end{array}
\qquad
\begin{array}{cc}
5 \\
+1 \\
\hline
\end{array}
\qquad
\begin{array}{cc}
8 \\
+1 \\
\hline
\end{array}
\qquad
\begin{array}{cc}
2 \\
+0 \\
\hline
\end{array}
$$

Practice reading and writing time

Make a calendar.

Month _____

Sunday	Monday	Tuesday	Wednesday	Thursday	Friday	Saturday

1. How many days are in a week? _____

2. How many school days are in a week? _____

3. How many days are in this month? _____

4. How many
    school days are in this month? _____

MAY

Sunday	Monday	Tuesday	Wednesday	Thursday	Friday	Saturday
			1	2	3	4
5	6	7	8	9	10	11
12	13	14	15	16	17	18
19	20	21	22	23	24	25
26	27	28	29	30	31	

Ring the day.

1. Mother's Day   Wednesday   Saturday   Sunday

2. Memorial Day   Thursday   Friday   Saturday

3. May 1   Sunday   Wednesday   Thursday

4. May 16   Tuesday   Wednesday   Thursday

5. May 5   Saturday   Sunday   Monday

Write the date.

6. first Saturday May 4

7. second Monday _____

8. last Sunday _____

9. third Tuesday _____

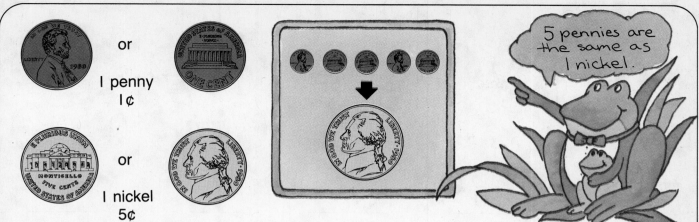

5 pennies are the same as 1 nickel.

or
I penny
I¢

or
I nickel
5¢

Count the money. Write the amount.

1.

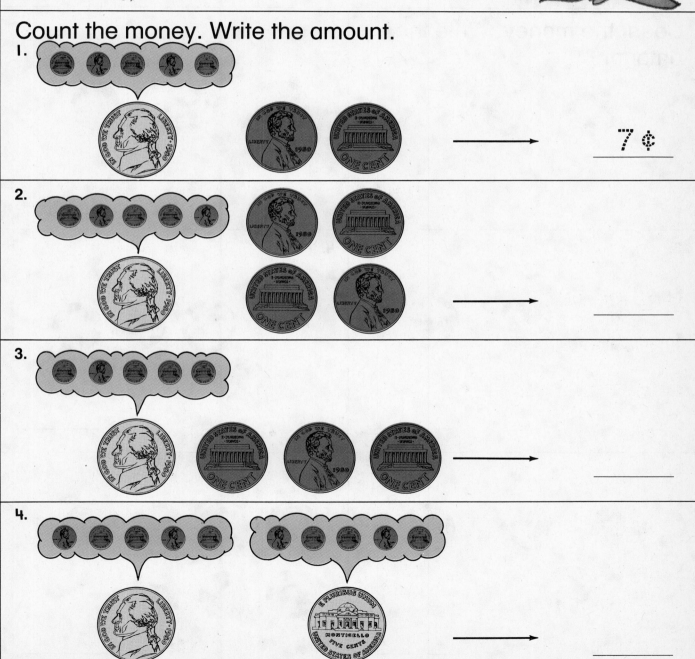

7 ¢

2.

_____

3.

_____

4.

_____

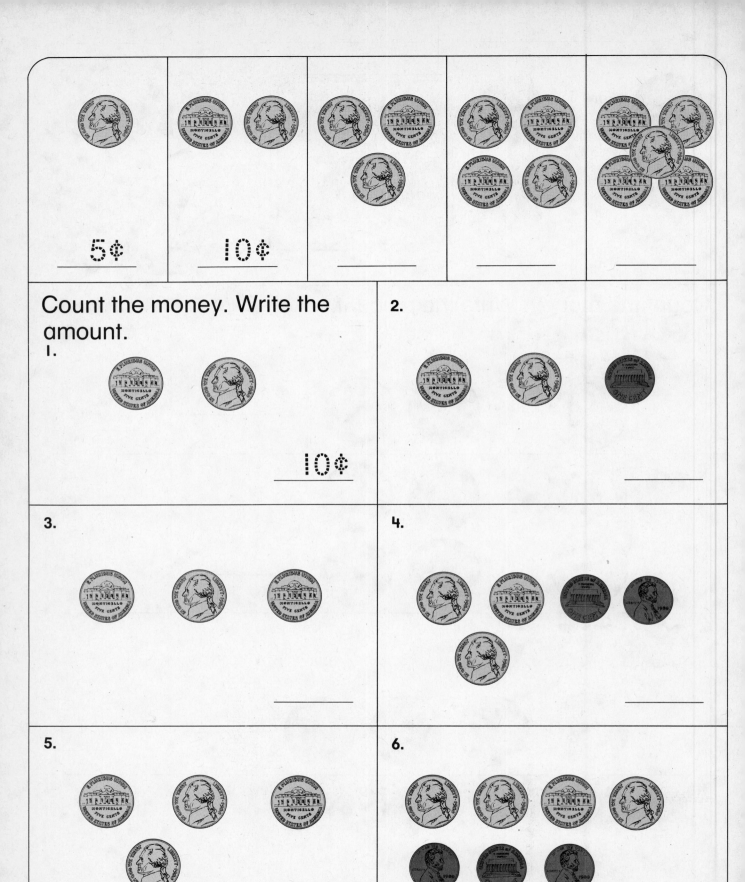

5¢   10¢   _____   _____   _____

Count the money. Write the amount.

1.

10¢

2.

_____

3.

_____

4.

_____

5.

_____

6.

_____

Counting nickels and pennies

Name _____

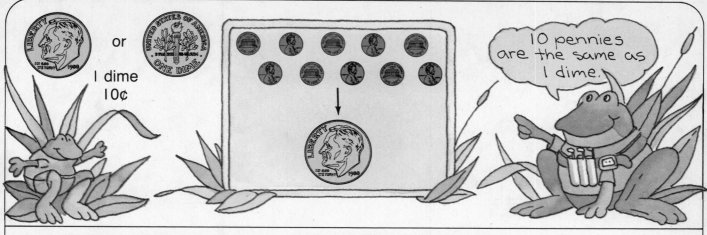

Count the money. How much money is there?

1.

_____ → 12¢

2.

_____ → _____

3.

_____ → _____

4.

_____ → _____

Counting dimes and pennies

10¢	20¢	_____	_____	_____

Count the money.
How much money is there?

1.

20¢

2.

_____

3.

_____

4.

_____

SKILLKEEPER

Subtract.

$$\begin{array}{r} 7 \\ -1 \\ \hline \end{array} \qquad \begin{array}{r} 4 \\ -2 \\ \hline \end{array} \qquad \begin{array}{r} 8 \\ -1 \\ \hline \end{array} \qquad \begin{array}{r} 9 \\ -2 \\ \hline \end{array} \qquad \begin{array}{r} 6 \\ -1 \\ \hline \end{array} \qquad \begin{array}{r} 5 \\ -2 \\ \hline \end{array}$$

Counting dimes and pennies

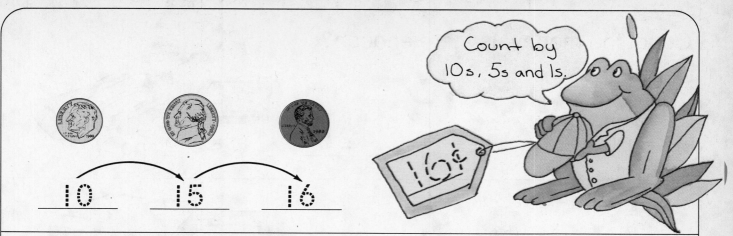

10   15   16

Count by 10s, 5s and 1s.

Count the money. Write the price.

1.

10   15

2.

___   ___   ___

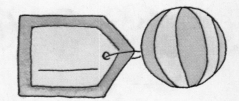

3.

_____

4.

Count the money. Is there enough?

1.

26¢ _____   yes   (no)

2.

_____   yes   no

3.

_____   yes   no

4.

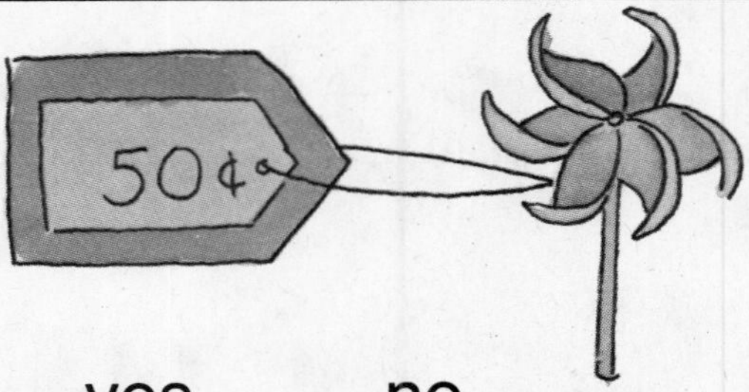

_____   yes   no

THINK MATH

Dotty has 2 pennies.

She has the same number of dimes.
How much money does she have? _____

Comparing amounts of money to price tags

Name _____

36¢

Match.

1. 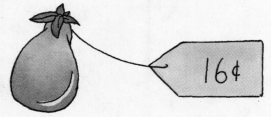 16¢

2. 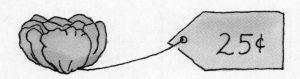 25¢

3. 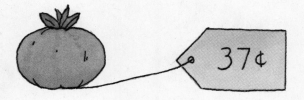 37¢

4.  19¢

5. 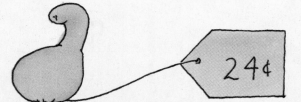 24¢

Matching coins and prices

(one hundred sixty-five) **165**

Ring the coins needed to pay the exact amount.

1. 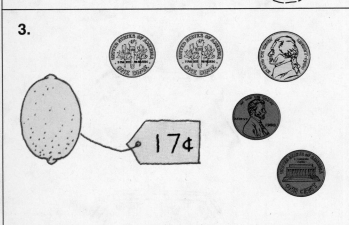 13¢

2.  31¢

3. 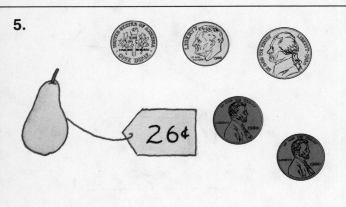 17¢

4. 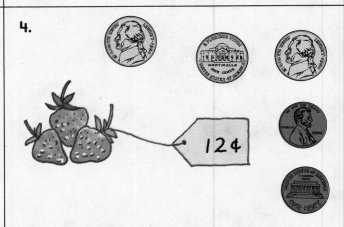 12¢

5. 26¢

6.  35¢

SKILLKEEPER

Add or subtract.

$$\begin{array}{r} 9 \\ +1 \\ \hline \end{array} \qquad \begin{array}{r} 8 \\ -2 \\ \hline \end{array} \qquad \begin{array}{r} 6 \\ +2 \\ \hline \end{array} \qquad \begin{array}{r} 5 \\ -1 \\ \hline \end{array} \qquad \begin{array}{r} 2 \\ +4 \\ \hline \end{array} \qquad \begin{array}{r} 8 \\ -1 \\ \hline \end{array}$$

Counting and matching amounts of money

Name _____

I quarter is the same as 25¢

or

I quarter
25¢

Count the money.

1.

25   26   27

→ 27¢

2.

→ _____

_____   _____   _____   _____   _____

3.

 _____

_____   _____   _____   _____

4.

 _____

_____   _____   _____   _____   _____

Introduction to quarters

Count the money. Write the price.

1.

25   30   31   32

2.

_____

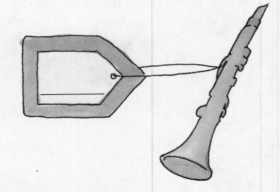

3.

_____

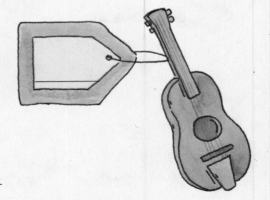

4.

_____

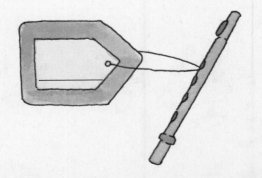

Counting with quarters

CHAPTER REVIEW/TEST

What time is it?

1.

___ : ___   ___ : ___   ___ : ___

2.

___ : ___   ___ : ___   ___ : ___

How much money is there?

3.

_____

4.

_____

5.

_____

6.

_____

CUMULATIVE REVIEW

Subtract.

1.
$$7$$
$$- 1$$
○ 3
○ 5
○ 6

2.
$$4$$
$$- 1$$
○ 3
○ 5
○ 2

3.
$$6$$
$$- 2$$
○ 4
○ 5
○ 8

4.
$$11$$
$$- 2$$
○ 8
○ 12
○ 9

How many are there?

5.
○ 33
○ 23
○ 13

6.
$$42$$
○ 3 tens 1 one
○ 4 tens 2 ones
○ 2 tens 4 ones

7. Finish the row.

51, 52, 53
○ 54, 55, 56
○ 55, 56, 57
○ 48, 49, 50

8. Count by twos.

2, 4, 6
○ 12
○ 10
○ 8

9. Choose the correct number sentence.

○ 8 − 2 = 6

○ 7 − 2 = 5

○ 5 − 1 = 4

ANOTHER LOOK

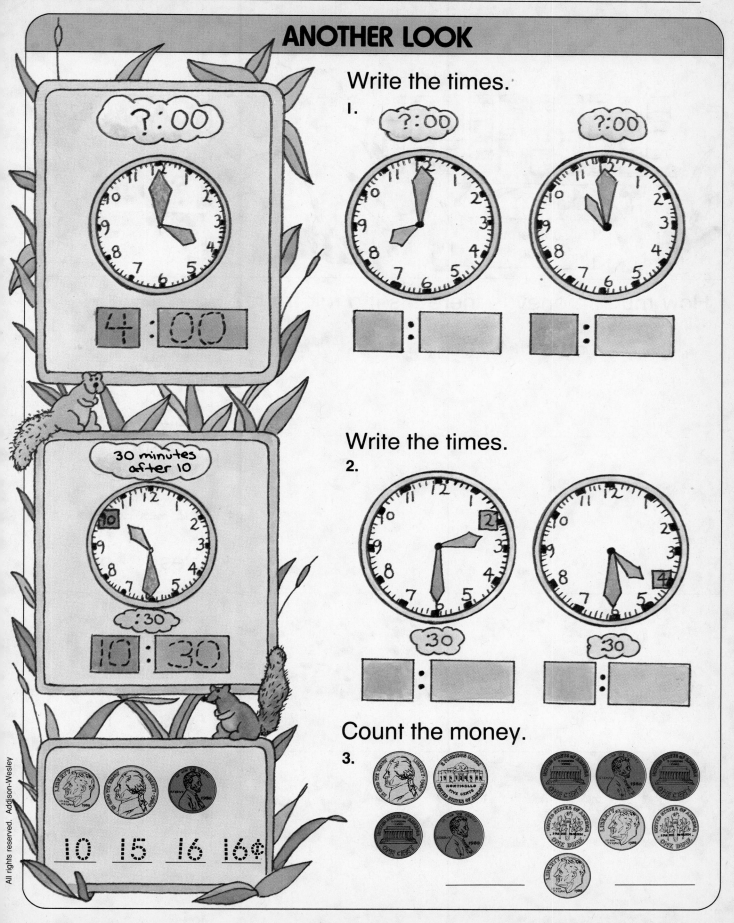

Write the times.

1.

Write the times.

2.

Count the money.

3.

Name _____

100 pennies
100¢

Fair trade

1 dollar
100¢

How much money is there? Is it a fair trade?

1.

100¢   (yes)   no

2.

_____   yes   no

3.

_____   yes   no

4.

    _____   yes   no

Enrichment—dollar bill

SUMS TO 12

Add.

1.

$$\begin{array}{r} 4 \\ +1 \\ \hline \end{array}$$
$$\begin{array}{r} 0 \\ +5 \\ \hline \end{array}$$
$$\begin{array}{r} 2 \\ +1 \\ \hline \end{array}$$
$$\begin{array}{r} 3 \\ +2 \\ \hline \end{array}$$

2.

$$\begin{array}{r} 1 \\ +1 \\ \hline \end{array}$$
$$\begin{array}{r} 2 \\ +3 \\ \hline \end{array}$$
$$\begin{array}{r} 1 \\ +2 \\ \hline \end{array}$$
$$\begin{array}{r} 3 \\ +1 \\ \hline \end{array}$$
$$\begin{array}{r} 2 \\ +2 \\ \hline \end{array}$$
$$\begin{array}{r} 1 \\ +4 \\ \hline \end{array}$$

3.

$$\begin{array}{r} 8 \\ +1 \\ \hline \end{array}$$
$$\begin{array}{r} 1 \\ +6 \\ \hline \end{array}$$
$$\begin{array}{r} 9 \\ +1 \\ \hline \end{array}$$
$$\begin{array}{r} 5 \\ +1 \\ \hline \end{array}$$
$$\begin{array}{r} 1 \\ +7 \\ \hline \end{array}$$
$$\begin{array}{r} 1 \\ +4 \\ \hline \end{array}$$

4.

$$\begin{array}{r} 2 \\ +5 \\ \hline \end{array}$$
$$\begin{array}{r} 8 \\ +2 \\ \hline \end{array}$$
$$\begin{array}{r} 4 \\ +2 \\ \hline \end{array}$$
$$\begin{array}{r} 7 \\ +2 \\ \hline \end{array}$$
$$\begin{array}{r} 2 \\ +9 \\ \hline \end{array}$$
$$\begin{array}{r} 6 \\ +2 \\ \hline \end{array}$$

5.

$$\begin{array}{r} 7 \\ +3 \\ \hline \end{array}$$
$$\begin{array}{r} 3 \\ +5 \\ \hline \end{array}$$
$$\begin{array}{r} 3 \\ +8 \\ \hline \end{array}$$
$$\begin{array}{r} 6 \\ +3 \\ \hline \end{array}$$
$$\begin{array}{r} 3 \\ +4 \\ \hline \end{array}$$
$$\begin{array}{r} 9 \\ +3 \\ \hline \end{array}$$

Add.

1.
$$3 + 6$$ $$7 + 1$$ $$1 + 4$$ $$6 + 0$$ $$2 + 7$$

2.
$$2 + 1$$ $$8 + 3$$ $$0 + 7$$ $$5 + 2$$ $$1 + 8$$ $$0 + 1$$

3.
$$3 + 3$$ $$9 + 1$$ $$2 + 8$$ $$3 + 7$$ $$1 + 1$$ $$4 + 2$$

4.
$$2 + 2$$ $$5 + 3$$ $$5 + 1$$ $$9 + 0$$ $$6 + 2$$ $$3 + 9$$

5.
$$3 + 1$$ $$0 + 8$$ $$2 + 9$$ $$1 + 6$$ $$3 + 4$$ $$4 + 0$$

THINK MATH

How many acorns are there in all?

5 acorns   5 acorns   5 acorns   5 acorns

_____ acorns

Facts review

$1 + 1 = \underline{2}$ $2 + 2 = \underline{4}$

Find the sums.

1.

$3 + 3 = \underline{\quad}$

2.

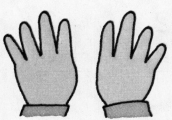

$4 + 4 = \underline{\quad}$

3.

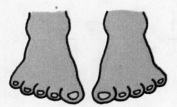

$5 + 5 = \underline{\quad}$

4.

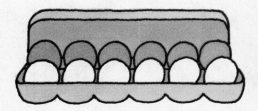

$6 + 6 = \underline{\quad}$

Add.

5.

$\begin{array}{r} 4 \\ +4 \\ \hline \end{array}$ $\begin{array}{r} 2 \\ +2 \\ \hline \end{array}$ $\begin{array}{r} 6 \\ +6 \\ \hline \end{array}$ $\begin{array}{r} 1 \\ +1 \\ \hline \end{array}$ $\begin{array}{r} 5 \\ +5 \\ \hline \end{array}$ $\begin{array}{r} 3 \\ +3 \\ \hline \end{array}$

6.

$\begin{array}{r} 6 \\ +6 \\ \hline \end{array}$ $\begin{array}{r} 3 \\ +3 \\ \hline \end{array}$ $\begin{array}{r} 1 \\ +1 \\ \hline \end{array}$ $\begin{array}{r} 4 \\ +4 \\ \hline \end{array}$ $\begin{array}{r} 2 \\ +2 \\ \hline \end{array}$ $\begin{array}{r} 5 \\ +5 \\ \hline \end{array}$

Doubles—1, 2, 3, 4, 5, 6

Add.

1. $2 + 2 =$ _____ $3 + 3 =$ _____

2. $4 + 4 =$ _____ $5 + 5 =$ _____ $6 + 6 =$ _____

3.
$$\begin{array}{r} 2 \\ +2 \\ \hline \end{array}$$
$$\begin{array}{r} 3 \\ +3 \\ \hline \end{array}$$
$$\begin{array}{r} 5 \\ +5 \\ \hline \end{array}$$
$$\begin{array}{r} 6 \\ +6 \\ \hline \end{array}$$
$$\begin{array}{r} 1 \\ +1 \\ \hline \end{array}$$
$$\begin{array}{r} 4 \\ +4 \\ \hline \end{array}$$

4.
$$\begin{array}{r} 3 \\ +3 \\ \hline \end{array}$$
$$\begin{array}{r} 5 \\ +5 \\ \hline \end{array}$$
$$\begin{array}{r} 1 \\ +1 \\ \hline \end{array}$$
$$\begin{array}{r} 4 \\ +4 \\ \hline \end{array}$$
$$\begin{array}{r} 2 \\ +2 \\ \hline \end{array}$$
$$\begin{array}{r} 6 \\ +6 \\ \hline \end{array}$$

5.
$$\begin{array}{r} 5 \\ +5 \\ \hline \end{array}$$
$$\begin{array}{r} 2 \\ +2 \\ \hline \end{array}$$
$$\begin{array}{r} 4 \\ +4 \\ \hline \end{array}$$
$$\begin{array}{r} 1 \\ +1 \\ \hline \end{array}$$
$$\begin{array}{r} 3 \\ +3 \\ \hline \end{array}$$
$$\begin{array}{r} 6 \\ +6 \\ \hline \end{array}$$

SKILLKEEPER

Write the times.

_ _ : _ _   _ _ : _ _   _ _ : _ _

Doubles—1, 2, 3, 4, 5, 6

This is one more than 3 + 3.

3 + 3 = 6   3 + 4 = 7

Add.

1.

$\begin{array}{r} 2 \\ + 2 \\ \hline 4 \end{array}$ ○○ ○○

$\begin{array}{r} 3 \\ + 2 \\ \hline 5 \end{array}$ ○○○● ○○

2.

$\begin{array}{r} 3 \\ + 3 \\ \hline \end{array}$ ○○○ ○○○

$\begin{array}{r} 3 \\ + 4 \\ \hline \end{array}$ ○○○ ○○○ ●

3.

$\begin{array}{r} 4 \\ + 4 \\ \hline \end{array}$ ○○ ○○ ○○

$\begin{array}{r} 4 \\ + 5 \\ \hline \end{array}$ ○○ ○○ ○○●

4.

$\begin{array}{r} 5 \\ + 5 \\ \hline \end{array}$ ○○○ ○○ ○○

$\begin{array}{r} 6 \\ + 5 \\ \hline \end{array}$ ○○○● ○○○ ○○

Add.

5.

$\begin{array}{r} 4 \\ + 4 \\ \hline \end{array}$ $\begin{array}{r} 5 \\ + 4 \\ \hline \end{array}$ $\begin{array}{r} 5 \\ + 5 \\ \hline \end{array}$ $\begin{array}{r} 5 \\ + 6 \\ \hline \end{array}$ $\begin{array}{r} 2 \\ + 2 \\ \hline \end{array}$ $\begin{array}{r} 2 \\ + 3 \\ \hline \end{array}$

6.

$\begin{array}{r} 3 \\ + 3 \\ \hline \end{array}$ $\begin{array}{r} 4 \\ + 3 \\ \hline \end{array}$ $\begin{array}{r} 1 \\ + 1 \\ \hline \end{array}$ $\begin{array}{r} 2 \\ + 1 \\ \hline \end{array}$ $\begin{array}{r} 5 \\ + 5 \\ \hline \end{array}$ $\begin{array}{r} 6 \\ + 5 \\ \hline \end{array}$

Add.

1.
$$
\begin{array}{r} 4 \\ +5 \\ \hline \end{array}
\quad
\begin{array}{r} 6 \\ +6 \\ \hline \end{array}
\quad
\begin{array}{r} 7 \\ +2 \\ \hline \end{array}
\quad
\begin{array}{r} 4 \\ +4 \\ \hline \end{array}
\quad
\begin{array}{r} 3 \\ +8 \\ \hline \end{array}
$$

2.
$$
\begin{array}{r} 2 \\ +6 \\ \hline \end{array}
\quad
\begin{array}{r} 6 \\ +5 \\ \hline \end{array}
\quad
\begin{array}{r} 5 \\ +1 \\ \hline \end{array}
\quad
\begin{array}{r} 5 \\ +4 \\ \hline \end{array}
\quad
\begin{array}{r} 2 \\ +7 \\ \hline \end{array}
\quad
\begin{array}{r} 5 \\ +5 \\ \hline \end{array}
$$

3.
$$
\begin{array}{r} 6 \\ +3 \\ \hline \end{array}
\quad
\begin{array}{r} 4 \\ +5 \\ \hline \end{array}
\quad
\begin{array}{r} 4 \\ +3 \\ \hline \end{array}
\quad
\begin{array}{r} 5 \\ +6 \\ \hline \end{array}
\quad
\begin{array}{r} 3 \\ +3 \\ \hline \end{array}
\quad
\begin{array}{r} 9 \\ +1 \\ \hline \end{array}
$$

4.
$$
\begin{array}{r} 3 \\ +9 \\ \hline \end{array}
\quad
\begin{array}{r} 2 \\ +2 \\ \hline \end{array}
\quad
\begin{array}{r} 6 \\ +5 \\ \hline \end{array}
\quad
\begin{array}{r} 8 \\ +1 \\ \hline \end{array}
\quad
\begin{array}{r} 5 \\ +4 \\ \hline \end{array}
\quad
\begin{array}{r} 2 \\ +3 \\ \hline \end{array}
$$

SKILLKEEPER

Count the money.

_____

_____

Doubles plus one

Name _____

Add.

1.

4	9	3	2	6
+ 5	+ 1	+ 3	+ 7	+ 5

2.

3	5	5	5	3	9
+ 8	+ 5	+ 6	+ 4	+ 4	+ 2

3.

2	4	3	2	6	3
+ 8	+ 5	+ 9	+ 2	+ 5	+ 5

4.

4	6	5	3	5	6
+ 3	+ 6	+ 6	+ 7	+ 4	+ 2

5.

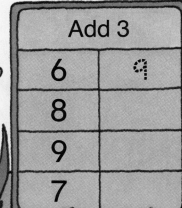

Add 3	
6	9
8	
9	
7	

Add 4	
2	
4	
5	
3	

Add 5	
4	
6	
3	
5	

Practice the facts

(one hundred seventy-nine) **179**

Solve.

1.

Jane got 4 fish.
Bill got 4 fish.
How many are there in all?

$$\begin{array}{r} 4 \\ +\ 4 \\ \hline 8 \end{array}$$

___8___ fish

2.

Dick has 5 birds.
Pat has 5 birds.
How many are there in all?

_____ birds

3.

Jim saw 6 dogs.
Then he saw 5 more.
How many are there in all?

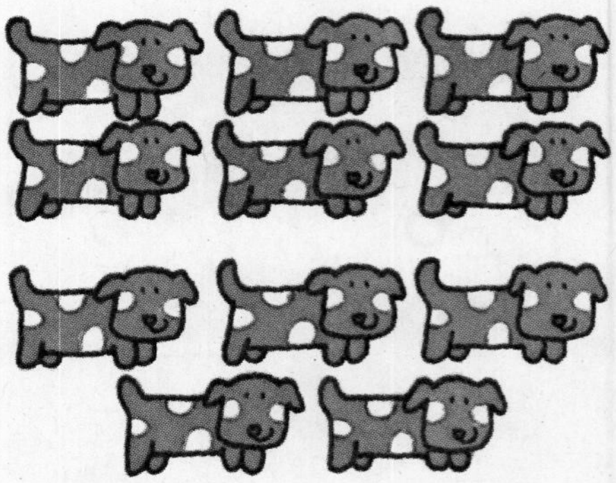

_____ dogs

4.

Ann found 4 bugs.
Don found 5 bugs.
How many are there in all?

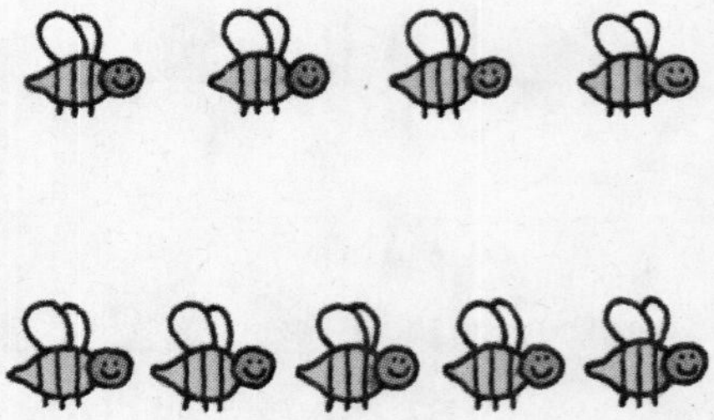

_____ bugs

Problem solving—short sentence

$$\begin{array}{r} 4 \\ +4 \\ \hline \end{array} \qquad \begin{array}{r} 4 \\ +5 \\ \hline \end{array} \qquad \begin{array}{r} 4 \\ +6 \\ \hline 10 \end{array} \qquad \begin{array}{r} 4 \\ +7 \\ \hline 11 \end{array}$$

These are new facts.

$$\begin{array}{r} 6 \\ +4 \\ \hline 10 \end{array}$$

Same as $\begin{array}{r} 4 \\ +6 \end{array}$

$$\begin{array}{r} 7 \\ +4 \\ \hline 11 \end{array}$$

Same as $\begin{array}{r} 4 \\ +7 \end{array}$

Add.

1.
$$\begin{array}{r} 6 \\ +4 \\ \hline \end{array} \qquad \begin{array}{r} 5 \\ +5 \\ \hline \end{array} \qquad \begin{array}{r} 4 \\ +6 \\ \hline \end{array} \qquad \begin{array}{r} 7 \\ +2 \\ \hline \end{array} \qquad \begin{array}{r} 7 \\ +4 \\ \hline \end{array} \qquad \begin{array}{r} 5 \\ +4 \\ \hline \end{array}$$

2.
$$\begin{array}{r} 6 \\ +5 \\ \hline \end{array} \qquad \begin{array}{r} 3 \\ +8 \\ \hline \end{array} \qquad \begin{array}{r} 4 \\ +7 \\ \hline \end{array} \qquad \begin{array}{r} 3 \\ +3 \\ \hline \end{array} \qquad \begin{array}{r} 6 \\ +4 \\ \hline \end{array} \qquad \begin{array}{r} 7 \\ +4 \\ \hline \end{array}$$

3.
$$\begin{array}{r} 4 \\ +3 \\ \hline \end{array} \qquad \begin{array}{r} 4 \\ +6 \\ \hline \end{array} \qquad \begin{array}{r} 6 \\ +6 \\ \hline \end{array} \qquad \begin{array}{r} 6 \\ +4 \\ \hline \end{array} \qquad \begin{array}{r} 7 \\ +4 \\ \hline \end{array} \qquad \begin{array}{r} 3 \\ +2 \\ \hline \end{array}$$

4.
$$\begin{array}{r} 4 \\ +7 \\ \hline \end{array} \qquad \begin{array}{r} 9 \\ +2 \\ \hline \end{array} \qquad \begin{array}{r} 4 \\ +4 \\ \hline \end{array} \qquad \begin{array}{r} 6 \\ +4 \\ \hline \end{array} \qquad \begin{array}{r} 4 \\ +7 \\ \hline \end{array} \qquad \begin{array}{r} 9 \\ +3 \\ \hline \end{array}$$

Add.

1.
$$7 + 4$$ $$2 + 9$$ $$6 + 3$$ $$4 + 6$$ $$6 + 6$$ $$2 + 8$$

2.
$$7 + 2$$ $$6 + 4$$ $$5 + 5$$ $$4 + 7$$ $$5 + 4$$ $$6 + 4$$

3.
$$3 + 4$$ $$7 + 4$$ $$7 + 3$$ $$9 + 1$$ $$4 + 6$$ $$4 + 7$$

4.
$$7 + 4$$ $$4 + 6$$ $$5 + 6$$ $$4 + 7$$ $$5 + 3$$ $$6 + 4$$

THINK MATH

Write the numbers in order.

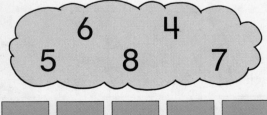

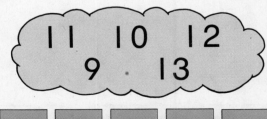

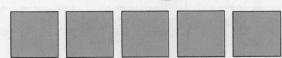

New facts

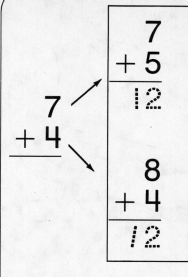

$$\begin{array}{r} 7 \\ +5 \\ \hline 12 \end{array}$$

$$\begin{array}{r} 5 \\ +7 \\ \hline 12 \end{array}$$

Same as $\begin{array}{r} 7 \\ +5 \end{array}$

$$\begin{array}{r} 8 \\ +4 \\ \hline 12 \end{array}$$

$$\begin{array}{r} 4 \\ +8 \\ \hline 12 \end{array}$$

Same as $\begin{array}{r} 8 \\ +4 \end{array}$

These are more new facts.

Add.

1. $\begin{array}{r} 4 \\ +6 \\ \hline \end{array}$ $\begin{array}{r} 7 \\ +5 \\ \hline \end{array}$ $\begin{array}{r} 6 \\ +5 \\ \hline \end{array}$ $\begin{array}{r} 9 \\ +3 \\ \hline \end{array}$ $\begin{array}{r} 4 \\ +8 \\ \hline \end{array}$ $\begin{array}{r} 5 \\ +4 \\ \hline \end{array}$

2. $\begin{array}{r} 5 \\ +5 \\ \hline \end{array}$ $\begin{array}{r} 8 \\ +4 \\ \hline \end{array}$ $\begin{array}{r} 8 \\ +2 \\ \hline \end{array}$ $\begin{array}{r} 5 \\ +7 \\ \hline \end{array}$ $\begin{array}{r} 6 \\ +4 \\ \hline \end{array}$ $\begin{array}{r} 4 \\ +8 \\ \hline \end{array}$

3. $\begin{array}{r} 8 \\ +4 \\ \hline \end{array}$ $\begin{array}{r} 7 \\ +5 \\ \hline \end{array}$ $\begin{array}{r} 7 \\ +4 \\ \hline \end{array}$ $\begin{array}{r} 3 \\ +9 \\ \hline \end{array}$ $\begin{array}{r} 4 \\ +8 \\ \hline \end{array}$ $\begin{array}{r} 6 \\ +2 \\ \hline \end{array}$

4. $\begin{array}{r} 6 \\ +6 \\ \hline \end{array}$ $\begin{array}{r} 8 \\ +4 \\ \hline \end{array}$ $\begin{array}{r} 3 \\ +7 \\ \hline \end{array}$ $\begin{array}{r} 5 \\ +7 \\ \hline \end{array}$ $\begin{array}{r} 4 \\ +7 \\ \hline \end{array}$ $\begin{array}{r} 4 \\ +3 \\ \hline \end{array}$

Finish each table.

1.

Add 7

3	
5	
2	
4	

Add 5

7	
5	
4	
6	

2.

Add 6

6	
4	
3	
5	

Add 3

6	
2	
9	
4	

Add 4

7	
5	
8	
6	

SKILLKEEPER

Subtract.

$$\begin{array}{r} 10 \\ -\ 3 \\ \hline \end{array} \qquad \begin{array}{r} 6 \\ -2 \\ \hline \end{array} \qquad \begin{array}{r} 9 \\ -1 \\ \hline \end{array} \qquad \begin{array}{r} 8 \\ -3 \\ \hline \end{array} \qquad \begin{array}{r} 4 \\ -2 \\ \hline \end{array} \qquad \begin{array}{r} 5 \\ -1 \\ \hline \end{array}$$

Practice the facts

Add.

1.
$$4 + 5$$ $$7 + 4$$ $$4 + 6$$ $$4 + 8$$ $$5 + 3$$ $$3 + 3$$

2.
$$6 + 3$$ $$6 + 2$$ $$3 + 8$$ $$5 + 2$$ $$5 + 5$$ $$6 + 6$$

3.
$$2 + 7$$ $$4 + 2$$ $$7 + 5$$ $$4 + 4$$ $$2 + 8$$ $$9 + 2$$

4.
$$3 + 4$$ $$9 + 3$$ $$2 + 6$$ $$3 + 2$$ $$5 + 6$$ $$8 + 1$$

Practice the facts

Add. Color.

$$3 + 8$$

$$4 + 3$$

$$4 + 4$$

$$4 + 6$$

$$5 + 4$$

$$3 + 9$$

$$7 + 5$$

$$6 + 6$$

$$7 + 4$$

$$6 + 3$$

$$8 + 2$$

$$7 + 3 = \rule{1cm}{0.4pt}$$

$$6 + 5 = \rule{1cm}{0.4pt}$$

$$5 + 5 = \rule{1cm}{0.4pt}$$

$$9 + 2 = \rule{1cm}{0.4pt}$$

     Practice the facts

Add.

1.
$$8 + 3$$ $$5 + 7$$ $$6 + 5$$

2.
$$9 + 2$$ $$4 + 7$$ $$2 + 8$$

3.
$$3 + 4$$ $$9 + 3$$ $$4 + 5$$ $$2 + 9$$ $$7 + 5$$ $$5 + 3$$

4.
$$5 + 6$$ $$8 + 4$$ $$3 + 6$$ $$8 + 3$$ $$3 + 9$$ $$6 + 4$$

5.
$$9 + 1$$ $$5 + 4$$ $$6 + 5$$ $$5 + 7$$ $$4 + 4$$ $$6 + 3$$

Practice the facts

Solve.

1.

Mark found 7 shells.
3 shells broke.
How many shells are left?

_____4_____ shells

7
− 3
‾‾‾
4

2.

9 nuts were on the ground.
Some squirrels ate 2.
How many nuts
are left?

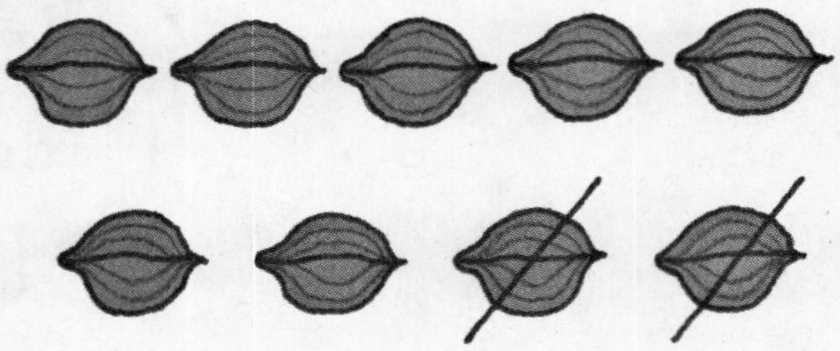

_____ nuts

3.

3 worms are crawling.
5 worms are eating.
How many worms
are there in all?

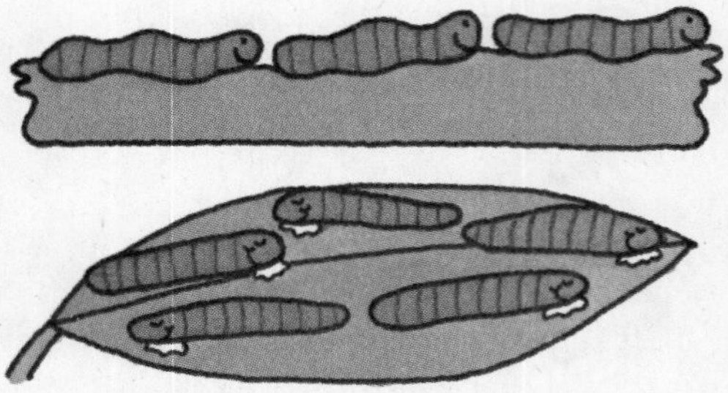

_____ worms

4.

6 rabbits are white.
6 rabbits are brown.
How many rabbits
are there in all?

_____ rabbits

Problem solving—short sentence

$$\begin{array}{r} 2 \\ 1 \\ +2 \\ \hline 5 \end{array}$$

Add.

1.

$$\begin{array}{r} 3 \\ 1 \\ +2 \\ \hline \end{array} \quad 4$$

$$\begin{array}{r} 2 \\ 3 \\ +2 \\ \hline \end{array} \quad 5$$

$$\begin{array}{r} 4 \\ 1 \\ +3 \\ \hline \end{array} \quad 5$$

$$\begin{array}{r} 1 \\ 5 \\ +1 \\ \hline \end{array} \quad 6$$

$$\begin{array}{r} 3 \\ 4 \\ +3 \\ \hline \end{array} \quad 7$$

2.

$$\begin{array}{r} 2 \\ 2 \\ +2 \\ \hline \end{array}$$

$$\begin{array}{r} 3 \\ 5 \\ +3 \\ \hline \end{array}$$

$$\begin{array}{r} 1 \\ 6 \\ +1 \\ \hline \end{array}$$

$$\begin{array}{r} 2 \\ 4 \\ +3 \\ \hline \end{array}$$

$$\begin{array}{r} 3 \\ 2 \\ +7 \\ \hline \end{array}$$

$$\begin{array}{r} 4 \\ 0 \\ +4 \\ \hline \end{array}$$

3.

$$\begin{array}{r} 5 \\ 2 \\ +3 \\ \hline \end{array}$$

$$\begin{array}{r} 3 \\ 2 \\ +4 \\ \hline \end{array}$$

$$\begin{array}{r} 4 \\ 1 \\ +4 \\ \hline \end{array}$$

$$\begin{array}{r} 2 \\ 5 \\ +3 \\ \hline \end{array}$$

$$\begin{array}{r} 6 \\ 0 \\ +6 \\ \hline \end{array}$$

$$\begin{array}{r} 3 \\ 2 \\ +3 \\ \hline \end{array}$$

Column addition　　　　　　　　　　(one hundred eighty-nine) **189**

Add.

1.

$$
\begin{array}{r} 2 \\ 1 \\ +\ 1 \\ \hline \end{array}
\qquad
\begin{array}{r} 1 \\ 2 \\ +\ 3 \\ \hline \end{array}
\qquad
\begin{array}{r} 2 \\ 4 \\ +\ 3 \\ \hline \end{array}
\qquad
\begin{array}{r} 1 \\ 2 \\ +\ 5 \\ \hline \end{array}
\qquad
\begin{array}{r} 2 \\ 2 \\ +\ 3 \\ \hline \end{array}
$$

2.

$$
\begin{array}{r} 3 \\ 4 \\ +\ 2 \\ \hline \end{array}
\qquad
\begin{array}{r} 6 \\ 3 \\ +\ 2 \\ \hline \end{array}
\qquad
\begin{array}{r} 2 \\ 1 \\ +\ 5 \\ \hline \end{array}
\qquad
\begin{array}{r} 5 \\ 2 \\ +\ 2 \\ \hline \end{array}
\qquad
\begin{array}{r} 2 \\ 3 \\ +\ 5 \\ \hline \end{array}
\qquad
\begin{array}{r} 2 \\ 4 \\ +\ 4 \\ \hline \end{array}
$$

3.

$$
\begin{array}{r} 3 \\ 4 \\ +\ 3 \\ \hline \end{array}
\qquad
\begin{array}{r} 2 \\ 5 \\ +\ 4 \\ \hline \end{array}
\qquad
\begin{array}{r} 5 \\ 2 \\ +\ 4 \\ \hline \end{array}
\qquad
\begin{array}{r} 4 \\ 2 \\ +\ 4 \\ \hline \end{array}
\qquad
\begin{array}{r} 5 \\ 3 \\ +\ 4 \\ \hline \end{array}
\qquad
\begin{array}{r} 3 \\ 2 \\ +\ 3 \\ \hline \end{array}
$$

THINK MATH

How far from Nale to Rale?

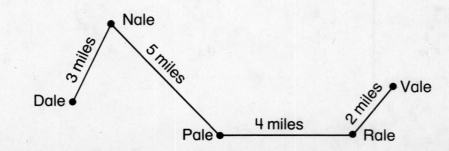

_____ miles

Column addition

QUESTION
DATA
PLAN
ANSWER
CHECK

Name _____

Draw more pictures or mark out some.

1.

Dan has 5 red apples.
Sue has 5 yellow apples.
How many apples are
there in all?

$$\begin{array}{r} 5 \\ + 5 \\ \hline 10 \end{array}$$

____10____ apples

2.

Alan had 8 crackers.
He ate 2.
How many crackers does
he have now?

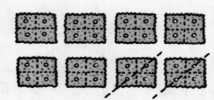

$$\begin{array}{r} 8 \\ - 2 \\ \hline 6 \end{array}$$

____6____ crackers

3.

Vera had 4 lemons.
Sal had 2. Chip had 5.
How many lemons
are there in all?

_____ lemons

4.

Karen had 9 cherries.
She gave away 3.
How many cherries
does she have left?

_____ cherries

Problem solving—short sentence

1. Maria spent 9¢. What did she buy?

2. Jack spent 7¢. What did he buy?

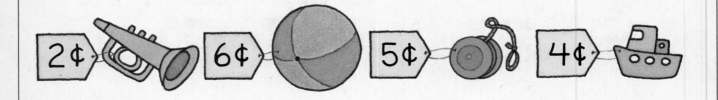

3. Jane spent 12¢. What did she buy?

4. Tom spent 11¢. What did he buy?

Problem solving strategy—guess and check

Name _____

Add.

1.

0	2	1	4	9	7
+5	+1	+3	+0	+1	+2

2.

5	4	1	3	6	2
+5	+4	+1	+3	+6	+2

3.

6	3	4	3	1	6
+5	+2	+5	+4	+2	+5

4.

2	2	4	3	2	3
5	4	3	4	1	2
+4	+4	+5	+2	+3	+4

5. Solve.

Ellen saw 5 rabbits.
2 ran away.
How many rabbits were left?

_____ rabbits

Name _____

CUMULATIVE REVIEW

How many are there?

1.
- ○ 15
- ○ 12
- ○ 13

2. | 4
- ○ 4 tens, 2 ones
- ○ 2 tens, 4 tens
- ○ 1 ten, 4 ones

Finish the row.

3. 46, 47, 48
- ○ 55, 56, 58
- ○ 49, 50, 51
- ○ 46, 47, 48

Count by twos.

4. 4, 6, 8, __?__
- ○ 12
- ○ 10
- ○ 14

What time is it?

5.
- ○ 3:00 o'clock
- ○ 2:00 o'clock
- ○ 4:00 o'clock

6.
- ○ 9:30
- ○ 10:30
- ○ 11:30

How much money is there?

7.
- ○ 5¢
- ○ 8¢
- ○ 7¢

8.
- ○ 20¢
- ○ 15¢
- ○ 10¢

Choose the correct number sentence.

9.
- ○ 6 + 2 = 8
- ○ 5 + 3 = 8
- ○ 7 + 2 = 9

Cumulative review

ANOTHER LOOK

Add.

These are doubles facts.

| 1 + 1 = 2 | 2 + 2 = 4 | 3 + 3 = 6 |

1. 2   5
   +2   +5
   ___   ___

| 4 + 4 = 8 | 5 + 5 = 10 | 6 + 6 = 12 |

2. 4   3
   +5   +4
   ___   ___

The doubles help with these.

3   4   4   5
+3   +3   +4   +4
___   ___   ___   ___
6 (one more) 7   8 (one more) 9

3. 6   7
   +4   +5
   ___   ___

        5   6
       +5   +5
       ___   ___
       10 (one more) 11

4. 6   4
   +6   +8
   ___   ___

5. 4   3
   +7   +3
   ___   ___

6   7   7   8
+4   +4   +5   +4
___   ___   ___   ___
10   11   12   12

6. 4   5
   +4   +7
   ___   ___

ENRICHMENT

Finish the table.

	Ticket Sales			
	Jean	Mike	Ann	In All
Monday	4	3	2	
Tuesday	2		3	8
Wednesday	3	5		12
Thursday	5		3	10
Friday		4	4	11

DIFFERENCES TO 12

How many are there in each part?	Subtract. Find the missing part.

Parts of 6

1.

_5_   _1_

$6 - 1 = \underline{5}$

$6 - 5 = \underline{1}$

2.

_____   _____

$6 - 2 = \underline{\hspace{1cm}}$

$6 - 4 = \underline{\hspace{1cm}}$

3.

_____   _____

$6 - 3 = \underline{\hspace{1cm}}$

4. Subtract.

$$\begin{array}{cccccc} 6 & 6 & 6 & 6 & 6 & 6 \\ -2 & -5 & -1 & -3 & -4 & -0 \\ \end{array}$$

Subtract.

1.

6	4	6	5	3	6
−4	−2	−3	−2	−2	−2

2.

4	6	5	6	6	2
−3	−1	−4	−6	−5	−1

3.

6	5	6	3	6	5
−2	−5	−5	−1	−0	−1

4.

4	6	5	6	6	3
−1	−0	−3	−4	−3	−0

5.

6	5	4	6	6	5
−1	−4	−2	−4	−5	−0

6.

5	6	6	3	5	6
−3	−0	−3	−1	−3	−6

Name _____

How many are there in each part?	Subtract. Find the missing part.
1. 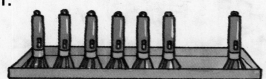 ___6___ ___1___	 Parts of 7 $7 - 1 = \underline{6}$ $7 - 6 = \underline{1}$
2.  _____ _____	$7 - 2 = \underline{}$ $7 - 5 = \underline{}$
3. 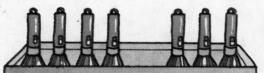 _____ _____	$7 - 3 = \underline{}$ $7 - 4 = \underline{}$

4. Subtract.

$$\begin{array}{cccccc} 7 & 7 & 7 & 7 & 7 & 7 \\ -\,2 & -\,4 & -\,1 & -\,5 & -\,3 & -\,6 \\ \hline \end{array}$$

Subtract.

1.
$$\begin{array}{r} 7 \\ -3 \\ \hline \end{array}$$
$$\begin{array}{r} 6 \\ -4 \\ \hline \end{array}$$
$$\begin{array}{r} 4 \\ -2 \\ \hline \end{array}$$
$$\begin{array}{r} 7 \\ -5 \\ \hline \end{array}$$
$$\begin{array}{r} 5 \\ -1 \\ \hline \end{array}$$
$$\begin{array}{r} 6 \\ -2 \\ \hline \end{array}$$

2.
$$\begin{array}{r} 3 \\ -2 \\ \hline \end{array}$$
$$\begin{array}{r} 7 \\ -0 \\ \hline \end{array}$$
$$\begin{array}{r} 5 \\ -3 \\ \hline \end{array}$$
$$\begin{array}{r} 6 \\ -6 \\ \hline \end{array}$$
$$\begin{array}{r} 2 \\ -1 \\ \hline \end{array}$$
$$\begin{array}{r} 7 \\ -1 \\ \hline \end{array}$$

3.
$$\begin{array}{r} 4 \\ -3 \\ \hline \end{array}$$
$$\begin{array}{r} 6 \\ -3 \\ \hline \end{array}$$
$$\begin{array}{r} 7 \\ -6 \\ \hline \end{array}$$
$$\begin{array}{r} 5 \\ -2 \\ \hline \end{array}$$
$$\begin{array}{r} 7 \\ -7 \\ \hline \end{array}$$
$$\begin{array}{r} 6 \\ -5 \\ \hline \end{array}$$

4.
$$\begin{array}{r} 5 \\ -0 \\ \hline \end{array}$$
$$\begin{array}{r} 7 \\ -2 \\ \hline \end{array}$$
$$\begin{array}{r} 6 \\ -1 \\ \hline \end{array}$$
$$\begin{array}{r} 4 \\ -1 \\ \hline \end{array}$$
$$\begin{array}{r} 7 \\ -4 \\ \hline \end{array}$$
$$\begin{array}{r} 5 \\ -4 \\ \hline \end{array}$$

5.
$$\begin{array}{r} 5 \\ -1 \\ \hline \end{array}$$
$$\begin{array}{r} 7 \\ -3 \\ \hline \end{array}$$
$$\begin{array}{r} 6 \\ -4 \\ \hline \end{array}$$
$$\begin{array}{r} 7 \\ -1 \\ \hline \end{array}$$
$$\begin{array}{r} 5 \\ -4 \\ \hline \end{array}$$
$$\begin{array}{r} 4 \\ -3 \\ \hline \end{array}$$

6.
$$\begin{array}{r} 7 \\ -4 \\ \hline \end{array}$$
$$\begin{array}{r} 6 \\ -2 \\ \hline \end{array}$$
$$\begin{array}{r} 7 \\ -5 \\ \hline \end{array}$$
$$\begin{array}{r} 7 \\ -6 \\ \hline \end{array}$$
$$\begin{array}{r} 6 \\ -3 \\ \hline \end{array}$$
$$\begin{array}{r} 4 \\ -4 \\ \hline \end{array}$$

Name _____

How many are there in each part?	Subtract. Find the missing part.

Parts of 8

1.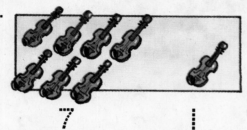

_7_ _1_

$8 - 1 = 7$

$8 - 7 = 1$

2.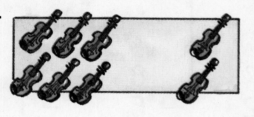

____ ____

$8 - 2 = $ ____

$8 - 6 = $ ____

3.

____ ____

$8 - 3 = $ ____

$8 - 5 = $ ____

4.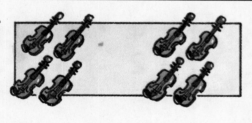

____ ____

$8 - 4 = $ ____

5. Subtract.

$$\begin{array}{cccccc} 8 & 8 & 8 & 8 & 8 & 8 \\ -4 & -2 & -5 & -6 & -7 & -3 \\ \hline \end{array}$$

Subtract.

1.
$$8 - 3$$ $$7 - 5$$ $$5 - 3$$ $$8 - 1$$ $$6 - 3$$ $$7 - 3$$

2.
$$4 - 3$$ $$8 - 6$$ $$6 - 5$$ $$7 - 2$$ $$8 - 5$$ $$6 - 1$$

3.
$$8 - 8$$ $$6 - 4$$ $$8 - 0$$ $$7 - 6$$ $$5 - 2$$ $$8 - 4$$

4.
$$8 - 7$$ $$6 - 2$$ $$7 - 4$$ $$8 - 2$$ $$4 - 2$$ $$7 - 1$$

SKILLKEEPER

Add.

$$3 + 3$$ $$3 + 4$$ $$5 + 5$$ $$6 + 5$$ $$4 + 4$$ $$4 + 5$$

Subtracting from 8

Subtract.

1.
$$
\begin{array}{r} 6 \\ -2 \\ \hline \end{array}
\qquad
\begin{array}{r} 6 \\ -4 \\ \hline \end{array}
\qquad
\begin{array}{r} 7 \\ -4 \\ \hline \end{array}
\qquad
\begin{array}{r} 7 \\ -3 \\ \hline \end{array}
\qquad
\begin{array}{r} 8 \\ -2 \\ \hline \end{array}
\qquad
\begin{array}{r} 8 \\ -6 \\ \hline \end{array}
$$

2.
$$
\begin{array}{r} 6 \\ -1 \\ \hline \end{array}
\qquad
\begin{array}{r} 5 \\ -2 \\ \hline \end{array}
\qquad
\begin{array}{r} 7 \\ -5 \\ \hline \end{array}
\qquad
\begin{array}{r} 6 \\ -3 \\ \hline \end{array}
\qquad
\begin{array}{r} 8 \\ -1 \\ \hline \end{array}
\qquad
\begin{array}{r} 7 \\ -6 \\ \hline \end{array}
$$

3.
$$
\begin{array}{r} 8 \\ -4 \\ \hline \end{array}
\qquad
\begin{array}{r} 6 \\ -0 \\ \hline \end{array}
\qquad
\begin{array}{r} 5 \\ -3 \\ \hline \end{array}
\qquad
\begin{array}{r} 7 \\ -1 \\ \hline \end{array}
\qquad
\begin{array}{r} 6 \\ -5 \\ \hline \end{array}
\qquad
\begin{array}{r} 8 \\ -6 \\ \hline \end{array}
$$

4.
$$
\begin{array}{r} 7 \\ -4 \\ \hline \end{array}
\qquad
\begin{array}{r} 8 \\ -7 \\ \hline \end{array}
\qquad
\begin{array}{r} 6 \\ -2 \\ \hline \end{array}
\qquad
\begin{array}{r} 4 \\ -2 \\ \hline \end{array}
\qquad
\begin{array}{r} 8 \\ -2 \\ \hline \end{array}
\qquad
\begin{array}{r} 7 \\ -3 \\ \hline \end{array}
$$

5.
$$
\begin{array}{r} 7 \\ -2 \\ \hline \end{array}
\qquad
\begin{array}{r} 6 \\ -4 \\ \hline \end{array}
\qquad
\begin{array}{r} 8 \\ -3 \\ \hline \end{array}
\qquad
\begin{array}{r} 7 \\ -4 \\ \hline \end{array}
\qquad
\begin{array}{r} 6 \\ -6 \\ \hline \end{array}
\qquad
\begin{array}{r} 8 \\ -5 \\ \hline \end{array}
$$

Finish each table.

Subtract 4

6	2
8	
5	
7	

Subtract 3

7	
8	
10	
9	

Subtract 5

6	
8	
5	
7	

Subtract 1

9	
7	
10	
8	

Subtract 3

6	
11	
12	
5	

Subtract 2

9	
10	
8	
11	

Practice the facts

How many are there in each part?	Subtract. Find the missing part.

1.

_____ 8 _____   _____ 1 _____

9 − 1 = _____ 8

9 − 8 = _____ 1

Parts of 9

2.

_____   _____

9 − 2 = _____

9 − 7 = _____

3.

_____   _____

9 − 3 = _____

9 − 6 = _____

4.

_____   _____

9 − 4 = _____

9 − 5 = _____

5. Subtract.

$$\begin{array}{cc} 9 \\ -5 \\ \hline \end{array} \qquad \begin{array}{cc} 9 \\ -3 \\ \hline \end{array} \qquad \begin{array}{cc} 9 \\ -7 \\ \hline \end{array} \qquad \begin{array}{cc} 9 \\ -4 \\ \hline \end{array} \qquad \begin{array}{cc} 9 \\ -2 \\ \hline \end{array} \qquad \begin{array}{cc} 9 \\ -6 \\ \hline \end{array}$$

Subtract.

1. $9 - 3$ $8 - 5$ $7 - 5$ $9 - 1$ $6 - 5$ $8 - 3$

2. $5 - 3$ $9 - 6$ $7 - 4$ $8 - 4$ $9 - 0$ $6 - 3$

3. $9 - 7$ $7 - 3$ $9 - 8$ $8 - 6$ $6 - 4$ $9 - 5$

4. $9 - 4$ $8 - 2$ $9 - 2$ $7 - 2$ $9 - 9$ $6 - 2$

THINK MATH

Rita is 2 years younger than Ed.
Ed is 9. How old is Rita?

_____ years old

Name _____

How many are there in each part?	Subtract. Find the missing part.

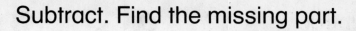

1.

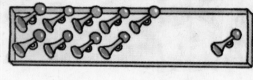

___9___ ___1___

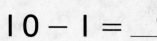

$10 - 1 = \underline{9}$

$10 - 9 = \underline{1}$

2.

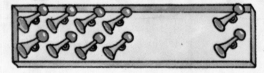

_____ _____

$10 - 2 = \underline{}$

$10 - 8 = \underline{}$

3.

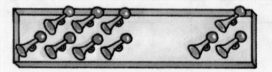

_____ _____

$10 - 3 = \underline{}$

$10 - 7 = \underline{}$

4.

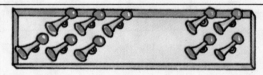

_____ _____

$10 - 4 = \underline{}$

$10 - 6 = \underline{}$

5.

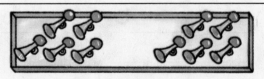

_____ _____

$10 - 5 = \underline{}$

6. Subtract.

$$\begin{array}{cc} 10 \\ -\ 3 \\ \hline \end{array} \qquad \begin{array}{cc} 10 \\ -\ 5 \\ \hline \end{array} \qquad \begin{array}{cc} 10 \\ -\ 8 \\ \hline \end{array} \qquad \begin{array}{cc} 10 \\ -\ 6 \\ \hline \end{array} \qquad \begin{array}{cc} 10 \\ -\ 4 \\ \hline \end{array} \qquad \begin{array}{cc} 10 \\ -\ 7 \\ \hline \end{array}$$

Subtract.

1.

10
− 3
_____

8
− 5
_____

10
− 7
_____

9
− 4
_____

10
− 4
_____

7
− 4
_____

2.

9
− 7
_____

10
− 6
_____

6
− 5
_____

9
− 2
_____

10
− 1
_____

8
− 6
_____

3.

10
− 8
_____

7
− 6
_____

9
− 3
_____

7
− 5
_____

8
− 4
_____

10
− 9
_____

4.

9
− 6
_____

6
− 4
_____

10
− 2
_____

8
− 7
_____

10
− 5
_____

9
− 8
_____

5.

10
− 4
_____

7
− 3
_____

8
− 4
_____

10
− 6
_____

7
− 5
_____

9
− 3
_____

6.

8
− 2
_____

10
− 7
_____

9
− 4
_____

10
− 4
_____

8
− 5
_____

8
− 1
_____

Subtracting from 10

Name _____

 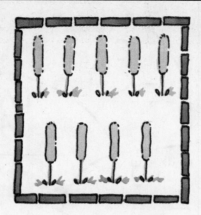 

Subtract.

1.
$$\begin{array}{r} 10 \\ -\ 3 \\ \hline \end{array}$$
$$\begin{array}{r} 10 \\ -\ 7 \\ \hline \end{array}$$
$$\begin{array}{r} 9 \\ -4 \\ \hline \end{array}$$
$$\begin{array}{r} 9 \\ -5 \\ \hline \end{array}$$
$$\begin{array}{r} 10 \\ -\ 6 \\ \hline \end{array}$$
$$\begin{array}{r} 10 \\ -\ 4 \\ \hline \end{array}$$

2.
$$\begin{array}{r} 9 \\ -3 \\ \hline \end{array}$$
$$\begin{array}{r} 8 \\ -4 \\ \hline \end{array}$$
$$\begin{array}{r} 10 \\ -\ 3 \\ \hline \end{array}$$
$$\begin{array}{r} 7 \\ -5 \\ \hline \end{array}$$
$$\begin{array}{r} 9 \\ -5 \\ \hline \end{array}$$
$$\begin{array}{r} 10 \\ -\ 7 \\ \hline \end{array}$$

3.
$$\begin{array}{r} 6 \\ -4 \\ \hline \end{array}$$
$$\begin{array}{r} 10 \\ -\ 5 \\ \hline \end{array}$$
$$\begin{array}{r} 8 \\ -7 \\ \hline \end{array}$$
$$\begin{array}{r} 10 \\ -\ 9 \\ \hline \end{array}$$
$$\begin{array}{r} 9 \\ -7 \\ \hline \end{array}$$
$$\begin{array}{r} 8 \\ -6 \\ \hline \end{array}$$

4.
$$\begin{array}{r} 10 \\ -\ 6 \\ \hline \end{array}$$
$$\begin{array}{r} 7 \\ -4 \\ \hline \end{array}$$
$$\begin{array}{r} 9 \\ -4 \\ \hline \end{array}$$
$$\begin{array}{r} 10 \\ -\ 2 \\ \hline \end{array}$$
$$\begin{array}{r} 8 \\ -5 \\ \hline \end{array}$$
$$\begin{array}{r} 9 \\ -2 \\ \hline \end{array}$$

5.
$$\begin{array}{r} 7 \\ -3 \\ \hline \end{array}$$
$$\begin{array}{r} 10 \\ -\ 4 \\ \hline \end{array}$$
$$\begin{array}{r} 8 \\ -3 \\ \hline \end{array}$$
$$\begin{array}{r} 9 \\ -6 \\ \hline \end{array}$$
$$\begin{array}{r} 10 \\ -\ 8 \\ \hline \end{array}$$
$$\begin{array}{r} 6 \\ -3 \\ \hline \end{array}$$

Practice the facts

Color.

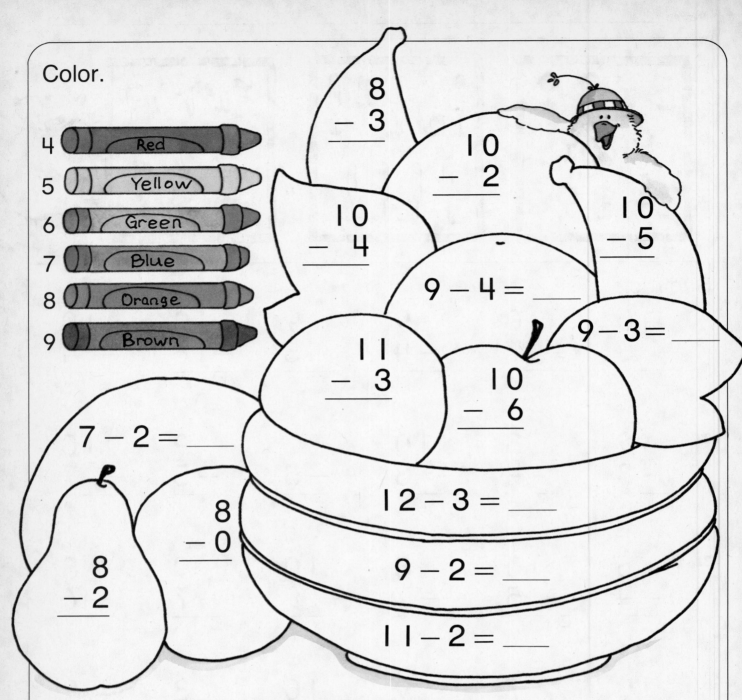

4 [Red]
5 [Yellow]
6 [Green]
7 [Blue]
8 [Orange]
9 [Brown]

$$8 - 3$$

$$10 - 2$$

$$10 - 4$$

$$10 - 5$$

$$9 - 4 = \underline{}$$

$$9 - 3 = \underline{}$$

$$11 - 3$$

$$10 - 6$$

$$7 - 2 = \underline{}$$

$$8 - 0$$

$$8 - 2$$

$$12 - 3 = \underline{}$$

$$9 - 2 = \underline{}$$

$$11 - 2 = \underline{}$$

SKILLKEEPER

How many are there?

37

____ tens

____ ones

84

____ tens

____ ones

65

____ tens

____ ones

Practice the facts

Name _____

Subtract.

1.

9	7	10	8
− 6	− 4	− 8	− 6

2.

8	10	7	9	10	8
− 7	− 5	− 5	− 4	− 3	− 4

3.

10	8	9	10	6	7
− 6	− 3	− 5	− 9	− 4	− 3

4.

8	10	7	9	10	6
− 5	− 7	− 6	− 8	− 4	− 3

5.

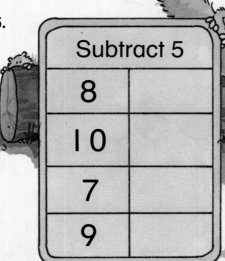
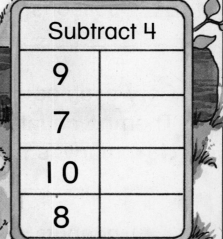

Subtract 5	
8	
10	
7	
9	

Subtract 3	
9	
12	
8	
10	

Subtract 4	
9	
7	
10	
8	

Solve.
Draw more pictures or mark out some.

6
+ 5

11

1. Lana saw 6 cars.
Then she saw 5 more.
How many did she see in all?

_____ cars

2. Rafer has 9 keys.
He lost 4 keys.
How many does he have left?

_____ keys

3. Barb has 10 balloons.
She gave away 6 of them.
How many balloons
does she have now?

_____ balloons

4. Cory counted 5 peanuts.
Then he counted 4 more.
How many is this in all?

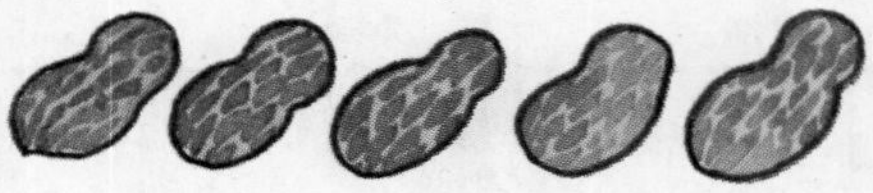

_____ peanuts

Problem solving—short sentence

Name _____

How many are there in each part?	Subtract. Find the missing part.

1.

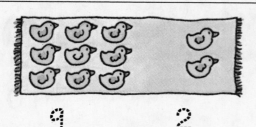

____9____   ____2____

Parts of 11

$11 - 2 = \underline{\quad 9 \quad}$

$11 - 9 = \underline{\quad 2 \quad}$

2.

_____   _____

$11 - 3 = \underline{\quad\quad}$

$11 - 8 = \underline{\quad\quad}$

3.

_____   _____

$11 - 4 = \underline{\quad\quad}$

$11 - 7 = \underline{\quad\quad}$

4.

_____   _____

$11 - 5 = \underline{\quad\quad}$

$11 - 6 = \underline{\quad\quad}$

5. Subtract.

$$\begin{array}{cccccc} 11 & 11 & 11 & 11 & 11 & 11 \\ -\,5 & -\,9 & -\,6 & -\,8 & -\,7 & -\,4 \\ \hline \end{array}$$

Subtracting from 11   (two hundred thirteen) **213**

Subtract.

1.
11	10	8	11	9	10
− 5	− 5	− 5	− 3	− 5	− 3

2.
7	11	9	8	10	11
− 5	− 7	− 6	− 6	− 8	− 8

3.
11	9	11	10	8	10
− 9	− 7	− 2	− 9	− 4	− 7

4.
7	11	10	11	9	10
− 4	− 6	− 4	− 4	− 4	− 6

THINK MATH

3 of the ducks did not run away.
How many ran away?

_____ ducks

Name _____

How many are there in each part?	Subtract. Find the missing part.

1.

_9_   _3_

$12 - 3 =$ _9_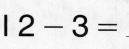

$12 - 9 =$ _3_

2.

_____   _____

$12 - 4 =$ _____

$12 - 8 =$ _____

3.

_____   _____

$12 - 5 =$ _____

$12 - 7 =$ _____

4.

_____   _____

$12 - 6 =$ _____

5. Subtract.

$$\begin{array}{cccccc} 12 & 12 & 12 & 12 & 12 & 12 \\ -\ 5 & -\ 7 & -\ 9 & -\ 4 & -\ 8 & -\ 6 \\ \hline \end{array}$$

Subtract.

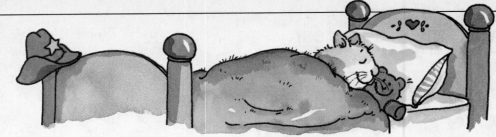

1.
$$12 \atop -\,7$$
$$9 \atop -\,6$$
$$11 \atop -\,7$$
$$12 \atop -\,5$$
$$8 \atop -\,5$$
$$10 \atop -\,7$$

2.
$$7 \atop -\,5$$
$$11 \atop -\,5$$
$$9 \atop -\,5$$
$$10 \atop -\,6$$
$$12 \atop -\,9$$
$$11 \atop -\,9$$

3.
$$12 \atop -\,3$$
$$10 \atop -\,5$$
$$11 \atop -\,8$$
$$12 \atop -\,4$$
$$9 \atop -\,7$$
$$10 \atop -\,4$$

4.
$$8 \atop -\,6$$
$$12 \atop -\,6$$
$$11 \atop -\,6$$
$$10 \atop -\,8$$
$$11 \atop -\,4$$
$$12 \atop -\,8$$

SKILLKEEPER

Write the times.

_____ : _____

_____ : _____

_____ : _____

Subtract.

1.
$$10 - 7 \qquad 12 - 5 \qquad 8 - 5 \qquad 11 - 7$$

2.
$$11 - 6 \qquad 7 - 4 \qquad 10 - 5 \qquad 12 - 7 \qquad 9 - 6 \qquad 11 - 4$$

3.
$$10 - 6 \qquad 12 - 6 \qquad 8 - 6 \qquad 11 - 9 \qquad 12 - 4 \qquad 7 - 5$$

4.
$$11 - 8 \qquad 9 - 7 \qquad 12 - 9 \qquad 10 - 8 \qquad 6 - 4 \qquad 11 - 5$$

5.

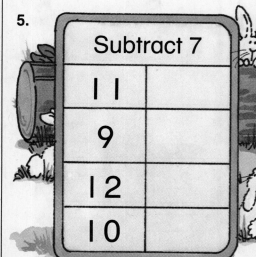
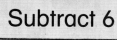
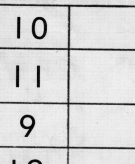

Subtract 7	
11	
9	
12	
10	

Subtract 6	
10	
11	
9	
12	

Subtract 8	
12	
9	
10	
11	

Practice the facts

Name _____

Subtract. Color.

3   Orange
4   Blue
5   Yellow
6   Red

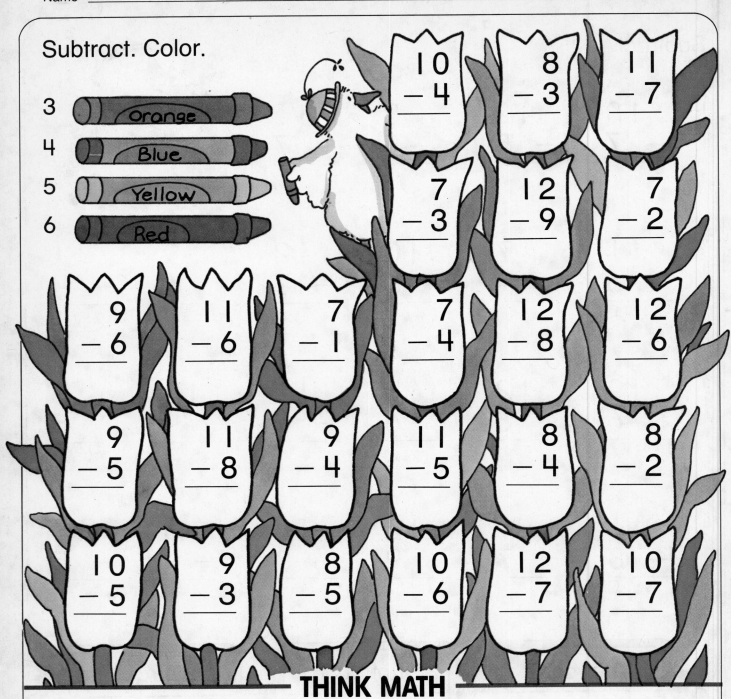

```
 10      8     11
- 4     -3     -7
____    ____   ____

  7     12      7
- 3     -9     -2
____    ____   ____

  9     11      7     12     12
- 6     -6     -4     -8     -6
____    ____   ____   ____   ____
```

```
  9     11      9     11      8      8
- 5     -8     -4     -5     -4     -2
____    ____   ____   ____   ____   ____
```

```
 10      9      8     10     12     10
- 5     -3     -5     -6     -7     -7
____    ____   ____   ____   ____   ____
```

THINK MATH

Jenny bought 5 toy cars.
Ring what she bought.

4 Toy Cars   2 Toy Cars   3 Toy Cars

Practice the facts

Name _____

Add or subtract.

1.

$$7 + 4$$
$$5 + 4$$
$$8 + 4$$
$$3 + 4$$
$$3 + 7$$
$$3 + 5$$

2.

$$10 - 8$$
$$12 - 6$$
$$8 - 2$$
$$9 - 4$$
$$11 - 4$$
$$7 - 3$$

3.

$$6 + 2$$
$$7 - 5$$
$$5 + 7$$
$$12 - 8$$
$$10 - 5$$
$$8 + 2$$

4.

$$9 - 6$$
$$7 + 2$$
$$11 - 6$$
$$2 + 5$$
$$3 + 8$$
$$8 - 5$$

5.

$$10 - 2$$
$$8 - 4$$
$$9 - 9$$
$$12 - 7$$
$$10 - 6$$
$$6 - 2$$

6.

$$7 - 0$$
$$5 - 3$$
$$12 - 9$$
$$11 - 4$$
$$9 - 5$$
$$8 - 3$$

Practice the facts

Solve.

1. Mary had 11¢.

She bought a .

How much does she have left?

11¢
− 4¢
────
7¢

___7___ ¢

2. Jim bought an

and a .

How much is it for both?

_____ ¢

3. Pam bought a

and a .

How much did she spend?

_____ ¢

4. Ann has 10¢.

She bought a .

How much does she have left?

_____ ¢

5. Ted bought a

and an .

How much is it for both?

_____ ¢

6. Joe has 12¢.

He bought a .

How much does he have left?

_____ ¢

Problem solving—using data from a price tag

Ring names for the number.

1.  **7** (3+4) 5+3 (2+5) 3+3

2.  **9** 4+4 5+4 2+7 6+2 3+6

3. **6** 10−4 9−3 11−2 10−5 12−6

4. **11** 5+5 7+5 8+3 4+7 5+6

5. **5** 12−7 11−4 10−5 9−4 11−7

6.  **12** 6+4 4+8 3+9 2+7 7+5

7.  **8** 4+4 1+9 3+5 6+2 2+9

8.  **10** 8+2 3+7 6+3 5+5 7+2

Solve. Draw more pictures or mark out some.

1. 11 bees were on a flower.
5 flew away.
How many bees were left?

_____6_____ bees

$$\begin{array}{r} 11 \\ -5 \\ \hline 6 \end{array}$$

2. 7 ladybugs were on a rock.
5 ladybugs were on the grass.
How many is this in all?

_____ ladybugs

3. 4 beetles were green.
5 beetles were black.
How many beetles is this in all?

_____ beetles

4. 12 fireflies were in the yard.
4 flew away.
How many were left?

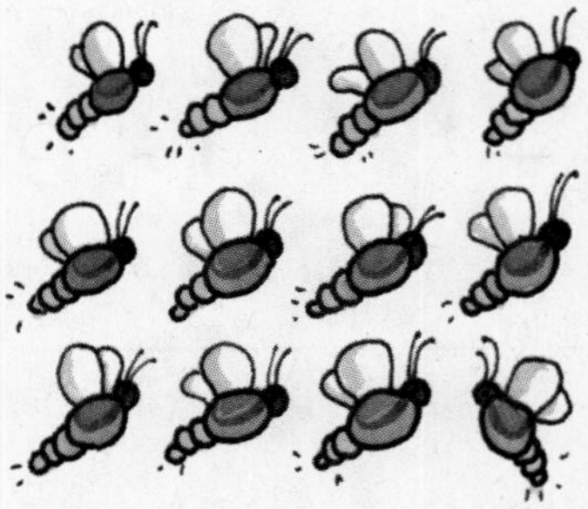

_____ fireflies

Problem solving—short sentence

Name _____

CHAPTER REVIEW/TEST

Subtract.

1.
$$\begin{array}{r} 9 \\ -5 \\ \hline \end{array} \qquad \begin{array}{r} 12 \\ -7 \\ \hline \end{array} \qquad \begin{array}{r} 10 \\ -8 \\ \hline \end{array} \qquad \begin{array}{r} 11 \\ -5 \\ \hline \end{array} \qquad \begin{array}{r} 7 \\ -4 \\ \hline \end{array} \qquad \begin{array}{r} 8 \\ -5 \\ \hline \end{array}$$

2.
$$\begin{array}{r} 10 \\ -5 \\ \hline \end{array} \qquad \begin{array}{r} 6 \\ -4 \\ \hline \end{array} \qquad \begin{array}{r} 12 \\ -8 \\ \hline \end{array} \qquad \begin{array}{r} 8 \\ -6 \\ \hline \end{array} \qquad \begin{array}{r} 9 \\ -6 \\ \hline \end{array} \qquad \begin{array}{r} 11 \\ -7 \\ \hline \end{array}$$

3.
$$\begin{array}{r} 12 \\ -5 \\ \hline \end{array} \qquad \begin{array}{r} 7 \\ -5 \\ \hline \end{array} \qquad \begin{array}{r} 10 \\ -7 \\ \hline \end{array} \qquad \begin{array}{r} 9 \\ -4 \\ \hline \end{array} \qquad \begin{array}{r} 11 \\ -4 \\ \hline \end{array} \qquad \begin{array}{r} 10 \\ -6 \\ \hline \end{array}$$

4.
$$\begin{array}{r} 9 \\ -7 \\ \hline \end{array} \qquad \begin{array}{r} 12 \\ -9 \\ \hline \end{array} \qquad \begin{array}{r} 10 \\ -4 \\ \hline \end{array} \qquad \begin{array}{r} 11 \\ -6 \\ \hline \end{array} \qquad \begin{array}{r} 8 \\ -4 \\ \hline \end{array} \qquad \begin{array}{r} 12 \\ -6 \\ \hline \end{array}$$

5. Solve. Draw more pictures or mark out some.

11 birds were on a rock.
5 flew away.
How many birds were left?

_____ birds

CUMULATIVE REVIEW

Give the times.

1.
- ○ 3:00
- ○ 4:00
- ○ 5:00

2.
- ○ 2:30
- ○ 6:30
- ○ 1:30

Count the money.

3.
- ○ 12¢
- ○ 14¢
- ○ 16¢

4.
- ○ 40¢
- ○ 35¢
- ○ 31¢

Add.

5.
$$\begin{array}{r} 5 \\ +\,4 \\ \hline \end{array}$$
- ○ 7
- ○ 8
- ○ 9

6.
$$\begin{array}{r} 6 \\ +\,6 \\ \hline \end{array}$$
- ○ 10
- ○ 12
- ○ 14

7.
$$\begin{array}{r} 8 \\ +\,4 \\ \hline \end{array}$$
- ○ 11
- ○ 12
- ○ 13

8.
$$\begin{array}{r} 5 \\ 2 \\ +\,3 \\ \hline \end{array}$$
- ○ 10
- ○ 8
- ○ 9

9. Draw or mark out to solve.

Vince saw 5 butterflies.
Then he saw 6 more.
How many butterflies
did Vince see?

- ○ 9
- ○ 10
- ○ 11

ANOTHER LOOK

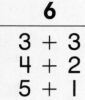

6	**7**
3 + 3	4 + 3
4 + 2	5 + 2
5 + 1	6 + 1

8	**9**
4 + 4	5 + 4
5 + 3	6 + 3
6 + 2	7 + 2
7 + 1	8 + 1

10	**11**
5 + 5	6 + 5
6 + 4	7 + 4
7 + 3	8 + 3
8 + 2	9 + 2
9 + 1	

12
6 + 6
7 + 5
8 + 4
9 + 3

Subtract.

1.
$$\begin{array}{r} 9 \\ -6 \\ \hline \end{array} \qquad \begin{array}{r} 11 \\ -6 \\ \hline \end{array} \qquad \begin{array}{r} 10 \\ -2 \\ \hline \end{array}$$

2.
$$\begin{array}{r} 7 \\ -5 \\ \hline \end{array} \qquad \begin{array}{r} 12 \\ -6 \\ \hline \end{array} \qquad \begin{array}{r} 8 \\ -4 \\ \hline \end{array}$$

3.
$$\begin{array}{r} 11 \\ -4 \\ \hline \end{array} \qquad \begin{array}{r} 9 \\ -4 \\ \hline \end{array} \qquad \begin{array}{r} 10 \\ -4 \\ \hline \end{array}$$

4.
$$\begin{array}{r} 12 \\ -5 \\ \hline \end{array} \qquad \begin{array}{r} 8 \\ -1 \\ \hline \end{array} \qquad \begin{array}{r} 9 \\ -8 \\ \hline \end{array}$$

5.
$$\begin{array}{r} 6 \\ -2 \\ \hline \end{array} \qquad \begin{array}{r} 10 \\ -9 \\ \hline \end{array} \qquad \begin{array}{r} 11 \\ -2 \\ \hline \end{array}$$

6.
$$\begin{array}{r} 10 \\ -5 \\ \hline \end{array} \qquad \begin{array}{r} 8 \\ -6 \\ \hline \end{array} \qquad \begin{array}{r} 12 \\ -8 \\ \hline \end{array}$$

7.
$$\begin{array}{r} 7 \\ -0 \\ \hline \end{array} \qquad \begin{array}{r} 11 \\ -8 \\ \hline \end{array} \qquad \begin{array}{r} 10 \\ -7 \\ \hline \end{array}$$

Name _____

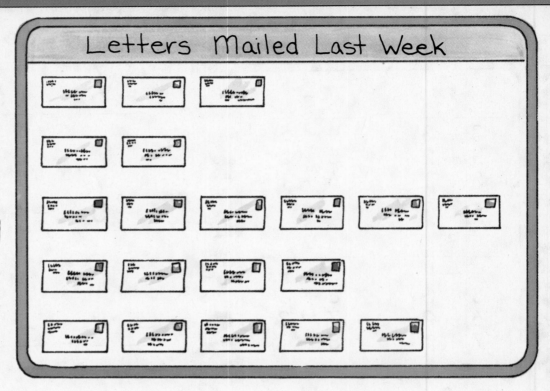

Letters Mailed Last Week

Monday

Tuesday

Wednesday

Thursday

Friday

Each [✉] means 2 letters.

How many letters were mailed?

1. Monday ____6____

2. Tuesday _____

3. Wednesday _____

4. Thursday _____

5. Friday _____

Enrichment—graphing

GEOMETRY AND GRAPHING

Match.

sphere

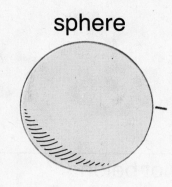

cube

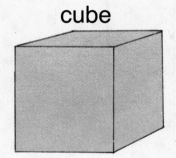

cylinder

cone

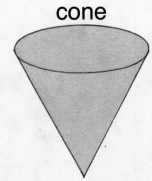

Space figures

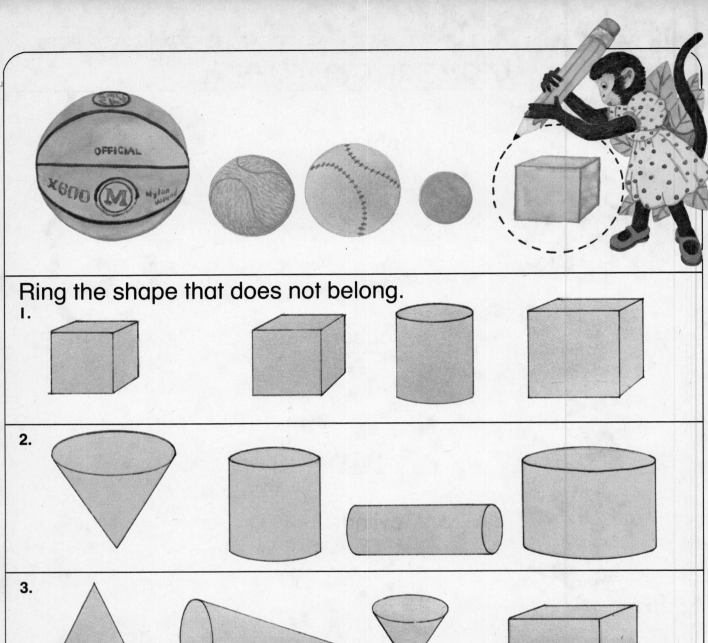

Ring the shape that does not belong.

1.

2.

3.

THINK MATH

Ring Jo's dog.
She is standing.
She has spots.

Space figures

Match.

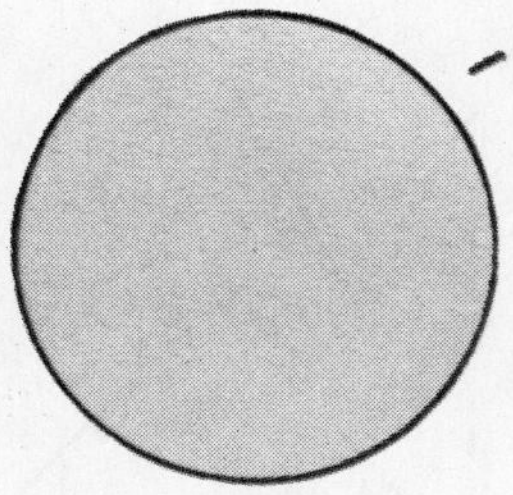

circle

square

TOYS

A B

Plane shapes—circles and squares

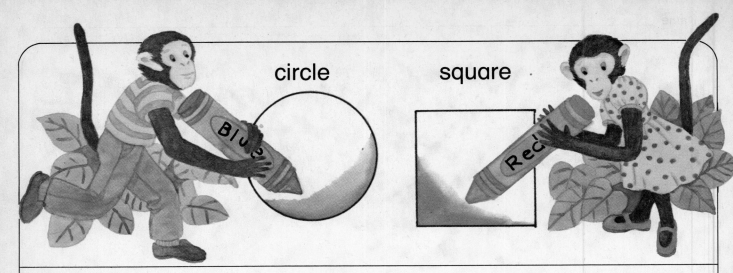

circle　　　square

Color.

Add.

$$
\begin{array}{r} 5 \\ +2 \\ \hline \end{array}
\qquad
\begin{array}{r} 4 \\ +3 \\ \hline \end{array}
\qquad
\begin{array}{r} 8 \\ +2 \\ \hline \end{array}
\qquad
\begin{array}{r} 1 \\ +6 \\ \hline \end{array}
\qquad
\begin{array}{r} 2 \\ +9 \\ \hline \end{array}
\qquad
\begin{array}{r} 3 \\ +8 \\ \hline \end{array}
$$

　　　　　　　　　Plane shapes—circles and squares

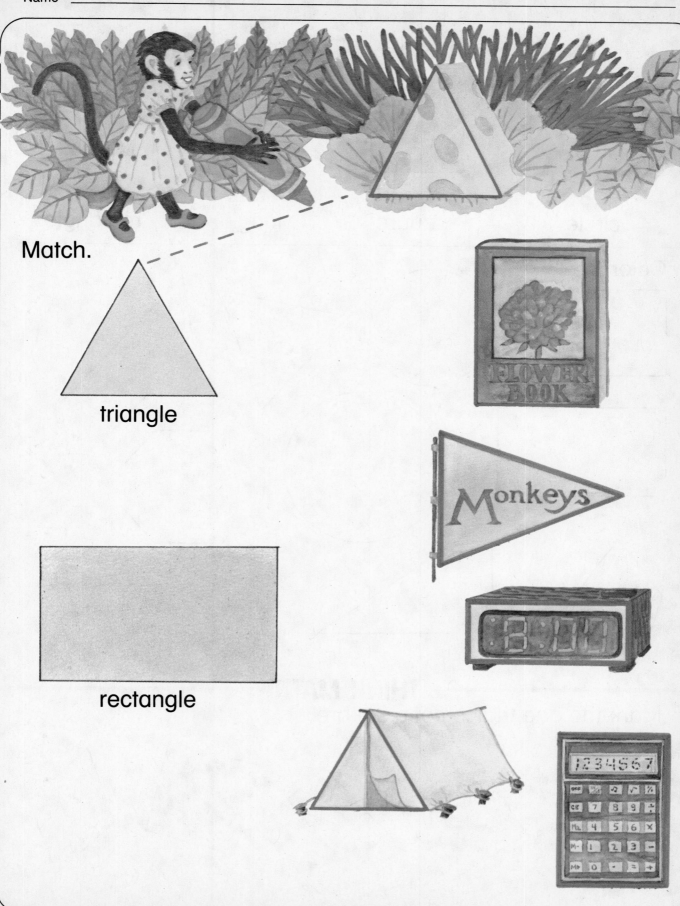

Match.

triangle

rectangle

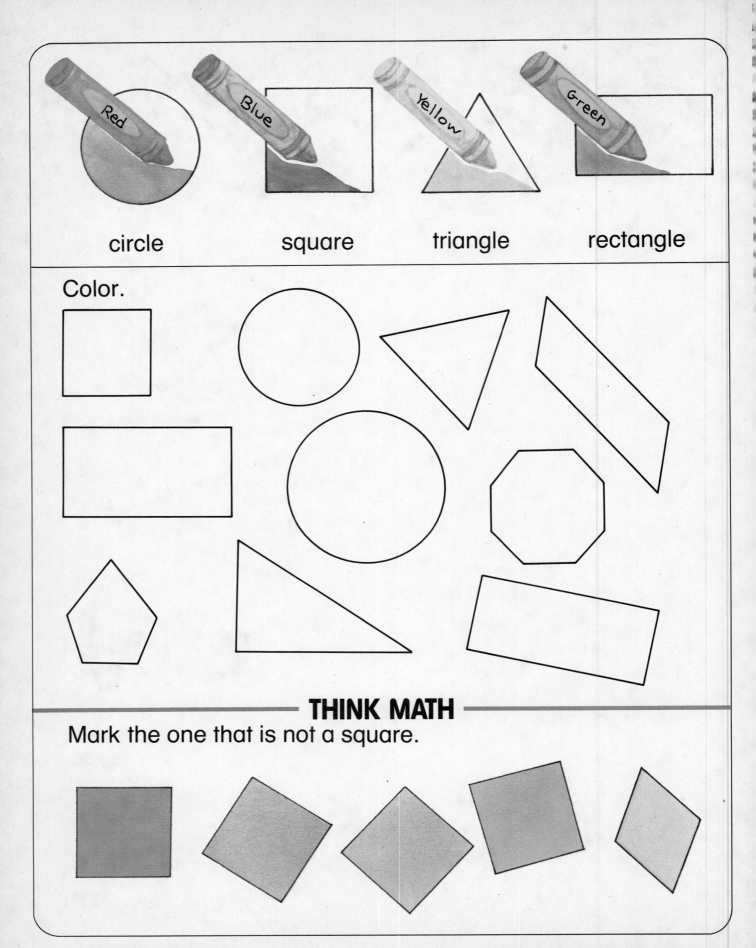

circle   square   triangle   rectangle

Color.

THINK MATH

Mark the one that is not a square.

Recognizing circles, squares, triangles, and rectangles

Name _____

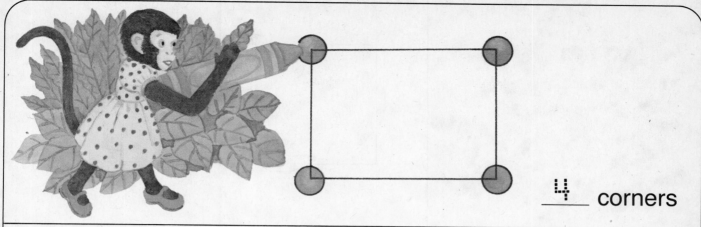

_4_ corners

Color the ◯ on each corner.
How many corners are there?

1.

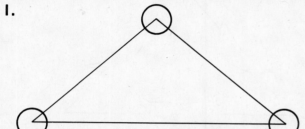

_____ corners

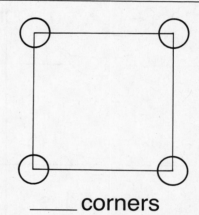

_____ corners

2.

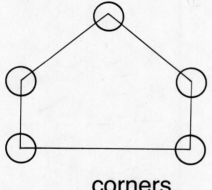

_____ corners

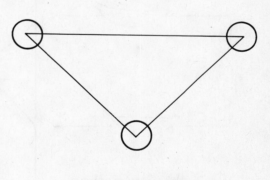

_____ corners

3.

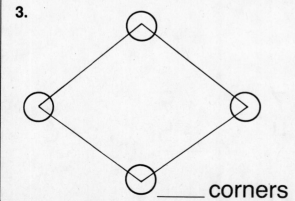

_____ corners

_____ corners

Counting corners

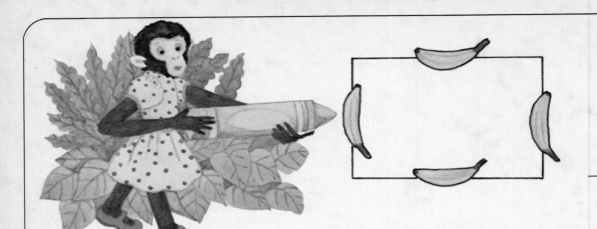

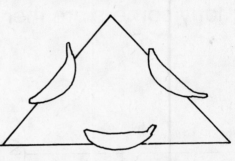

_____4 sides

Color the  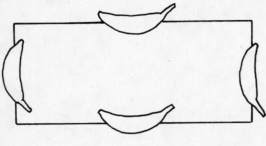 on each side. How many sides are there?

1.

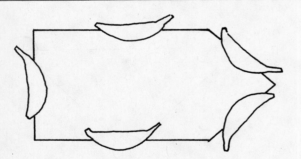

_____ sides   _____ sides

2.

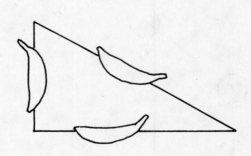

_____ sides   _____ sides

SKILLKEEPER

Subtract.

$$
\begin{array}{cccccc}
8 & 7 & 9 & 7 & 9 & 8 \\
-3 & -1 & -2 & -4 & -5 & -6 \\
\hline
\end{array}
$$

Counting sides

Name _____

Copy each shape.

1.

rectangle

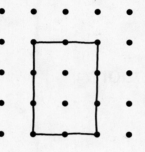

2.

triangle

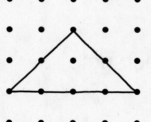

3.

square

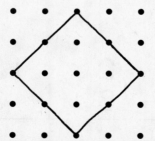

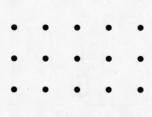

Copying shapes

rectangle

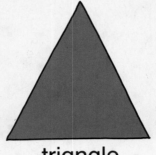
triangle

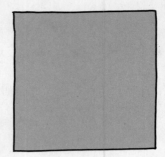
square

Draw each shape.

1.

rectangle

2.

square

3.

triangle

4.

rectangle

SKILLKEEPER

Subtract.

$$
\begin{array}{r} 11 \\ -\ 4 \\ \hline \end{array}
\qquad
\begin{array}{r} 11 \\ -\ 8 \\ \hline \end{array}
\qquad
\begin{array}{r} 11 \\ -\ 6 \\ \hline \end{array}
\qquad
\begin{array}{r} 12 \\ -\ 8 \\ \hline \end{array}
\qquad
\begin{array}{r} 12 \\ -\ 3 \\ \hline \end{array}
\qquad
\begin{array}{r} 12 \\ -\ 7 \\ \hline \end{array}
$$

Drawing shapes

Name _____

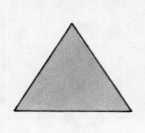 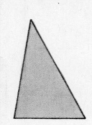 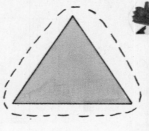 

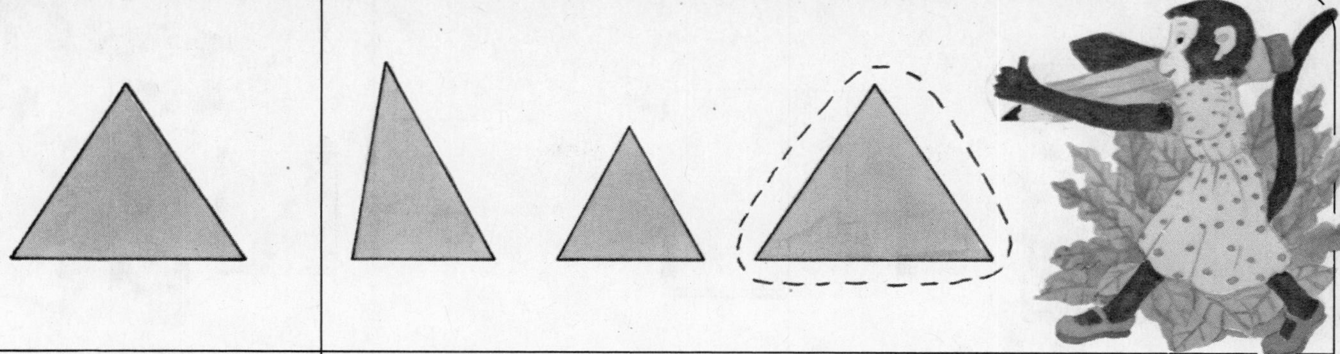

1. Ring the picture that is the same size and shape as the first.

2.

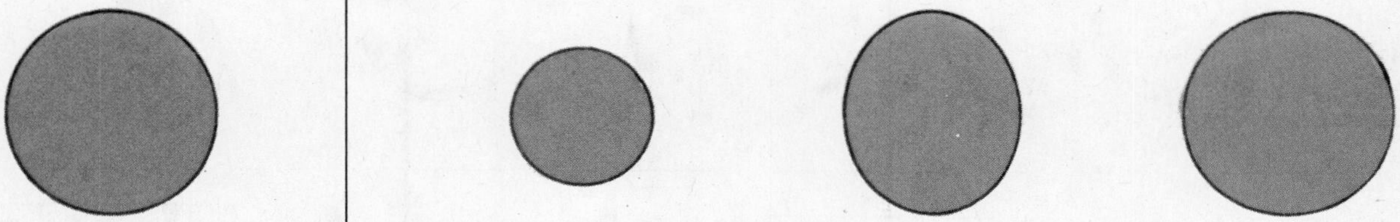

3.

4.

5.

Congruence—same size and shape

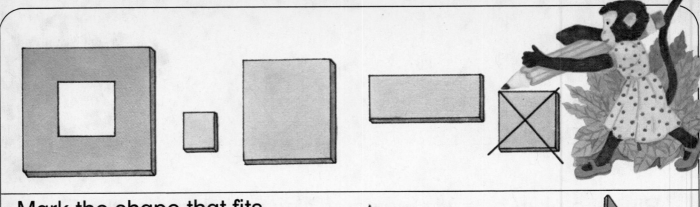

Mark the shape that fits.

1.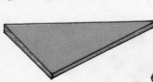

2.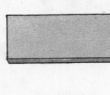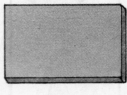

3.

4.

SKILLKEEPER

Add or subtract.

$$\begin{array}{r} 8 \\ +4 \\ \hline \end{array} \qquad \begin{array}{r} 11 \\ -5 \\ \hline \end{array} \qquad \begin{array}{r} 9 \\ +3 \\ \hline \end{array} \qquad \begin{array}{r} 12 \\ -6 \\ \hline \end{array} \qquad \begin{array}{r} 6 \\ +4 \\ \hline \end{array} \qquad \begin{array}{r} 11 \\ -7 \\ \hline \end{array}$$

Congruence—same size and shape

Name _____

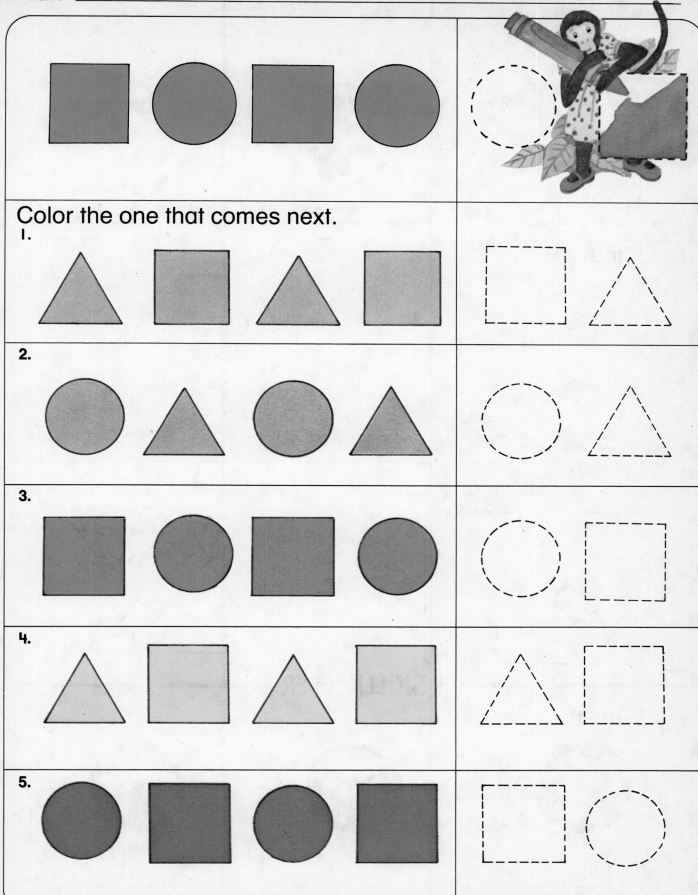

Color the one that comes next.

1.

2.

3.

4.

5.

Shape patterns

(two hundred thirty-nine)   **239**

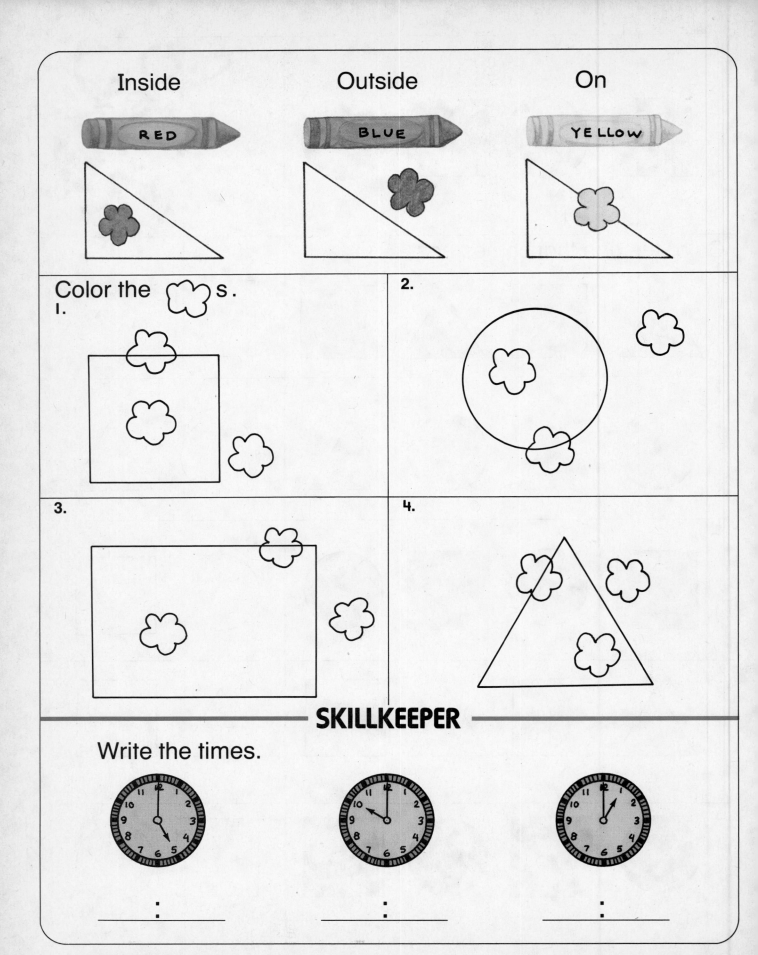

Inside   Outside   On

RED   BLUE   YELLOW

Color the 🌸 s.

1.

2.

3.

4.

SKILLKEEPER

Write the times.

_____ : _____   _____ : _____   _____ : _____

     Inside, outside, on

Name _____

Color a [ ] for each tally mark.

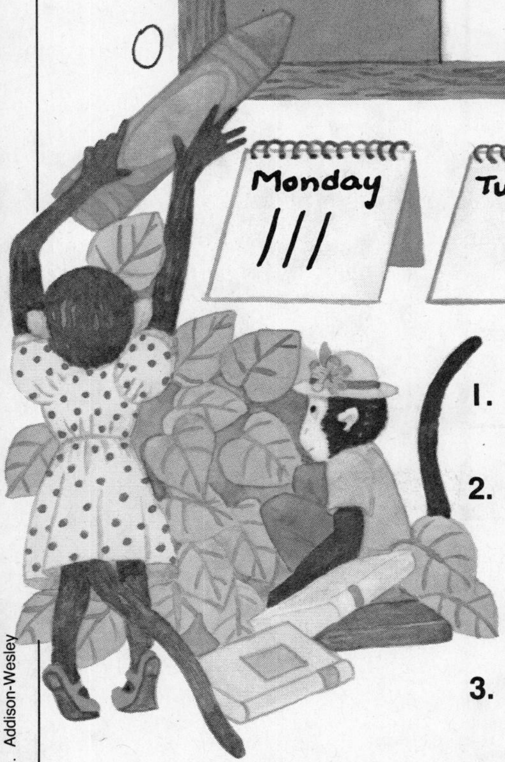

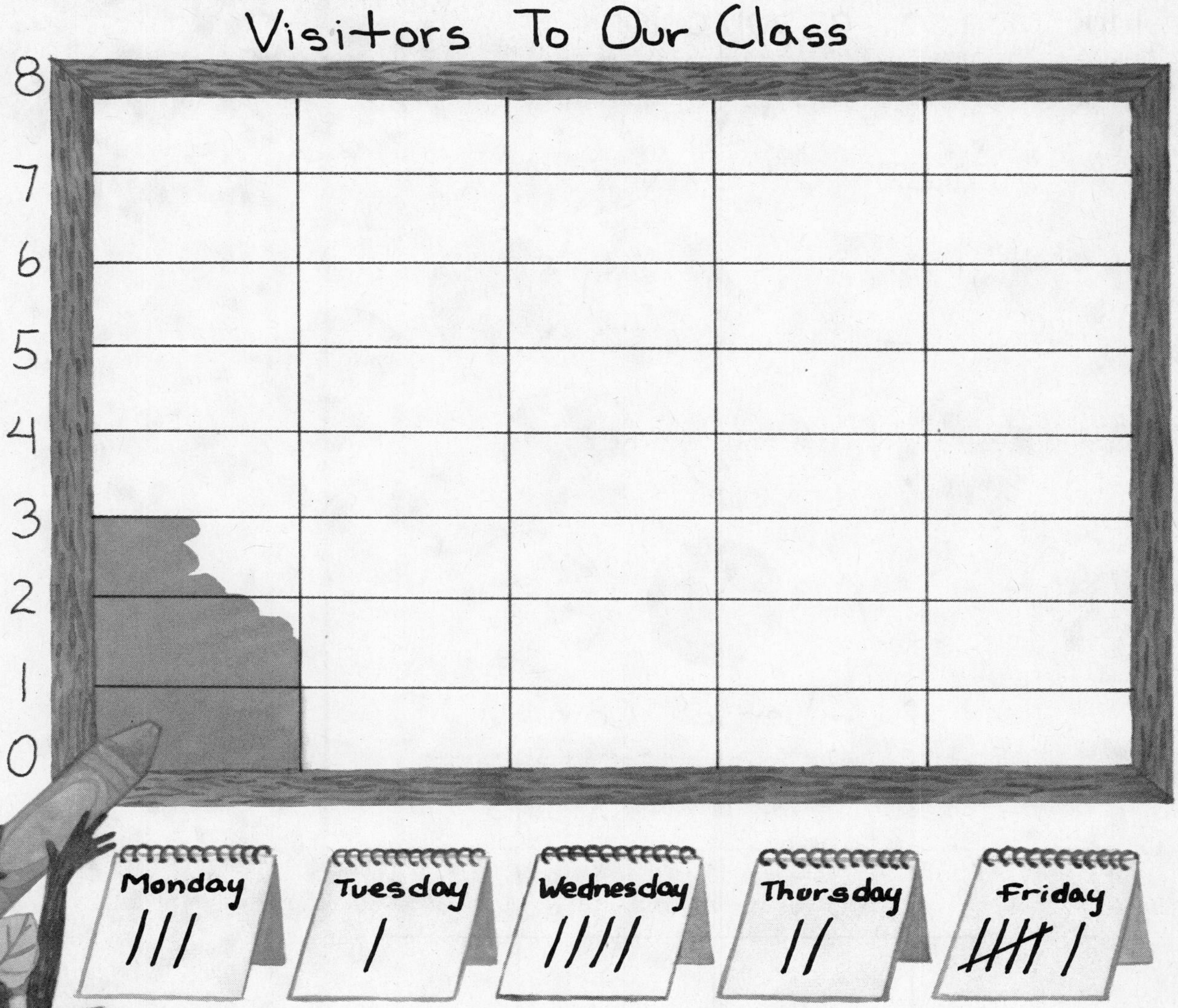

Visitors To Our Class

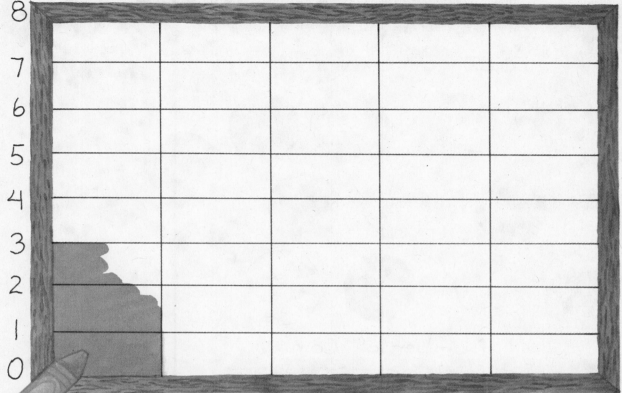

8
7
6
5
4
3
2
1
0

Monday | Tuesday | Wednesday | Thursday | Friday
/// | / | //// | // | ℍℍ I

1. How many visited on Monday? ____

2. How many visited on Wednesday? ____

3. Ring the day with the most visitors.

Monday   Tuesday   Wednesday

Thursday   Friday

Bar graph—counting tallies

Color a [ ] for each coin.
Mark each coin as you color.

Number of Coins

6
5
4
3
2
1
0

How many coins are there in all? _____

Bar graph—recognizing and counting coins

1. **Color each picture.**

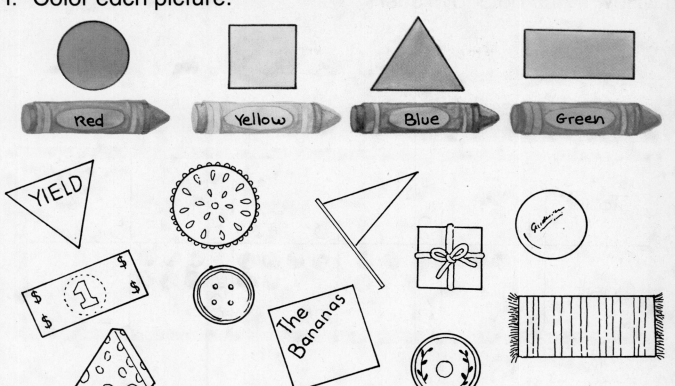

2. **Color a** ▢ **for each picture above.**

Number of Shapes

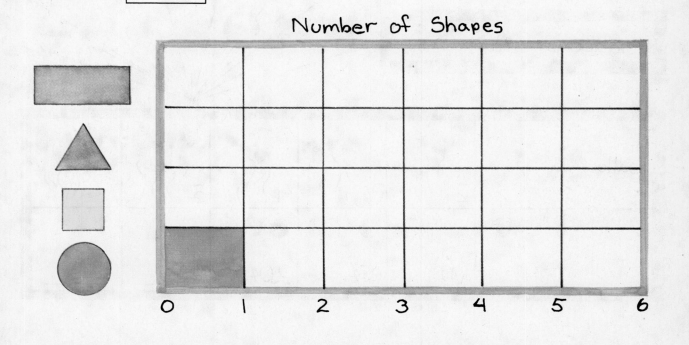

Bar graph—classifying shapes

1. How much do 5 toys cost?

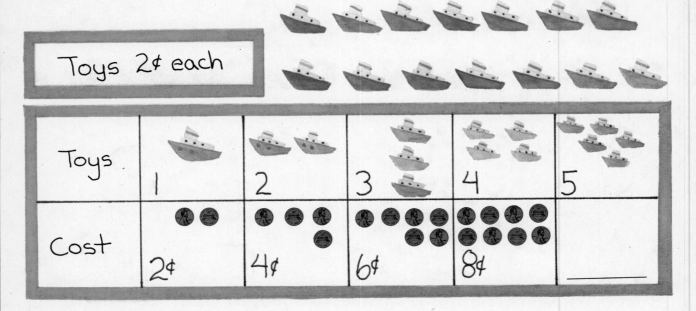

Toys 2¢ each

Toys	1	2	3	4	5
Cost	2¢	4¢	6¢	8¢	

5 toys cost __10¢__ .

2. How much do 6 balloons cost?

Balloons 5¢ each

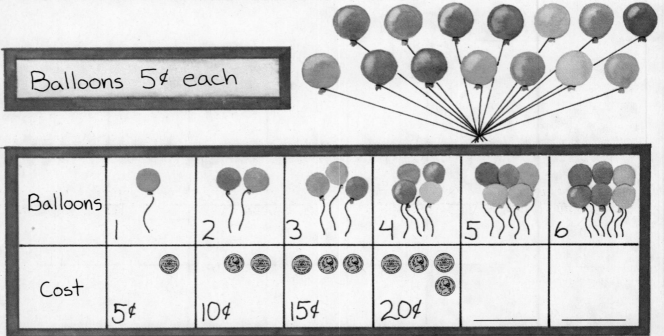

Balloons	1	2	3	4	5	6
Cost	5¢	10¢	15¢	20¢		

6 balloons cost _____ .

Problem solving strategy—make a table

CHAPTER REVIEW/TEST

1. Match.

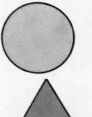

2. How many corners and sides are there?

Corners _____   Sides _____

3. Ring the shape that fits.

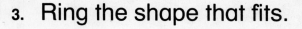
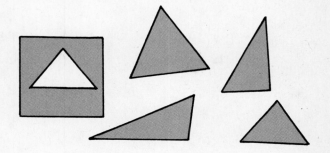

4. Ring the shape that is outside.

5. Color a ☐ for each fish.

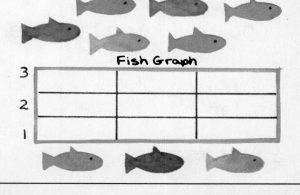

CUMULATIVE REVIEW

Add.

1.
$$\begin{array}{r} 4 \\ +4 \\ \hline \end{array}$$
○ 7
○ 8
○ 9

2.
$$\begin{array}{r} 6 \\ +6 \\ \hline \end{array}$$
○ 13
○ 14
○ 12

3.
$$\begin{array}{r} 6 \\ +4 \\ \hline \end{array}$$
○ 10
○ 11
○ 12

4.
$$\begin{array}{r} 6 \\ +5 \\ \hline \end{array}$$
○ 11
○ 13
○ 12

Subtract.

5.
$$\begin{array}{r} 7 \\ -4 \\ \hline \end{array}$$
○ 4
○ 3
○ 6

6.
$$\begin{array}{r} 9 \\ -7 \\ \hline \end{array}$$
○ 1
○ 3
○ 2

7.
$$\begin{array}{r} 11 \\ -8 \\ \hline \end{array}$$
○ 3
○ 4
○ 5

8.
$$\begin{array}{r} 12 \\ -4 \\ \hline \end{array}$$
○ 8
○ 7
○ 5

9. Solve.

10 apples were on the table.
Barb gave away 4.
How many apples
were left?

_____ apples

ANOTHER LOOK

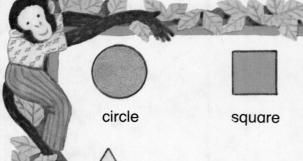

circle   square

triangle   rectangle

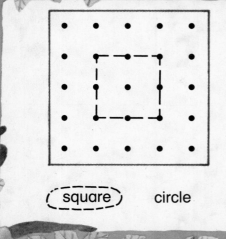

(square)   circle

Each [ ] means 1.

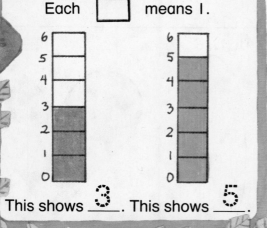

This shows _3_. This shows _5_.

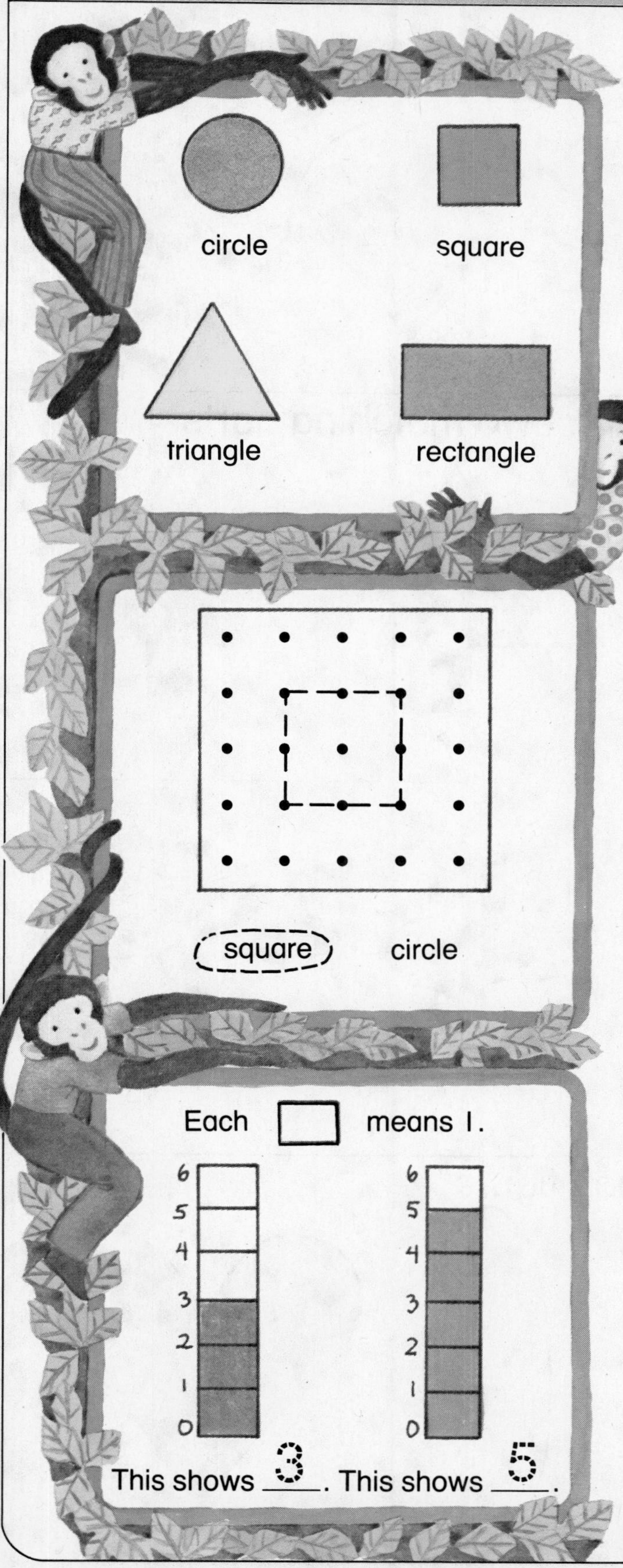

1. Color the shapes.

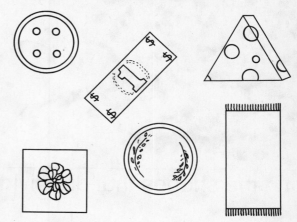

2. Trace the shapes. Ring the name.

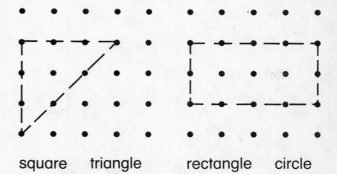

square   triangle   rectangle   circle

3. Color a [ ] for each 👕.

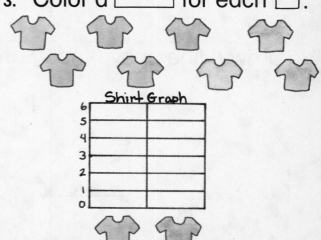

Shirt Graph

ENRICHMENT

 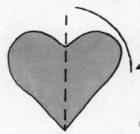

Line of Symmetry

Ring the shapes that are divided into two matching parts.

1.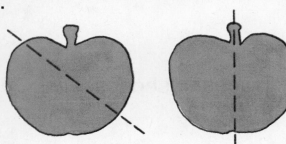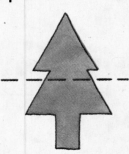

2.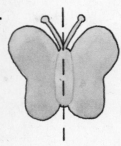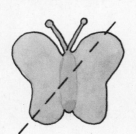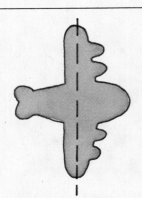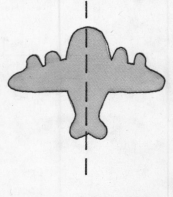

3. Draw a line of symmetry on each figure.

 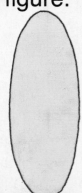  

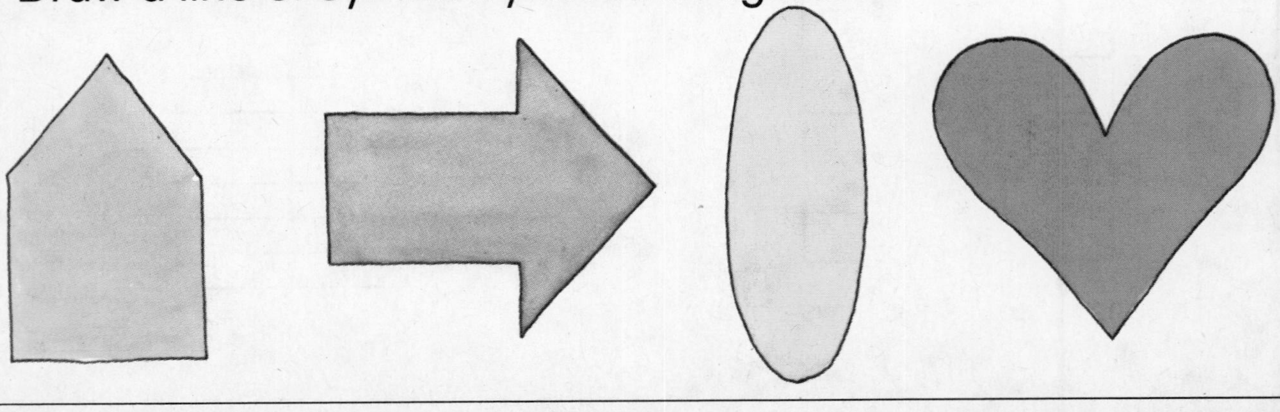

Enrichment—symmetry

Name _____

ADDITION AND SUBTRACTION : 2-DIGIT NUMBERS

How far is it from the town
to the lake?

Town
12   Lake
34

Add the ones.

↓

Add the tens.

Tens	Ones
3	4
+ 1	2
	6
3	4
+ 1	2
4	6

It is 46 miles from the town to the lake.

First add the ones. Then add the tens.

1.

Tens	Ones
2	5
+ 1	3

Tens	Ones
3	2
+	5

2.

Tens	Ones
1	2
+ 3	6

Tens	Ones
4	2
+ 1	4

Tens	Ones
5	0
+ 2	7

Tens	Ones
3	1
+ 2	8

3.

Tens	Ones
1	9
+ 1	0

Tens	Ones
6	3
+	2

Tens	Ones
4	2
+ 4	6

Tens	Ones
4	1
+ 5	7

Adding 2-digit numbers without trading

Add the ones. → Add the tens.

$$\begin{array}{r} 2\,1 \\ +\,4\,6 \\ \hline 7 \end{array}$$
$$\begin{array}{r} 2\,1 \\ +\,4\,6 \\ \hline 6\,7 \end{array}$$

Add.

1.
$$\begin{array}{r} 47 \\ +22 \end{array}$$
$$\begin{array}{r} 14 \\ +33 \end{array}$$
$$\begin{array}{r} 25 \\ +10 \end{array}$$
$$\begin{array}{r} 26 \\ +42 \end{array}$$
$$\begin{array}{r} 74 \\ +\ 5 \end{array}$$
$$\begin{array}{r} 43 \\ +16 \end{array}$$

2.
$$\begin{array}{r} 53 \\ +15 \end{array}$$
$$\begin{array}{r} 40 \\ +40 \end{array}$$
$$\begin{array}{r} 32 \\ +17 \end{array}$$
$$\begin{array}{r} 62 \\ +\ 2 \end{array}$$
$$\begin{array}{r} 13 \\ +50 \end{array}$$
$$\begin{array}{r} 27 \\ +11 \end{array}$$

3.
$$\begin{array}{r} 50 \\ +20 \end{array}$$
$$\begin{array}{r} 55 \\ +\ 3 \end{array}$$
$$\begin{array}{r} 63 \\ +25 \end{array}$$
$$\begin{array}{r} 33 \\ +43 \end{array}$$
$$\begin{array}{r} 12 \\ +17 \end{array}$$
$$\begin{array}{r} 30 \\ +20 \end{array}$$

THINK MATH

Jenny's apple is red.
It has a leaf on it.
Ring Jenny's apple.

Adding two-digit numbers without trading

How much money is there altogether?

$$\begin{array}{r} 16¢ \\ + 32¢ \\ \hline 48¢ \end{array}$$

Altogether there is 48¢.

Add.

1.
$$\begin{array}{r} 23¢ \\ +21¢ \\ \hline \end{array}$$
$$\begin{array}{r} 34¢ \\ +44¢ \\ \hline \end{array}$$
$$\begin{array}{r} 60¢ \\ +27¢ \\ \hline \end{array}$$
$$\begin{array}{r} 32¢ \\ + 5¢ \\ \hline \end{array}$$
$$\begin{array}{r} 15¢ \\ +21¢ \\ \hline \end{array}$$

2.
$$\begin{array}{r} 54¢ \\ +15¢ \\ \hline \end{array}$$
$$\begin{array}{r} 32¢ \\ +64¢ \\ \hline \end{array}$$
$$\begin{array}{r} 20¢ \\ +30¢ \\ \hline \end{array}$$
$$\begin{array}{r} 51¢ \\ +28¢ \\ \hline \end{array}$$
$$\begin{array}{r} 84¢ \\ + 3¢ \\ \hline \end{array}$$

3.
$$\begin{array}{r} 46¢ \\ + 3¢ \\ \hline \end{array}$$
$$\begin{array}{r} 33¢ \\ +53¢ \\ \hline \end{array}$$
$$\begin{array}{r} 76¢ \\ +10¢ \\ \hline \end{array}$$
$$\begin{array}{r} 95¢ \\ + 3¢ \\ \hline \end{array}$$
$$\begin{array}{r} 30¢ \\ +30¢ \\ \hline \end{array}$$

4.
$$\begin{array}{r} 40¢ \\ +48¢ \\ \hline \end{array}$$
$$\begin{array}{r} 52¢ \\ +23¢ \\ \hline \end{array}$$
$$\begin{array}{r} 51¢ \\ +12¢ \\ \hline \end{array}$$
$$\begin{array}{r} 76¢ \\ + 3¢ \\ \hline \end{array}$$
$$\begin{array}{r} 61¢ \\ +24¢ \\ \hline \end{array}$$

Adding money

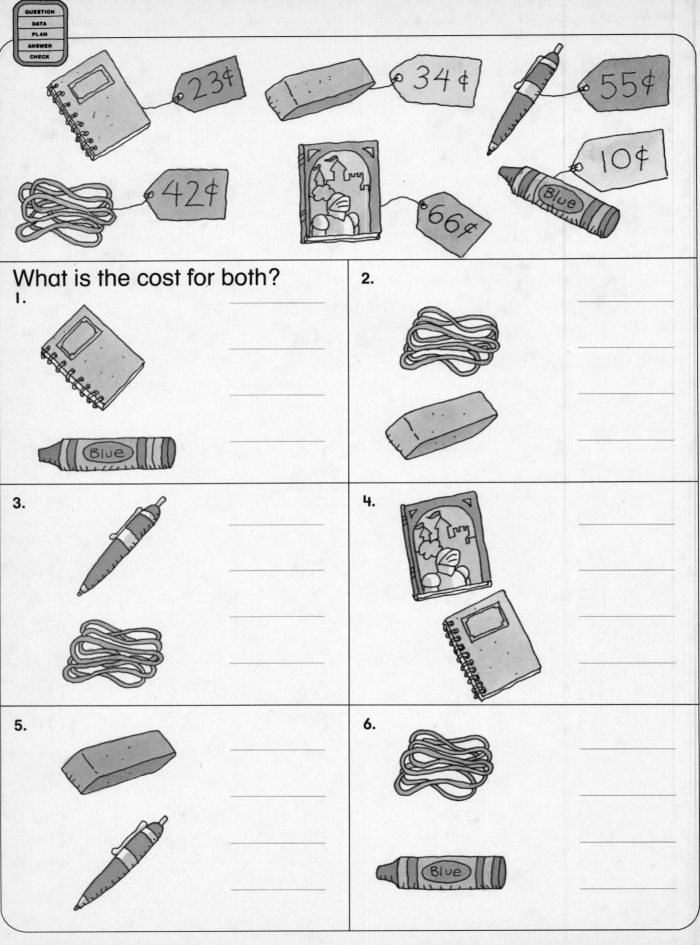

What is the cost for both?

1.

2.

3.

4.

5.

6.

Problem solving—using data from a price tag

Name _____

The total score is 68.

Add.

1.

12	32	24	66	70	41
40	51	30	11	10	4
+26	+ 5	+23	+22	+10	+44

2.

30	14	54	73	28	20
17	10	20	12	20	50
+21	+43	+11	+ 2	+10	+10

3.

3	55	23	15	6	31
4	11	33	14	21	17
+12	+12	+42	+10	+32	+21

Add.

1.

12	23	50	13	4	30
5	4	18	13	42	10
+31	+61	+21	+13	+31	+20

2.

31	44	6	13	54	3
14	20	31	43	21	4
+23	+ 5	+30	+23	+14	+11

3.

50	62	25	37	41	12
10	16	24	42	12	11
+ 8	+ 1	+20	+10	+12	+13

39 birds are on a fence.
22 fly away.
How many birds are left?

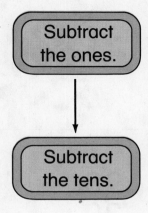

Subtract
the ones.

↓

Subtract
the tens.

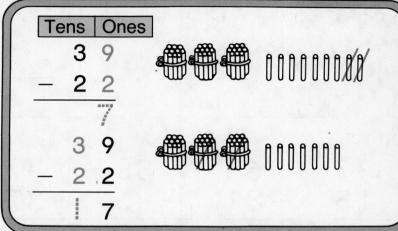

Tens	Ones
3	9
− 2	2
	7
3	9
− 2	2
1	7

There are 16 birds left.

First subtract the ones. Then subtract the tens.

1.

Tens	Ones
3	6
− 1	4
2	2

Tens	Ones
2	8
− 1	6

2.

Tens	Ones
7	5
− 3	0

Tens	Ones
8	8
− 4	4

Tens	Ones
6	3
− 2	3

Tens	Ones
9	8
− 4	3

3.

Tens	Ones
4	9
− 2	5

Tens	Ones
6	6
− 3	5

Tens	Ones
7	4
− 5	0

Tens	Ones
9	7
− 2	5

Subtract the ones. → Subtract the tens.

$$\begin{array}{r} 8\,5 \\ -\,2\,3 \\ \hline 2 \end{array}$$
$$\begin{array}{r} 8\,5 \\ -\,2\,3 \\ \hline 6\,2 \end{array}$$

Subtract.

1.
$$\begin{array}{r} 37 \\ -15 \\ \hline \end{array}$$
$$\begin{array}{r} 64 \\ -31 \\ \hline \end{array}$$
$$\begin{array}{r} 88 \\ -46 \\ \hline \end{array}$$
$$\begin{array}{r} 47 \\ -37 \\ \hline \end{array}$$
$$\begin{array}{r} 93 \\ -20 \\ \hline \end{array}$$
$$\begin{array}{r} 47 \\ -\,6 \\ \hline \end{array}$$

2.
$$\begin{array}{r} 57 \\ -43 \\ \hline \end{array}$$
$$\begin{array}{r} 38 \\ -\,3 \\ \hline \end{array}$$
$$\begin{array}{r} 75 \\ -14 \\ \hline \end{array}$$
$$\begin{array}{r} 96 \\ -43 \\ \hline \end{array}$$
$$\begin{array}{r} 69 \\ -27 \\ \hline \end{array}$$
$$\begin{array}{r} 78 \\ -20 \\ \hline \end{array}$$

3.
$$\begin{array}{r} 88 \\ -50 \\ \hline \end{array}$$
$$\begin{array}{r} 27 \\ -\,4 \\ \hline \end{array}$$
$$\begin{array}{r} 94 \\ -22 \\ \hline \end{array}$$
$$\begin{array}{r} 78 \\ -42 \\ \hline \end{array}$$
$$\begin{array}{r} 60 \\ -20 \\ \hline \end{array}$$
$$\begin{array}{r} 81 \\ -21 \\ \hline \end{array}$$

THINK MATH

Who has between 40 and 50 cards?

_____

Roger · 43 cards

Jackie · 56 cards

Wendy · 39 cards

Subtracting 2-digit numbers without trading

Name _____

How much money is left?

$$\begin{array}{r} 27¢ \\ -\ 15¢ \\ \hline 12¢ \end{array}$$

15¢

There is 12¢ left.

Subtract.

1.
$$\begin{array}{r} 48¢ \\ -25¢ \\ \hline \end{array}$$
$$\begin{array}{r} 86¢ \\ -13¢ \\ \hline \end{array}$$
$$\begin{array}{r} 55¢ \\ -43¢ \\ \hline \end{array}$$
$$\begin{array}{r} 36¢ \\ -20¢ \\ \hline \end{array}$$
$$\begin{array}{r} 19¢ \\ -\ 7¢ \\ \hline \end{array}$$

2.
$$\begin{array}{r} 74¢ \\ -21¢ \\ \hline \end{array}$$
$$\begin{array}{r} 28¢ \\ -24¢ \\ \hline \end{array}$$
$$\begin{array}{r} 63¢ \\ -53¢ \\ \hline \end{array}$$
$$\begin{array}{r} 59¢ \\ -24¢ \\ \hline \end{array}$$
$$\begin{array}{r} 81¢ \\ -50¢ \\ \hline \end{array}$$

3.
$$\begin{array}{r} 57¢ \\ -42¢ \\ \hline \end{array}$$
$$\begin{array}{r} 74¢ \\ -34¢ \\ \hline \end{array}$$
$$\begin{array}{r} 98¢ \\ -25¢ \\ \hline \end{array}$$
$$\begin{array}{r} 66¢ \\ -62¢ \\ \hline \end{array}$$
$$\begin{array}{r} 29¢ \\ -\ 6¢ \\ \hline \end{array}$$

4.
$$\begin{array}{r} 42¢ \\ -11¢ \\ \hline \end{array}$$
$$\begin{array}{r} 39¢ \\ -\ 8¢ \\ \hline \end{array}$$
$$\begin{array}{r} 26¢ \\ -13¢ \\ \hline \end{array}$$
$$\begin{array}{r} 67¢ \\ -15¢ \\ \hline \end{array}$$
$$\begin{array}{r} 75¢ \\ -50¢ \\ \hline \end{array}$$

Subtracting money

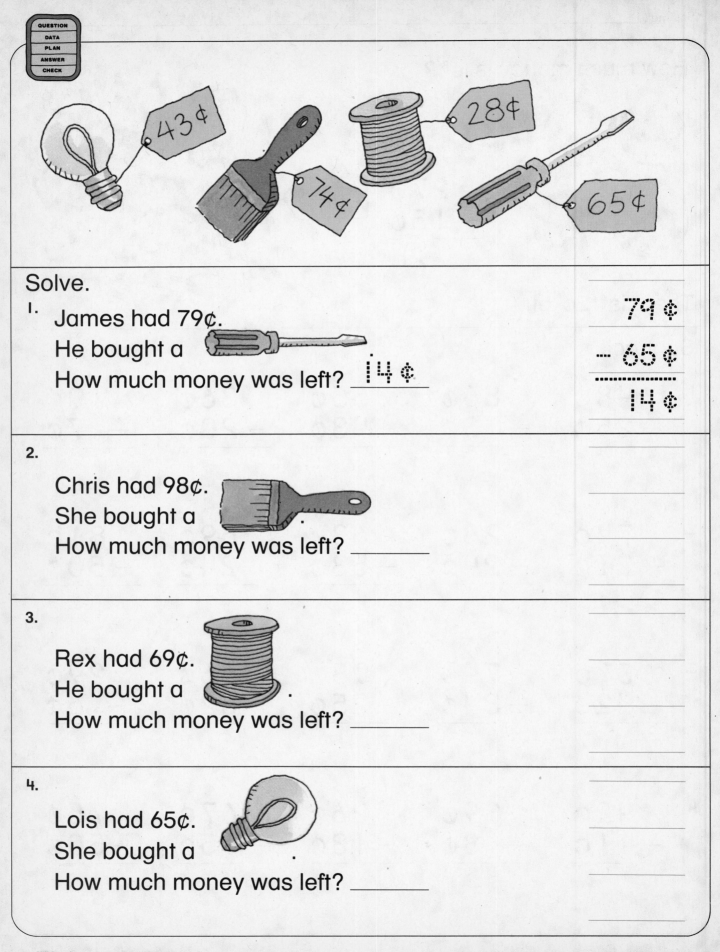

Solve.

1. James had 79¢.
He bought a ____.
How much money was left? __14¢__

$$\begin{array}{r} 79¢ \\ -\ 65¢ \\ \hline 14¢ \end{array}$$

2. Chris had 98¢.
She bought a ____.
How much money was left? _____

3. Rex had 69¢.
He bought a ____.
How much money was left? _____

4. Lois had 65¢.
She bought a ____.
How much money was left? _____

Problem solving—using data from a price tag

Name _____

Add or subtract.

1.

63	84	54	66	17	39
+ 21	− 32	+ 14	− 35	+ 62	− 15

2.

60	78	27	56	54	86
+ 28	− 34	+ 31	− 54	+ 15	− 36

3.

25	67	44	59	28	55
+ 3	− 4	+ 45	− 13	+ 61	− 34

4.

50	86	46	98	72	48
+ 40	− 66	+ 3	− 34	+ 7	− 28

5.

48	67	50	73	59	88
+ 51	− 25	+ 6	− 41	+ 30	− 17

6.

43	21	65	96	20	64
+ 46	− 11	+ 21	− 25	+ 78	− 12

Addition and subtraction practice

1. Katy had 14 shells.
She found 22 more.
How many shells did she find altogether?

$$\begin{array}{r} 14 \\ +22 \\ \hline 36 \end{array}$$

_____ shells

2. John had 79¢.
He spent 69¢ for a pen.
How much money did he have left?

_____

3. Kay picked 24 pears.
Kim picked 35 pears.
How many pears did they pick together?

_____ pears

4. Mary saw 48 bees.
Then 25 flew away.
How many bees were left?

_____ bees

Problem solving—story problems

CHAPTER REVIEW/TEST

Add or subtract.

1.
$$32 + 16$$
$$54 + 25$$
$$13 + 4$$
$$81 + 7$$
$$60 + 20$$

2.
$$48¢ + 21¢$$
$$23¢ + 5¢$$
$$40¢ + 36¢$$
$$73¢ + 16¢$$
$$44¢ + 34¢$$

3.
$$12 \\ 23 \\ +31$$
$$24 \\ 20 \\ +35$$
$$60 \\ 12 \\ +5$$
$$4 \\ 14 \\ +61$$
$$30 \\ 30 \\ +29$$

4.
$$77 - 42$$
$$89 - 67$$
$$68 - 13$$
$$96 - 50$$
$$67 - 5$$

5.
$$68¢ - 44¢$$
$$95¢ - 70¢$$
$$99¢ - 43¢$$
$$78¢ - 17¢$$
$$75¢ - 25¢$$

6. Solve.

Lori picked 24 pears.
She picked 25 more.
How many pears did
she pick altogether?

_____ pears

CUMULATIVE REVIEW

Subtract.

1.
$$\begin{array}{r} 8 \\ -\ 5 \\ \hline \end{array}$$
○ 2
○ 3
○ 4

2.
$$\begin{array}{r} 10 \\ -\ 4 \\ \hline \end{array}$$
○ 5
○ 6
○ 7

3.
$$\begin{array}{r} 11 \\ -\ 2 \\ \hline \end{array}$$
○ 9
○ 8
○ 7

4.
$$\begin{array}{r} 12 \\ -\ 5 \\ \hline \end{array}$$
○ 5
○ 6
○ 7

Choose the correct name.

5.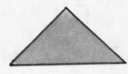
○ circle
○ square
○ triangle

6.
○ circle
○ triangle
○ rectangle

7.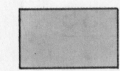
○ circle
○ rectangle
○ triangle

How many apples are there?

8.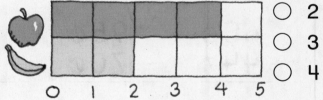
○ 2
○ 3
○ 4

9. **Solve.**

Randy had 9 tickets.
He used 6.
How many tickets does
he have left?

○ 2
○ 3
○ 4

ANOTHER LOOK

Add the ones. → Add the tens.

Tens	Ones
2	5
+3	2
	7

Tens	Ones
2	5
+3	2
5	7

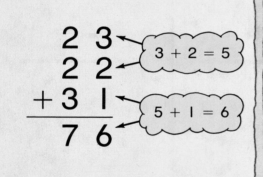

2 3
2 2   3 + 2 = 5
+3 1
7 6   5 + 1 = 6

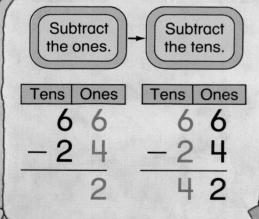

Subtract the ones. → Subtract the tens.

Tens	Ones
6	6
-2	4
	2

Tens	Ones
6	6
-2	4
4	2

Add.

1.
$$48 \quad 36 \quad 44¢$$
$$+11 \quad +43 \quad +53¢$$

2.
$$35 \quad 61 \quad 15$$
$$+42 \quad +37 \quad +31$$

3.
$$30 \quad 46 \quad 11$$
$$32 \quad 12 \quad 44$$
$$+15 \quad +21 \quad +3$$

Subtract.

4.
$$85 \quad 97 \quad 59¢$$
$$-52 \quad -33 \quad -19¢$$

5.
$$56 \quad 75 \quad 19$$
$$-13 \quad -34 \quad -12$$

ENRICHMENT

The Calculator Digits

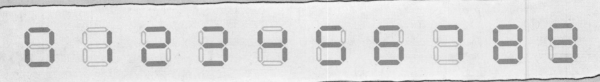

0 1 2 3 4 5 6 7 8 9

Add or subtract.
Color the "lights" to show
your answer.

I.
  +

2.
  −

3.
  +

4.
  −

5.
  +

6.
  −

7.
  +

8.
  −

Enrichment—calculator digit computation

MEASUREMENT-METRIC UNITS

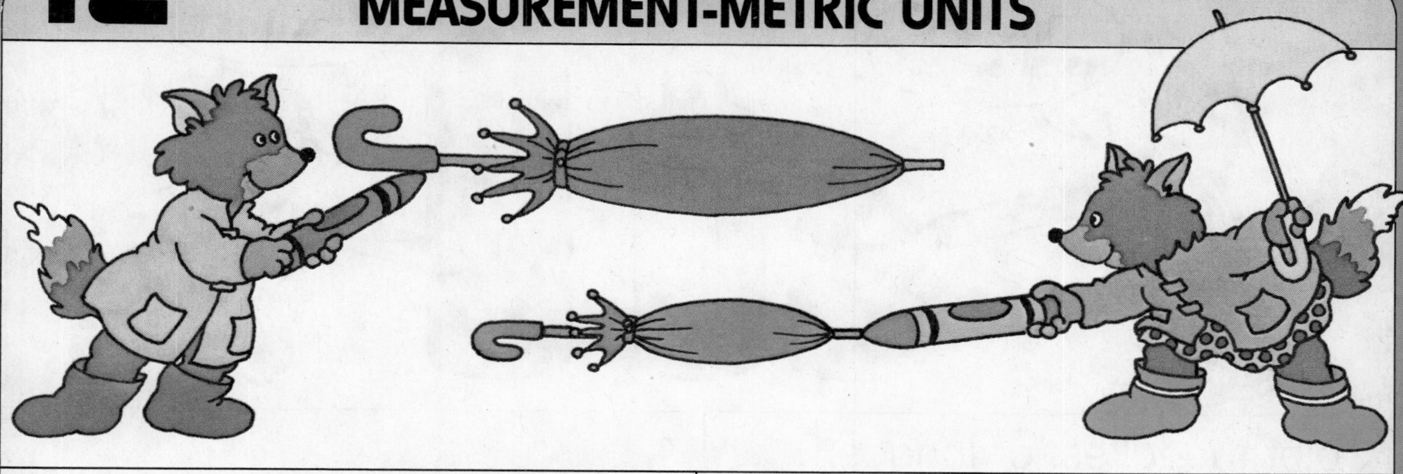

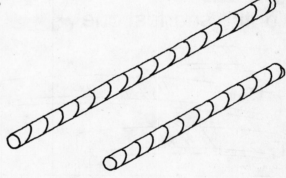

Color the longer one .
Color the shorter one .

1.

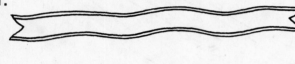

2.

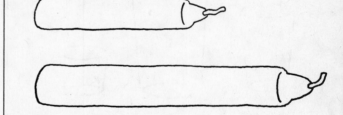

3.

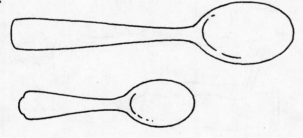

4.

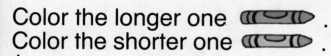

5.

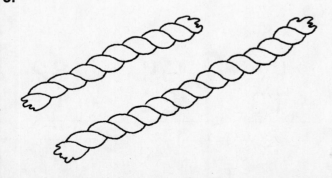

6.

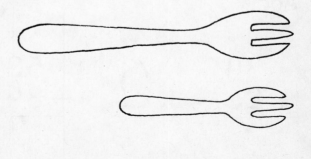

Comparison—longer, shorter

Color the tallest or longest one 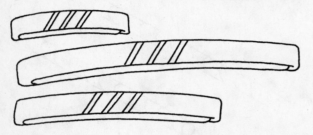.
Color the shortest one .

1.

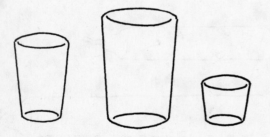

2.

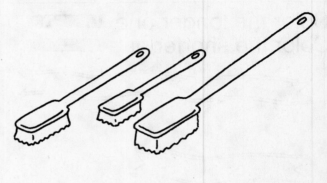

3.

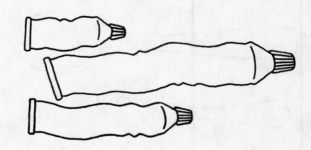

4.

SKILLKEEPER

Add.

34	71	53	46	64	82
+25	+26	+34	+13	+22	+11

Comparison—longest, shortest, tallest

Name _____

unit

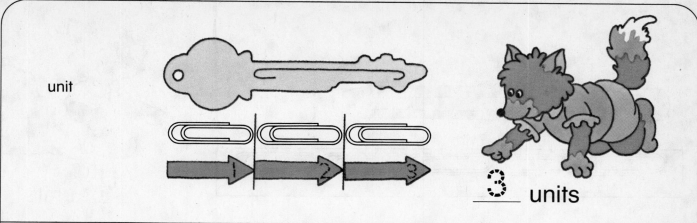

_____ units

Count the paper clips to find the length.

1.

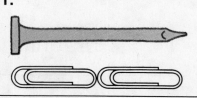

_____ units

2.

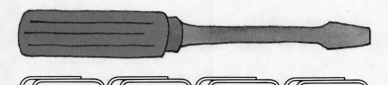

_____ units

3.

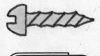

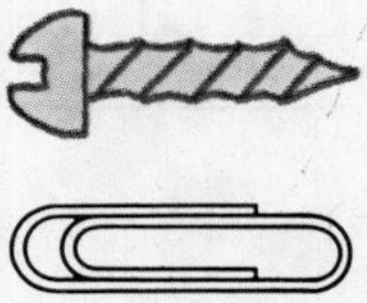

_____ unit

4.

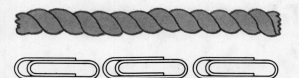

_____ units

5.

_____ units

Measuring length—nonstandard units

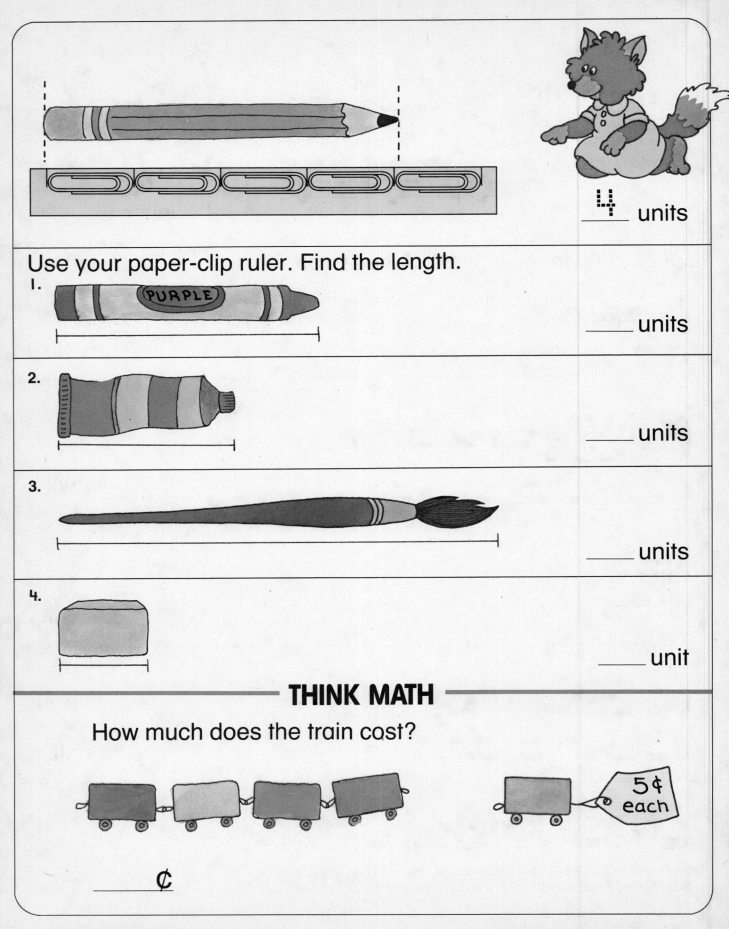

_4_ units

Use your paper-clip ruler. Find the length.

1. PURPLE

_____ units

2.

_____ units

3.

_____ units

4.

_____ unit

THINK MATH

How much does the train cost?

5¢
each

_____ ¢

Measuring length—nonstandard units

Name _____

unit

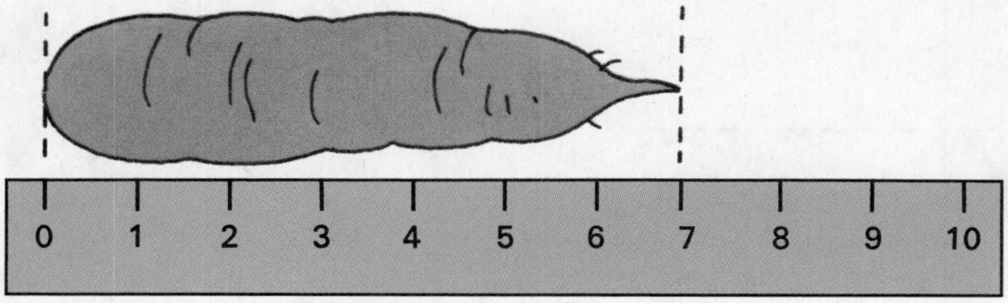

| 0 | 1 | 2 | 3 | 4 | 5 | 6 | 7 | 8 | 9 | 10 |

__7__ units

Write the number of units.

1.

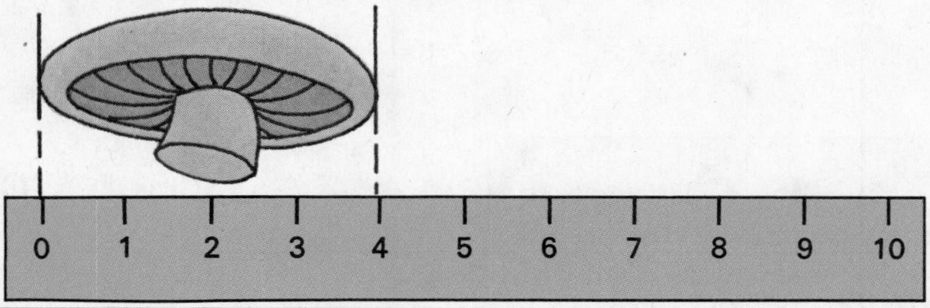

| 0 | 1 | 2 | 3 | 4 | 5 | 6 | 7 | 8 | 9 | 10 |

__4__ units

2.

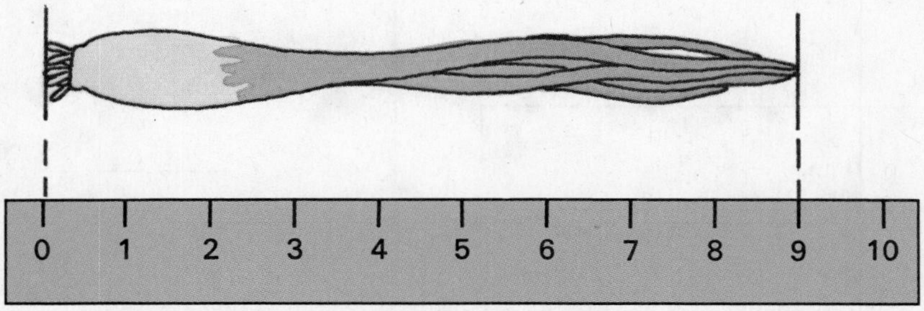

| 0 | 1 | 2 | 3 | 4 | 5 | 6 | 7 | 8 | 9 | 10 |

_____ units

3.

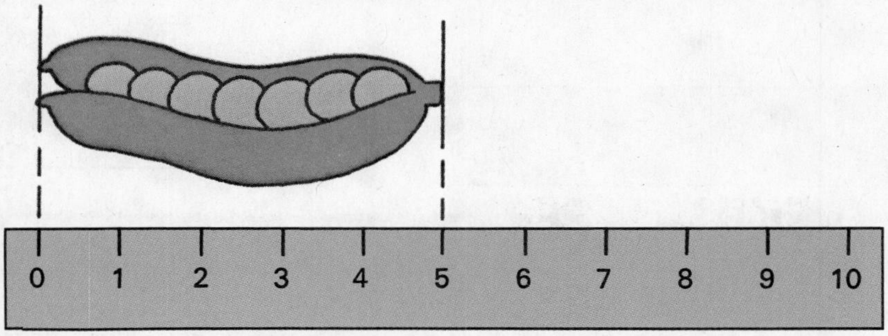

| 0 | 1 | 2 | 3 | 4 | 5 | 6 | 7 | 8 | 9 | 10 |

_____ units

4.

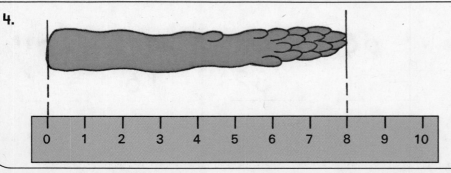

| 0 | 1 | 2 | 3 | 4 | 5 | 6 | 7 | 8 | 9 | 10 |

_____ units

Measuring length—standard units

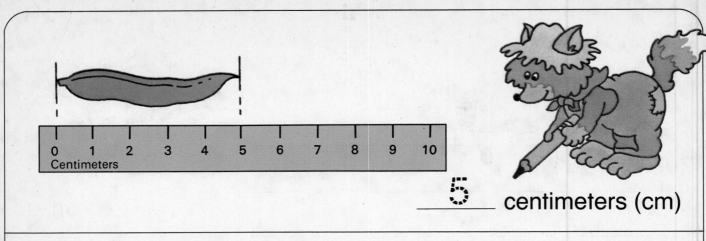

_____ **5** centimeters (cm)

How many centimeters for each?

1.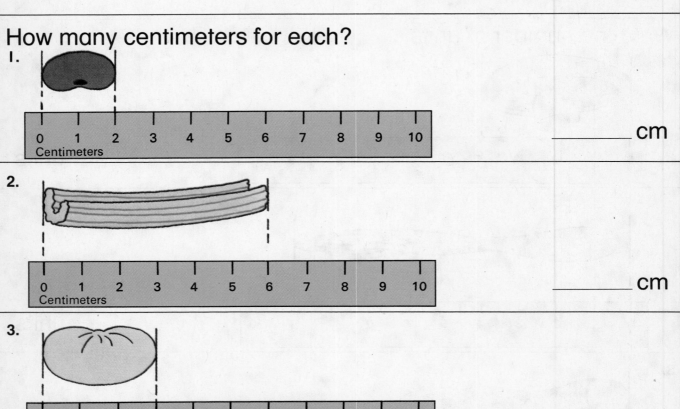

_____ cm

2.

_____ cm

3.

_____ cm

Subtract.

74	68	29	56	37	94
− 21	− 54	− 11	− 32	− 16	− 52

Measuring length—centimeter units

Name _____

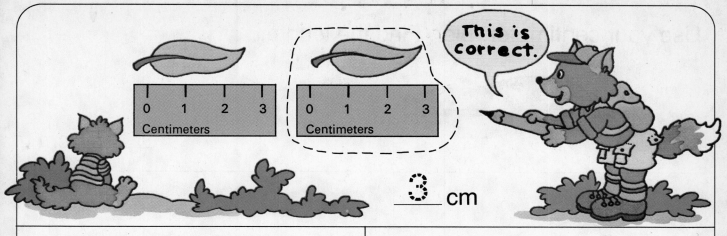

This is correct.

3 cm

Ring the correct one. Write the length.

1.

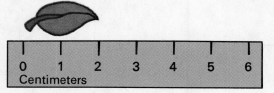

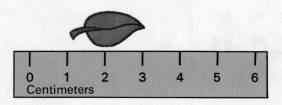

_____ cm

2.

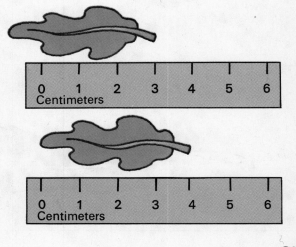

_____ cm

3.

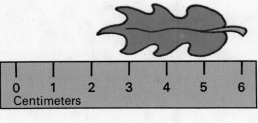

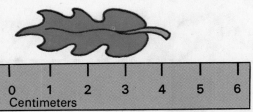

_____ cm

4.

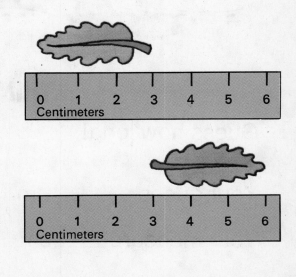

_____ cm

Using and reading a ruler

Use your centimeter ruler. Find the length.

1.

_____ cm

2.

_____ cm

3.

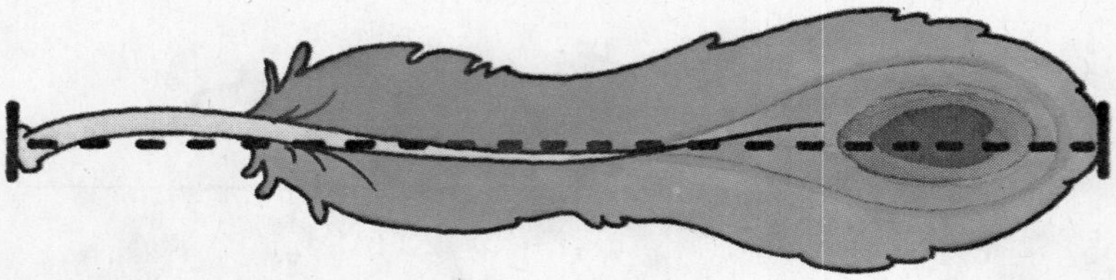

_____ cm

4.

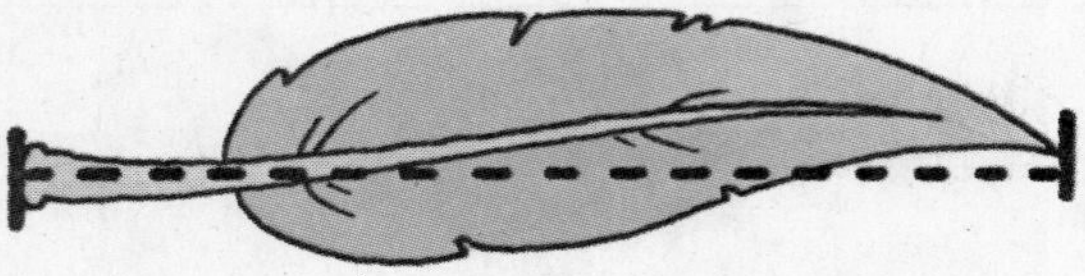

_____ cm

THINK MATH

Guess how long!

Your guess _____ cm

Your measure _____ cm

Difference _____ cm

Measuring practice

Name _____

Use your centimeter ruler.
Find the length.

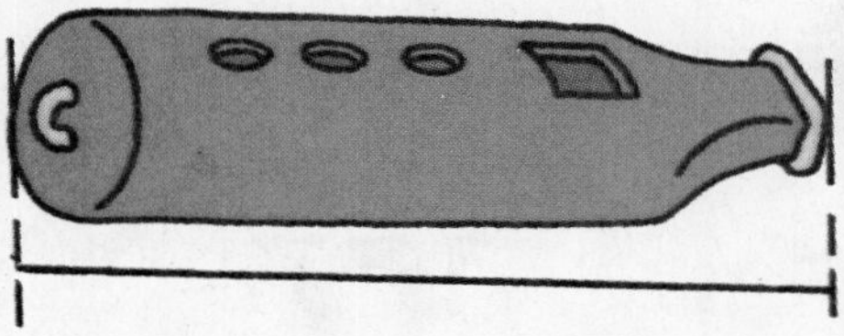

_____6_____ cm

_____ cm

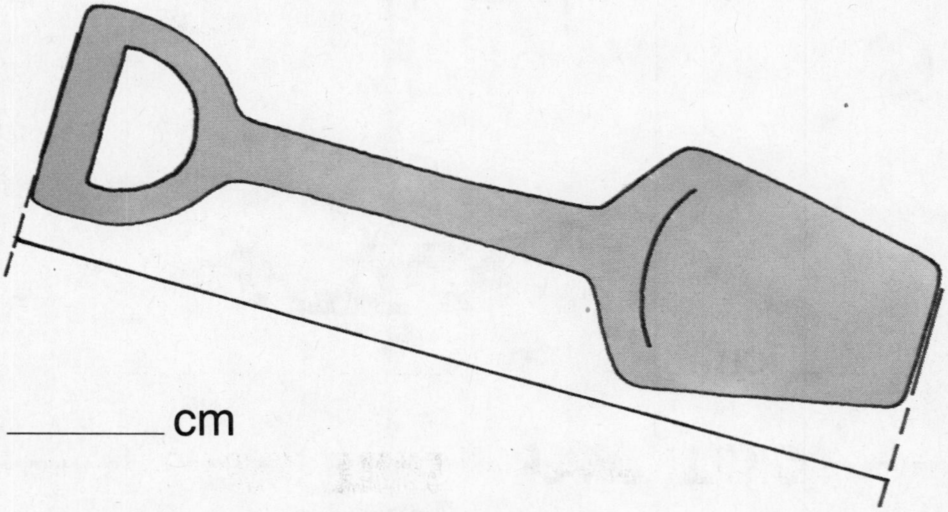

_____ cm

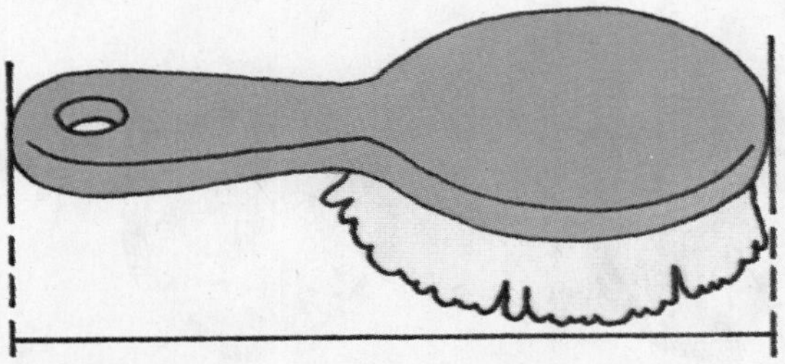

_____ cm

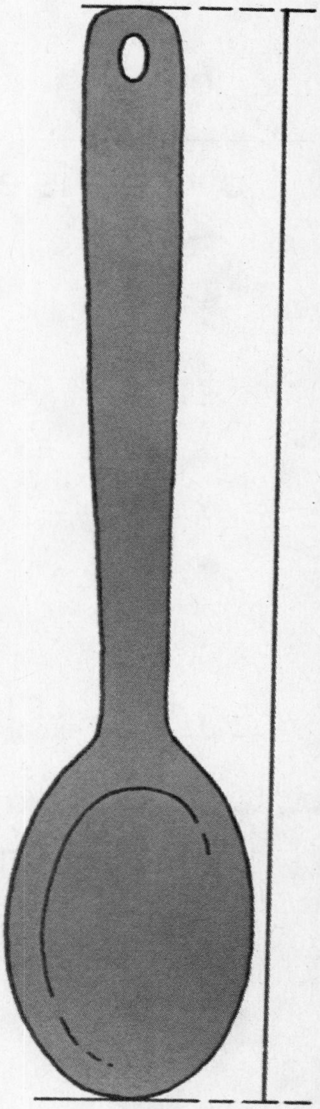

_____ cm

Use your ruler.

1. How long is each?

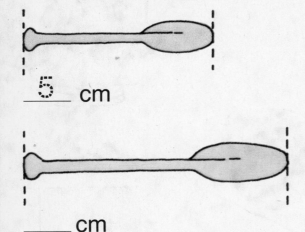

__5__ cm

_____ cm

2. How tall is each?

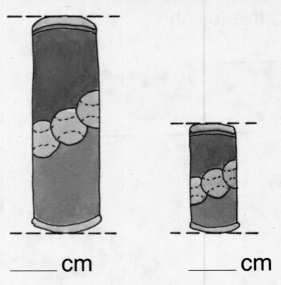

_____ cm   _____ cm

3. How high is each bounce?

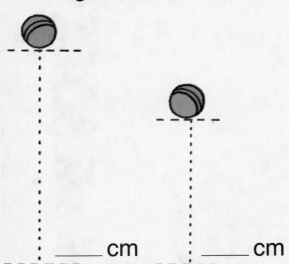

_____ cm   _____ cm

4. How long is each boat?

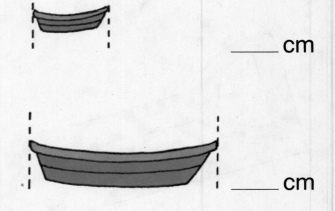

_____ cm

_____ cm

SKILLKEEPER

Write the times.

___:___   ___:___   ___:___   ___:___

Name _____

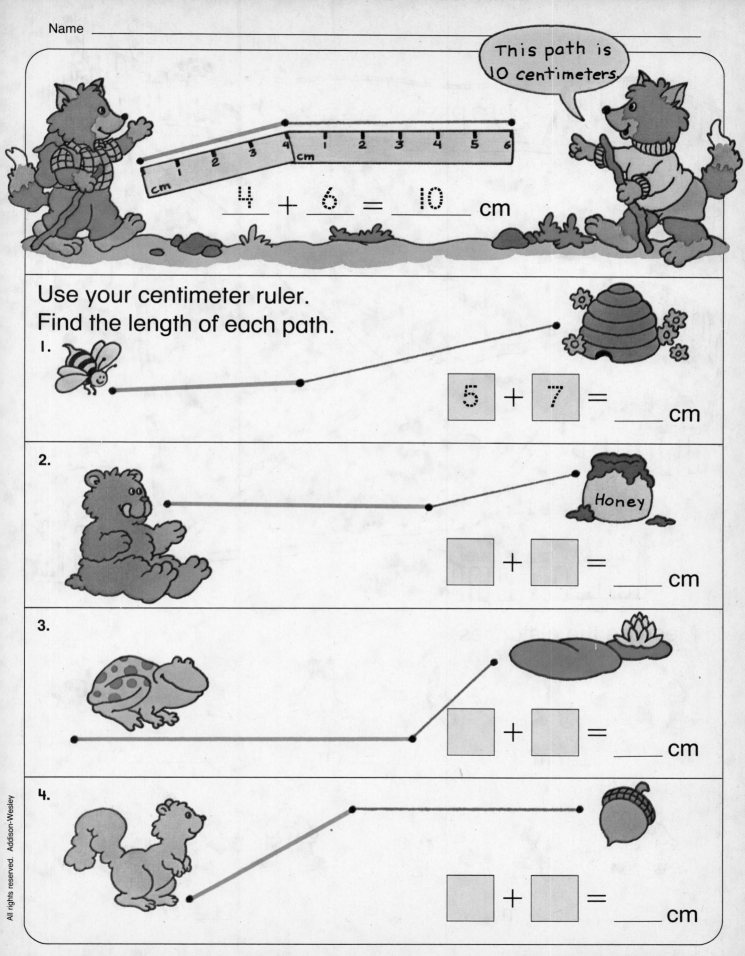

This path is 10 centimeters.

___4___ + ___6___ = ___10___ cm

Use your centimeter ruler.
Find the length of each path.

1. 5 + 7 = ____ cm

2. ☐ + ☐ = ____ cm

3. ☐ + ☐ = ____ cm

4. ☐ + ☐ = ____ cm

Length of paths

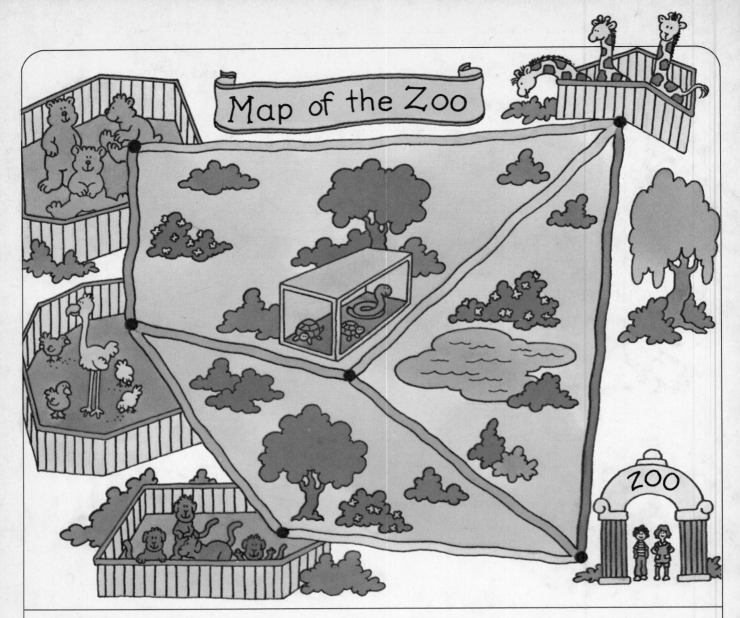

Map of the Zoo

Measure the distances.

 _____ cm

 _____ cm

 _____ cm

 _____ cm

 _____ cm

Name _____

1. Ring things that hold more than a liter.

2. Ring things that hold less than a liter.

Capacity—liter

(two hundred seventy-seven) **277**

It sure is cold.

Cold Day   Warm Day   Hot Day

Ring the correct one.

1.

2.

3.

SKILLKEEPER

Add.

21	53	41	22	13	34
34	12	20	56	42	43
+42	+34	+37	+11	+32	+22

Temperature—degrees Celsius

Name _____

1. Ring the objects that weigh more than a kilogram.

2. Ring the objects that weigh less than a kilogram.

Weight—kilograms

Look for a pattern. Write the missing numbers.

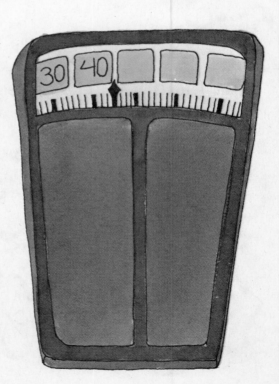

Problem solving strategy—find a pattern

CHAPTER REVIEW/TEST

Give the length.

1.  _____ cm

2. 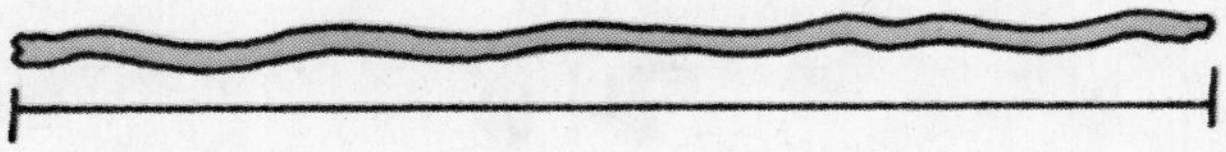 _____ cm

3.  _____ cm

4. 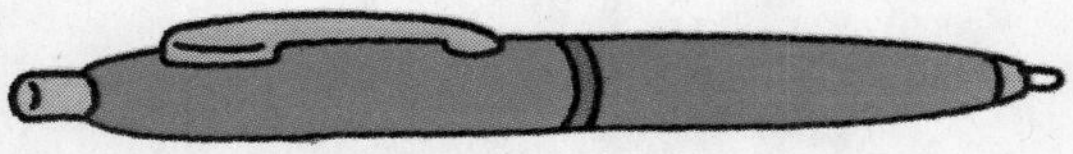 _____ cm

5. How long is the path?

$\boxed{} + \boxed{} = $ _____ cm

6. Ring objects that hold less than a liter.

7. Ring objects that weigh more than a kilogram.

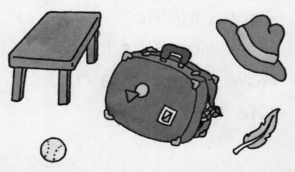

CUMULATIVE REVIEW

Choose the matching shape.

1.

○ ○
○ □
○ △

2.

○ ○
○ □
○ △

3. How many corners?
○ 3
○ 4
○ 5

4. How many sides?

○ 3
○ 4
○ 5

Add.

5.
$$\begin{array}{r} 23 \\ +52 \end{array}$$

○ 74
○ 65
○ 75

6.
$$\begin{array}{r} 54¢ \\ +35¢ \end{array}$$

○ 88¢
○ 89¢
○ 90¢

Subtract.

7.
$$\begin{array}{r} 63 \\ -21 \end{array}$$

○ 42
○ 32
○ 43

8.
$$\begin{array}{r} 78¢ \\ -52¢ \end{array}$$

○ 24¢
○ 25¢
○ 26¢

9. Solve.

Katy had 79¢.
She spent 30¢ for a toy.
How much money did
she have left?

○ 40¢

○ 49¢

○ 39¢

ANOTHER LOOK

_____6_____ units

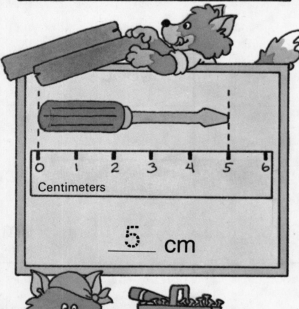

_____5_____ cm

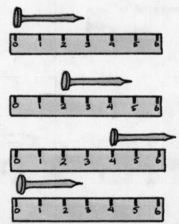

Count the units.

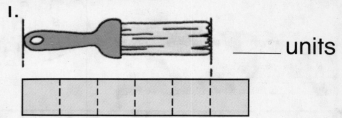

1. _____ units

2. _____ units

How long is each one?

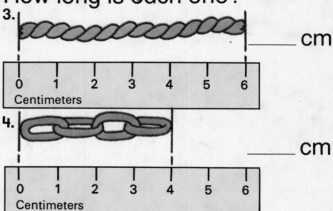

3. _____ cm

4. _____ cm

Which ones are correct?

5.

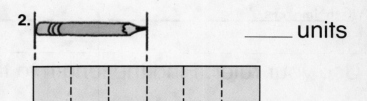

ENRICHMENT

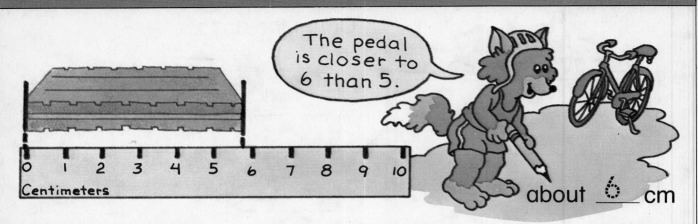

The pedal is closer to 6 than 5.

about __6__ cm

Use your ruler. Find the length to the nearest centimeter.

1.

about __4__ cm

2.

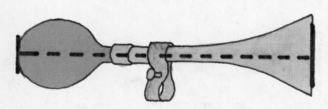

about _____ cm

3.

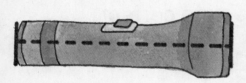

about _____ cm

4.

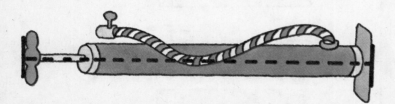

about _____ cm

Enrichment—measuring to the nearest centimeter

Name _____

Find the sums.

1.

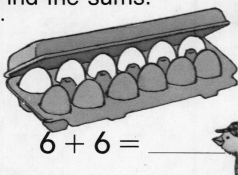

These are more doubles.

$6 + 6 =$ _____

2.

February						
1	2	3	4	5	6	7
8	9	10	11	12	13	14
15	16	17	18	19	20	21
22	23	24	25	26	27	28

$7 + 7 =$ _____

3.

CRAYONS 16

$8 + 8 =$ _____

4.

$9 + 9 =$ _____

Add.

5.

$$\begin{array}{r} 7 \\ + 7 \\ \hline \end{array}\quad \begin{array}{r} 4 \\ + 5 \\ \hline \end{array}\quad \begin{array}{r} 2 \\ + 5 \\ \hline \end{array}\quad \begin{array}{r} 6 \\ + 6 \\ \hline \end{array}\quad \begin{array}{r} 5 \\ + 6 \\ \hline \end{array}\quad \begin{array}{r} 9 \\ + 9 \\ \hline \end{array}$$

6.

$$\begin{array}{r} 6 \\ + 2 \\ \hline \end{array}\quad \begin{array}{r} 8 \\ + 8 \\ \hline \end{array}\quad \begin{array}{r} 4 \\ + 4 \\ \hline \end{array}\quad \begin{array}{r} 7 \\ + 7 \\ \hline \end{array}\quad \begin{array}{r} 2 \\ + 4 \\ \hline \end{array}\quad \begin{array}{r} 6 \\ + 6 \\ \hline \end{array}$$

7.

$$\begin{array}{r} 5 \\ + 5 \\ \hline \end{array}\quad \begin{array}{r} 9 \\ + 9 \\ \hline \end{array}\quad \begin{array}{r} 2 \\ + 3 \\ \hline \end{array}\quad \begin{array}{r} 4 \\ + 3 \\ \hline \end{array}\quad \begin{array}{r} 8 \\ + 8 \\ \hline \end{array}\quad \begin{array}{r} 3 \\ + 3 \\ \hline \end{array}$$

More doubles—6, 7, 8, 9

Add.

1.
$$\begin{array}{r} 6 \\ +\,6 \\ \hline \end{array}$$
$$\begin{array}{r} 3 \\ +\,4 \\ \hline \end{array}$$
$$\begin{array}{r} 2 \\ +\,5 \\ \hline \end{array}$$
$$\begin{array}{r} 8 \\ +\,8 \\ \hline \end{array}$$
$$\begin{array}{r} 5 \\ +\,3 \\ \hline \end{array}$$
$$\begin{array}{r} 6 \\ +\,1 \\ \hline \end{array}$$

2.
$$\begin{array}{r} 2 \\ +\,6 \\ \hline \end{array}$$
$$\begin{array}{r} 4 \\ +\,4 \\ \hline \end{array}$$
$$\begin{array}{r} 5 \\ +\,4 \\ \hline \end{array}$$
$$\begin{array}{r} 2 \\ +\,2 \\ \hline \end{array}$$
$$\begin{array}{r} 7 \\ +\,7 \\ \hline \end{array}$$
$$\begin{array}{r} 6 \\ +\,4 \\ \hline \end{array}$$

3.
$$\begin{array}{r} 9 \\ +\,9 \\ \hline \end{array}$$
$$\begin{array}{r} 2 \\ +\,3 \\ \hline \end{array}$$
$$\begin{array}{r} 8 \\ +\,0 \\ \hline \end{array}$$
$$\begin{array}{r} 3 \\ +\,3 \\ \hline \end{array}$$
$$\begin{array}{r} 1 \\ +\,5 \\ \hline \end{array}$$
$$\begin{array}{r} 4 \\ +\,2 \\ \hline \end{array}$$

4.
$$\begin{array}{r} 5 \\ +\,2 \\ \hline \end{array}$$
$$\begin{array}{r} 8 \\ +\,8 \\ \hline \end{array}$$
$$\begin{array}{r} 3 \\ +\,7 \\ \hline \end{array}$$
$$\begin{array}{r} 9 \\ +\,9 \\ \hline \end{array}$$
$$\begin{array}{r} 6 \\ +\,5 \\ \hline \end{array}$$
$$\begin{array}{r} 9 \\ +\,1 \\ \hline \end{array}$$

5.
$$\begin{array}{r} 5 \\ +\,5 \\ \hline \end{array}$$
$$\begin{array}{r} 7 \\ +\,2 \\ \hline \end{array}$$
$$\begin{array}{r} 7 \\ +\,7 \\ \hline \end{array}$$
$$\begin{array}{r} 0 \\ +\,9 \\ \hline \end{array}$$
$$\begin{array}{r} 6 \\ +\,6 \\ \hline \end{array}$$
$$\begin{array}{r} 6 \\ +\,3 \\ \hline \end{array}$$

THINK MATH

Wayne's money

How many toys can Wayne buy?

2 cents each   _____ toys

More doubles—6, 7, 8, 9

Name _____

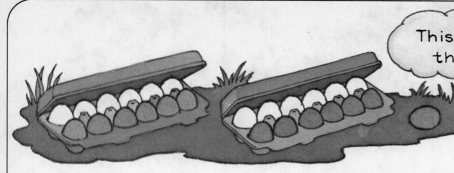

This is 1 more than 6+6

$6 + 6 = \underline{12}$ $6 + 7 = \underline{13}$

Add.

1.

$5 + 5 = \underline{10}$ $6 + 5 = \underline{11}$

2.

$4 + 4$ $4 + 5$

3.

$8 + 8$ $8 + 9$

4.

$7 + 7$ $8 + 7$

Add.

5.

$6 + 6$ $7 + 6$ $7 + 7$ $7 + 8$ $8 + 8$ $9 + 8$

6.

$6 + 7$ $5 + 6$ $8 + 7$ $4 + 5$ $8 + 9$ $4 + 3$

More doubles plus one   (two hundred eighty-seven) **287**

Add.

1.
$$7 + 7$$ 　 $$8 + 7$$ 　 $$9 + 9$$ 　 $$5 + 5$$ 　 $$6 + 5$$ 　 $$6 + 6$$

2.
$$8 + 8$$ 　 $$8 + 9$$ 　 $$9 + 8$$ 　 $$4 + 3$$ 　 $$5 + 4$$ 　 $$3 + 3$$

3.
$$3 + 4$$ 　 $$6 + 6$$ 　 $$7 + 6$$ 　 $$7 + 8$$ 　 $$4 + 4$$ 　 $$5 + 4$$

4.
$$9 + 9$$ 　 $$7 + 8$$ 　 $$7 + 7$$ 　 $$8 + 7$$ 　 $$8 + 8$$ 　 $$5 + 6$$

SKILLKEEPER

Subtract.

$$7 - 3$$ 　 $$10 - 4$$ 　 $$8 - 4$$ 　 $$9 - 2$$ 　 $$6 - 3$$ 　 $$10 - 5$$

　　　　More doubles plus one

Name _____

What is the total cost?

6¢
+ 6¢
12¢

6¢
+ 7¢
13¢

6¢ each

7¢ each

Add.

1.
8¢
+ 8¢

8¢
+ 9¢

9¢
+ 8¢

5¢
+ 5¢

6¢
+ 5¢

2.
4¢
+ 4¢

7¢
+ 2¢

7¢
+ 7¢

8¢
+ 7¢

7¢
+ 8¢

3.
5¢
+ 3¢

4¢
+ 6¢

6¢
+ 6¢

7¢
+ 6¢

9¢
+ 1¢

4.
9¢
+ 9¢

3¢
+ 8¢

9¢
+ 3¢

8¢
+ 8¢

7¢
+ 4¢

Add.

1.
$$\begin{array}{r} 7 \\ +7 \\ \hline \end{array}$$
$$\begin{array}{r} 7 \\ +8 \\ \hline \end{array}$$
$$\begin{array}{r} 8 \\ +2 \\ \hline \end{array}$$
$$\begin{array}{r} 8 \\ +3 \\ \hline \end{array}$$

2.
$$\begin{array}{r} 4 \\ +6 \\ \hline \end{array}$$
$$\begin{array}{r} 4 \\ +7 \\ \hline \end{array}$$
$$\begin{array}{r} 8 \\ +8 \\ \hline \end{array}$$
$$\begin{array}{r} 8 \\ +9 \\ \hline \end{array}$$
$$\begin{array}{r} 9 \\ +8 \\ \hline \end{array}$$
$$\begin{array}{r} 9 \\ +9 \\ \hline \end{array}$$

3.
$$\begin{array}{r} 7 \\ +3 \\ \hline \end{array}$$
$$\begin{array}{r} 3 \\ +6 \\ \hline \end{array}$$
$$\begin{array}{r} 6 \\ +6 \\ \hline \end{array}$$
$$\begin{array}{r} 6 \\ +7 \\ \hline \end{array}$$
$$\begin{array}{r} 7 \\ +6 \\ \hline \end{array}$$
$$\begin{array}{r} 4 \\ +4 \\ \hline \end{array}$$

4.
$$\begin{array}{r} 5 \\ +4 \\ \hline \end{array}$$
$$\begin{array}{r} 9 \\ +9 \\ \hline \end{array}$$
$$\begin{array}{r} 2 \\ +6 \\ \hline \end{array}$$
$$\begin{array}{r} 9 \\ +3 \\ \hline \end{array}$$
$$\begin{array}{r} 8 \\ +4 \\ \hline \end{array}$$
$$\begin{array}{r} 2 \\ +8 \\ \hline \end{array}$$

5.
$$\begin{array}{r} 8 \\ +7 \\ \hline \end{array}$$
$$\begin{array}{r} 9 \\ +8 \\ \hline \end{array}$$
$$\begin{array}{r} 7 \\ +7 \\ \hline \end{array}$$
$$\begin{array}{r} 3 \\ +7 \\ \hline \end{array}$$
$$\begin{array}{r} 8 \\ +8 \\ \hline \end{array}$$
$$\begin{array}{r} 9 \\ +9 \\ \hline \end{array}$$

THINK MATH

Give the missing number on the calculator key.

PRESS   READ

7	+	☐	=	→	13
9	−	☐	=	→	6
1	7	−	☐	=	→	9

Practice the facts

Name _____

How many are there in each part? Subtract.

1.

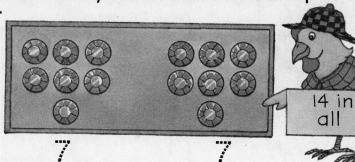

$$14 - 7 = \underline{\quad\quad}$$

7   7

2.

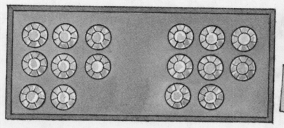

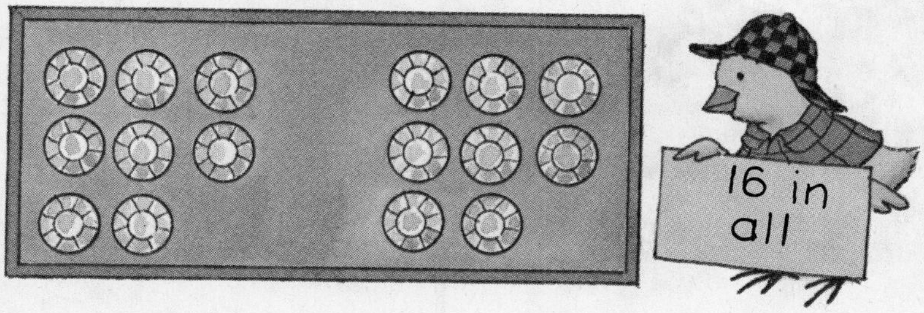

$$16 - 8 = \underline{\quad\quad}$$

_____   _____

3.

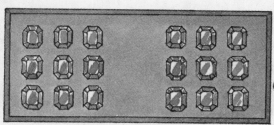 

$$18 - 9 = \underline{\quad\quad}$$

_____   _____

4. Subtract.

$$\begin{array}{cccccc}
16 & 14 & 12 & 18 & 10 & 8 \\
-\ 8 & -\ 7 & -\ 6 & -\ 9 & -\ 5 & -\ 4 \\
\hline
\end{array}$$

How many are there in each part? Subtract.

1.

_7_   _6_

$13 - 6 =$ _____

$13 - 7 =$ _____

2.

_____   _____

$15 - 7 =$ _____

$15 - 8 =$ _____

3.

_____   _____

$17 - 8 =$ _____

$17 - 9 =$ _____

4. Subtract.

$$\begin{array}{cccccc} 15 & 17 & 13 & 15 & 17 & 13 \\ -\ 8 & -\ 9 & -\ 6 & -\ 7 & -\ 8 & -\ 7 \\ \hline \end{array}$$

Related subtraction facts

Name _____

Use the numbers given. Complete the number sentences.

1.

13

8   5

$\underline{8} + \underline{5} = 13$ $\underline{13} - \underline{5} = 8$

$\underline{5} + \underline{8} = 13$ $\underline{13} - \underline{8} = 5$

2.

13

9   4

$\underline{} + \underline{} = 13$ $\underline{} - \underline{} = 9$

$\underline{} + \underline{} = 13$ $\underline{} - \underline{} = 4$

3.

14

8   6

$\underline{} + \underline{} = 14$ $\underline{} - \underline{} = 8$

$\underline{} + \underline{} = 14$ $\underline{} - \underline{} = 6$

4.

14

9   5

$\underline{} + \underline{} = 14$ $\underline{} - \underline{} = 9$

$\underline{} + \underline{} = 14$ $\underline{} - \underline{} = 5$

Last sums and differences

Use the numbers given. Complete the number sentences.

1.

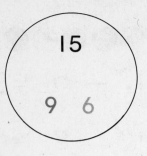

$\underline{9} + \underline{6} = 15$ $\underline{15} - \underline{6} = 9$

$\underline{6} + \underline{9} = 15$ $\underline{15} - \underline{9} = 6$

15
9 6

2.

$\underline{} + \underline{} = 16$ $\underline{} - \underline{} = 9$

$\underline{} + \underline{} = 16$ $\underline{} - \underline{} = 7$

16
9 7

Add or subtract.

3.

$\begin{array}{r}8\\+5\\\hline\end{array}$ $\begin{array}{r}5\\+9\\\hline\end{array}$ $\begin{array}{r}6\\+9\\\hline\end{array}$ $\begin{array}{r}8\\+6\\\hline\end{array}$ $\begin{array}{r}9\\+5\\\hline\end{array}$ $\begin{array}{r}9\\+7\\\hline\end{array}$

4.

$\begin{array}{r}13\\-9\\\hline\end{array}$ $\begin{array}{r}14\\-5\\\hline\end{array}$ $\begin{array}{r}16\\-7\\\hline\end{array}$ $\begin{array}{r}15\\-9\\\hline\end{array}$ $\begin{array}{r}14\\-8\\\hline\end{array}$ $\begin{array}{r}13\\-5\\\hline\end{array}$

5.

$\begin{array}{r}14\\-9\\\hline\end{array}$ $\begin{array}{r}16\\-9\\\hline\end{array}$ $\begin{array}{r}15\\-6\\\hline\end{array}$ $\begin{array}{r}13\\-8\\\hline\end{array}$ $\begin{array}{r}14\\-6\\\hline\end{array}$ $\begin{array}{r}13\\-4\\\hline\end{array}$

Last sums and differences

Name _____

Add or subtract.

1.
$$7 + 7$$ $$7 + 6$$ $$14 - 7$$ $$13 - 6$$

2.
$$8 + 8$$ $$8 + 9$$ $$16 - 8$$ $$17 - 8$$ $$17 - 9$$ $$9 + 8$$

3.
$$6 + 6$$ $$12 - 6$$ $$13 - 7$$ $$13 - 6$$ $$7 + 8$$ $$15 - 7$$

4.
$$9 + 9$$ $$18 - 9$$ $$8 + 7$$ $$15 - 8$$ $$5 + 5$$ $$10 - 5$$

5.
$$5¢ + 6¢$$ $$11¢ - 6¢$$ $$11¢ - 5¢$$ $$9¢ + 8¢$$ $$12¢ - 6¢$$ $$13¢ - 7¢$$

SKILLKEEPER

Write the times.

___:___   ___:___   ___:___   ___:___

Practice the facts

(two hundred ninety-five) **295**

Solve.

1. Luis saw 16 ladybugs.
   8 flew away.
   How many were left?

   _____8_____ ladybugs

   $$16$$
   $$-\ 8$$
   $$\overline{8}$$

2. Marta saw 7 roses in her yard.
   She saw 7 more next door.
   How many did she see in all?

   _____ roses

3. There were 9 children playing tag.
   9 more came.
   How many were there in all?

   _____ children

4. Brad saw 13 birds.
   7 flew away.
   How many were left?

   _____ birds

5. Mary had 15¢.
   She spent 7¢ for a pencil.
   How much did she have left?

   _____ ¢

Problem solving—story problems

Name _____

CHAPTER REVIEW/TEST

Add or subtract.

1.
$$\begin{array}{r} 7 \\ +7 \\ \hline \end{array}\qquad \begin{array}{r} 9 \\ +9 \\ \hline \end{array}\qquad \begin{array}{r} 6 \\ +6 \\ \hline \end{array}\qquad \begin{array}{r} 8 \\ +8 \\ \hline \end{array}\qquad \begin{array}{r} 7 \\ +8 \\ \hline \end{array}\qquad \begin{array}{r} 9 \\ +9 \\ \hline \end{array}$$

2.
$$\begin{array}{r} 6¢ \\ +7¢ \\ \hline \end{array}\qquad \begin{array}{r} 8¢ \\ +7¢ \\ \hline \end{array}\qquad \begin{array}{r} 8¢ \\ +9¢ \\ \hline \end{array}\qquad \begin{array}{r} 7¢ \\ +7¢ \\ \hline \end{array}\qquad \begin{array}{r} 9¢ \\ +9¢ \\ \hline \end{array}\qquad \begin{array}{r} 6¢ \\ +6¢ \\ \hline \end{array}$$

3.
$$\begin{array}{r} 13 \\ -6 \\ \hline \end{array}\qquad \begin{array}{r} 14 \\ -7 \\ \hline \end{array}\qquad \begin{array}{r} 12 \\ -6 \\ \hline \end{array}\qquad \begin{array}{r} 13 \\ -7 \\ \hline \end{array}\qquad \begin{array}{r} 16 \\ -8 \\ \hline \end{array}\qquad \begin{array}{r} 18 \\ -9 \\ \hline \end{array}$$

4.
$$\begin{array}{r} 17 \\ -9 \\ \hline \end{array}\qquad \begin{array}{r} 17 \\ -8 \\ \hline \end{array}\qquad \begin{array}{r} 15 \\ -8 \\ \hline \end{array}\qquad \begin{array}{r} 15 \\ -7 \\ \hline \end{array}$$

5.
$$\begin{array}{r} 5 \\ +8 \\ \hline \end{array}\qquad \begin{array}{r} 13 \\ -5 \\ \hline \end{array}\qquad \begin{array}{r} 6 \\ +8 \\ \hline \end{array}\qquad \begin{array}{r} 14 \\ -8 \\ \hline \end{array}\qquad \begin{array}{r} 9 \\ +6 \\ \hline \end{array}\qquad \begin{array}{r} 15 \\ -9 \\ \hline \end{array}$$

6. Solve.

Pat made 18 cards.
She gave away 9.
How many did she have left?

_____

_____

_____

_____

_____ cards

CUMULATIVE REVIEW

Add or subtract.

1.
$$\begin{array}{r} 23 \\ +66 \\ \hline \end{array}$$
○ 98
○ 89
○ 52

2.
$$\begin{array}{r} 14 \\ +33 \\ \hline \end{array}$$
○ 21
○ 56
○ 47

3.
$$\begin{array}{r} 97 \\ -17 \\ \hline \end{array}$$
○ 10
○ 26
○ 80

4.
$$\begin{array}{r} 50 \\ -20 \\ \hline \end{array}$$
○ 30
○ 70
○ 2

Find the length or height.

5.
○ 4 cm
○ 2 cm
○ 3 cm

6.
○ 1 cm
○ 4 cm
○ 6 cm

7.
○ 2 cm
○ 3 cm
○ 4 cm

8.
○ 5 cm
○ 4 cm
○ 3 cm

9. Solve.

Sean had 89¢.

He bought a .

○ 90¢

○ 68¢

○ 39¢

How much does he have left?

Cumulative review

ANOTHER LOOK

$$\begin{array}{r} 6 \\ +6 \\ \hline 12 \end{array} \qquad \begin{array}{r} 7 \\ +7 \\ \hline 14 \end{array}$$

$$\begin{array}{r} 8 \\ +8 \\ \hline 16 \end{array} \qquad \begin{array}{r} 9 \\ +9 \\ \hline 18 \end{array}$$

$$\begin{array}{r} 6 \\ +6 \\ \hline 12 \end{array} \quad \begin{array}{r} 6 \\ +7 \\ \hline 13 \end{array} \text{1 more} \quad \begin{array}{r} 7 \\ +7 \\ \hline 14 \end{array} \quad \begin{array}{r} 7 \\ +8 \\ \hline 15 \end{array} \text{1 more}$$

$$\begin{array}{r} 8 \\ +8 \\ \hline 16 \end{array} \quad \begin{array}{r} 8 \\ +9 \\ \hline 17 \end{array} \text{1 more}$$

$$\begin{array}{r} 6 \\ +6 \\ \hline 12 \end{array} \quad \begin{array}{r} 12 \\ -6 \\ \hline 6 \end{array} \quad \begin{array}{r} 7 \\ +7 \\ \hline 14 \end{array} \quad \begin{array}{r} 14 \\ -7 \\ \hline 7 \end{array}$$

$$\begin{array}{r} 8 \\ +8 \\ \hline 16 \end{array} \quad \begin{array}{r} 16 \\ -8 \\ \hline 8 \end{array} \quad \begin{array}{r} 9 \\ +9 \\ \hline 18 \end{array} \quad \begin{array}{r} 18 \\ -9 \\ \hline 9 \end{array}$$

Add.

1.
$$\begin{array}{r} 6 \\ +6 \\ \hline \end{array} \qquad \begin{array}{r} 8 \\ +8 \\ \hline \end{array} \qquad \begin{array}{r} 9 \\ +9 \\ \hline \end{array}$$

2.
$$\begin{array}{r} 7 \\ +7 \\ \hline \end{array} \qquad \begin{array}{r} 6 \\ +6 \\ \hline \end{array} \qquad \begin{array}{r} 8 \\ +8 \\ \hline \end{array}$$

3.
$$\begin{array}{r} 9 \\ +8 \\ \hline \end{array} \qquad \begin{array}{r} 7 \\ +6 \\ \hline \end{array} \qquad \begin{array}{r} 8 \\ +7 \\ \hline \end{array}$$

4.
$$\begin{array}{r} 7 \\ +8 \\ \hline \end{array} \qquad \begin{array}{r} 8 \\ +9 \\ \hline \end{array} \qquad \begin{array}{r} 6 \\ +7 \\ \hline \end{array}$$

5.
$$\begin{array}{r} 14 \\ -7 \\ \hline \end{array} \qquad \begin{array}{r} 18 \\ -9 \\ \hline \end{array} \qquad \begin{array}{r} 12 \\ -6 \\ \hline \end{array}$$

6.
$$\begin{array}{r} 16 \\ -8 \\ \hline \end{array} \qquad \begin{array}{r} 14 \\ -7 \\ \hline \end{array} \qquad \begin{array}{r} 18 \\ -9 \\ \hline \end{array}$$

Another look

Name _____

ENRICHMENT

TREASURE ISLAND

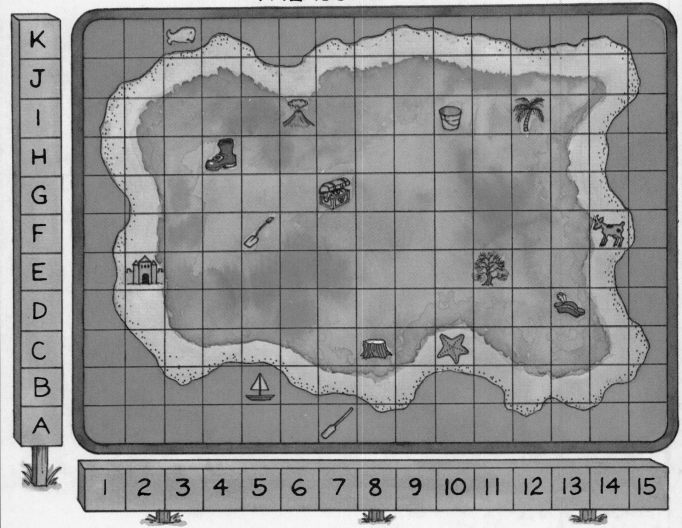

Where is each object?

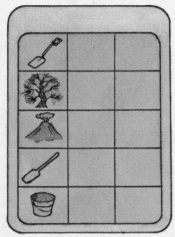

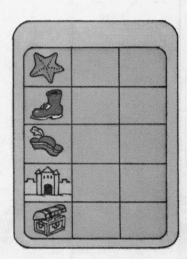

Enrichment—map locations

14 FRACTIONS AND CUSTOMARY MEASUREMENTS

Name _____

There are 2 equal parts.

2

How many equal parts are there?

1.

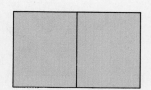 2 ___

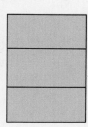 ___

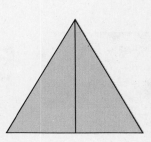 ___

2.

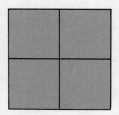 ___

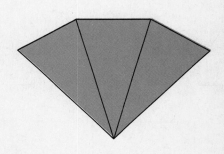

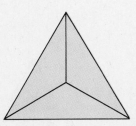 ___

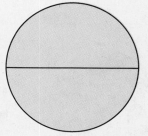 ___

3.

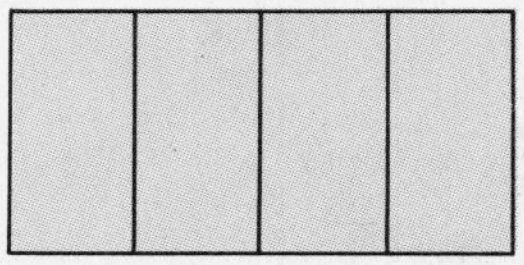

Concept of equal parts for fractions

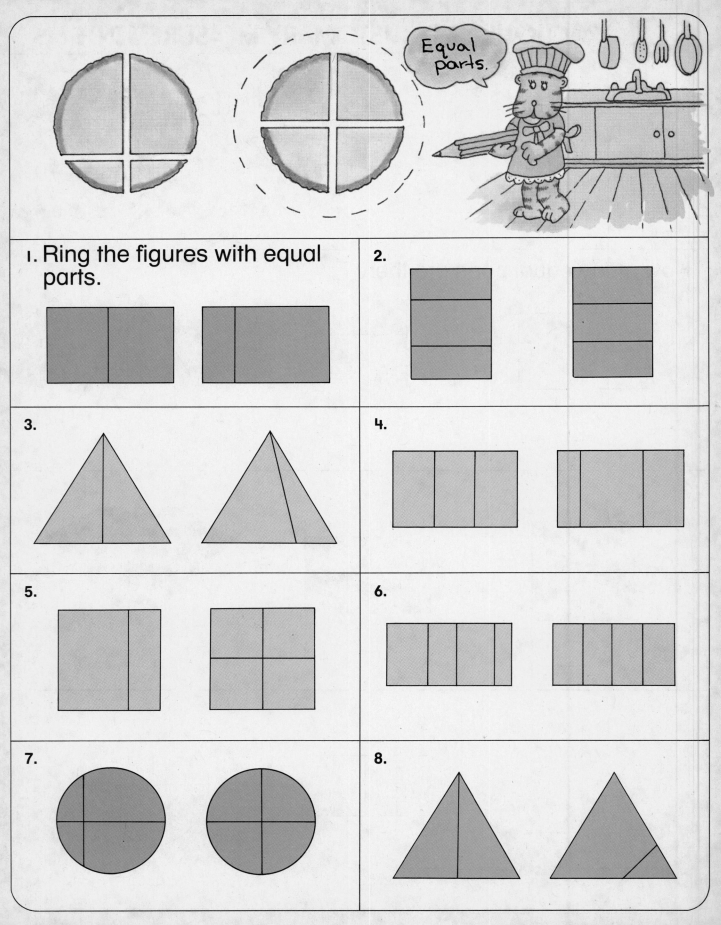

Equal parts.

1. Ring the figures with equal parts.

2.

3.

4.

5.

6.

7.

8.

Concept of equal parts for fractions

Name _____

2 equal parts

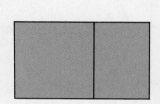

Each part is 1 half.

Ring the pictures that show halves.

1.

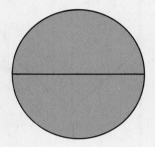 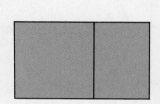 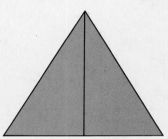

2.

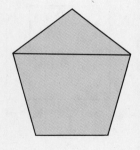 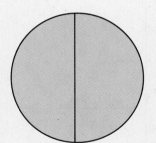 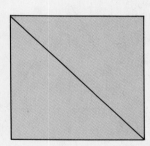

3.

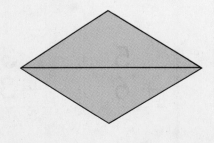 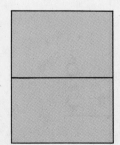 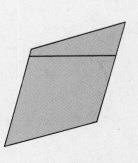

Halves

one half $\frac{1}{2}$

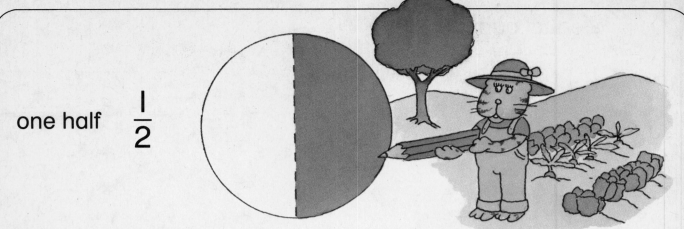

Color $\frac{1}{2}$.

1.

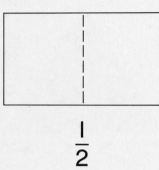

$\frac{1}{2}$ $\frac{1}{2}$ $\frac{1}{2}$

2.

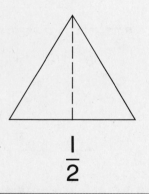

$\frac{1}{2}$ $\frac{1}{2}$ $\frac{1}{2}$

SKILLKEEPER

Add.

$$\begin{array}{r} 7 \\ +4 \\ \hline \end{array} \qquad \begin{array}{r} 8 \\ +3 \\ \hline \end{array} \qquad \begin{array}{r} 6 \\ +5 \\ \hline \end{array} \qquad \begin{array}{r} 9 \\ +2 \\ \hline \end{array} \qquad \begin{array}{r} 5 \\ +6 \\ \hline \end{array} \qquad \begin{array}{r} 3 \\ +8 \\ \hline \end{array}$$

One half

3 equal parts

Each part is 1 third.

Ring the pictures that show thirds.

1.

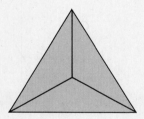 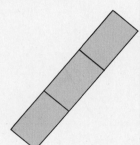 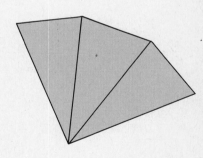

2.

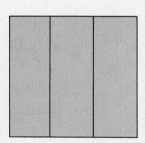 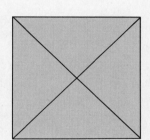 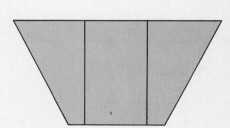

3.

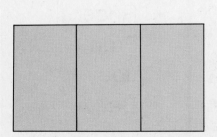 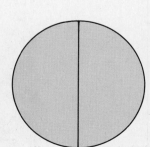 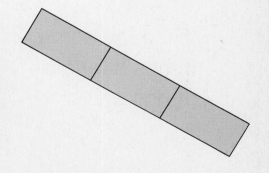

Thirds

one third $\dfrac{1}{3}$

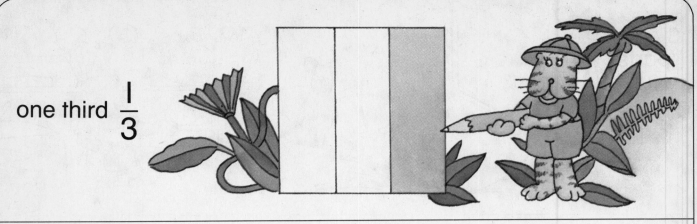

Color $\dfrac{1}{3}$.

1.

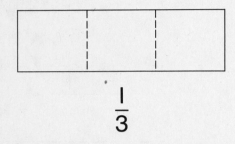

$\dfrac{1}{3}$

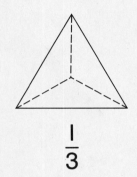

$\dfrac{1}{3}$

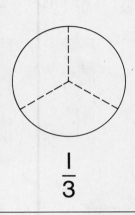

$\dfrac{1}{3}$

2.

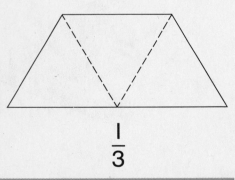

$\dfrac{1}{3}$

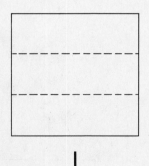

$\dfrac{1}{3}$

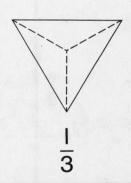

$\dfrac{1}{3}$

THINK MATH

Ring my name.
It has 4 letters.
It has an e.

Roger
Fran
Joey
Betty

One third

4 equal parts

Each part is 1 fourth.

Ring the figures that show fourths.

1.

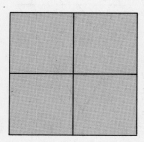 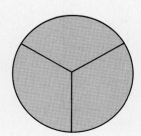 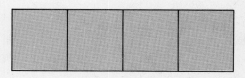

2.

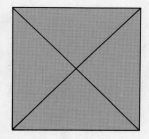 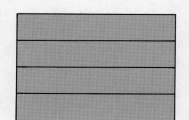 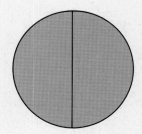

3.

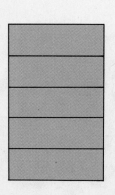 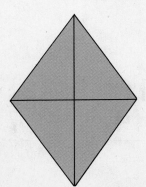 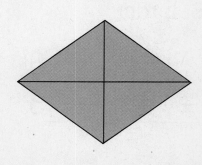

Fourths

one fourth $\frac{1}{4}$

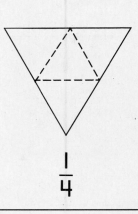

1. Color $\frac{1}{4}$.

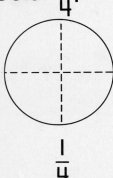 $\frac{1}{4}$

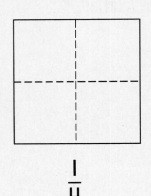 $\frac{1}{4}$

$\frac{1}{4}$

2.

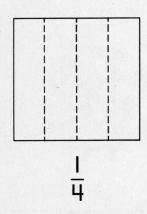 $\frac{1}{4}$

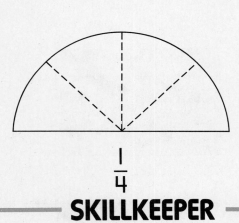 $\frac{1}{4}$

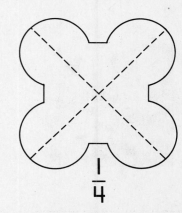 $\frac{1}{4}$

SKILLKEEPER

Subtract.

$$\begin{array}{r} 12 \\ -\ 4 \\ \hline \end{array} \qquad \begin{array}{r} 9 \\ -\ 3 \\ \hline \end{array} \qquad \begin{array}{r} 10 \\ -\ 4 \\ \hline \end{array} \qquad \begin{array}{r} 11 \\ -\ 7 \\ \hline \end{array} \qquad \begin{array}{r} 12 \\ -\ 3 \\ \hline \end{array} \qquad \begin{array}{r} 9 \\ -\ 5 \\ \hline \end{array}$$

One fourth

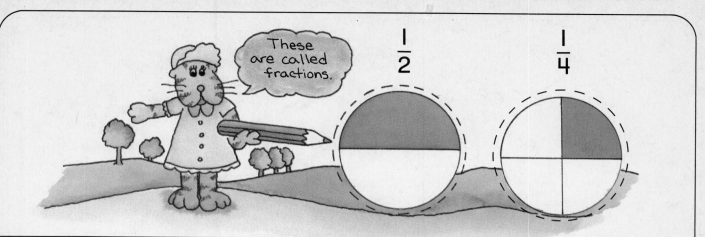

These are called fractions.

$\frac{1}{2}$ $\frac{1}{4}$

Ring the figure that shows the fraction.

1. $\frac{1}{2}$

2. $\frac{1}{3}$

3. $\frac{1}{4}$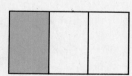

4. $\frac{1}{2}$

Ring the fraction.

5.

$\frac{1}{2}$ $\frac{1}{3}$ $\frac{1}{4}$

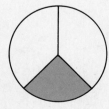

$\frac{1}{2}$ $\frac{1}{3}$ $\frac{1}{4}$

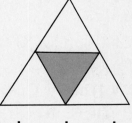

$\frac{1}{2}$ $\frac{1}{3}$ $\frac{1}{4}$

Fractional parts of regions

1. Color $\frac{1}{2}$.

2. Color $\frac{1}{4}$.

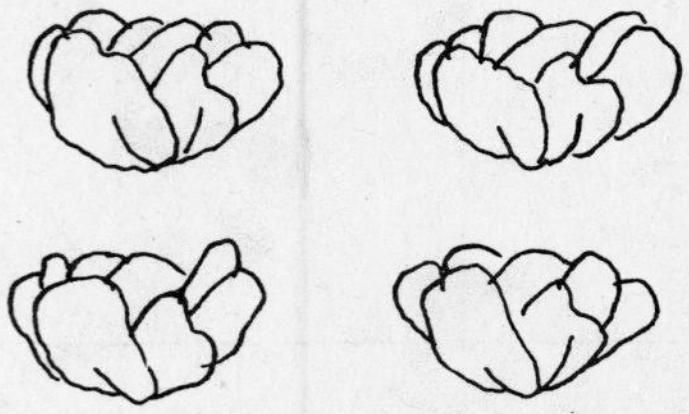

3. Color $\frac{1}{3}$.

4. Color $\frac{1}{4}$.

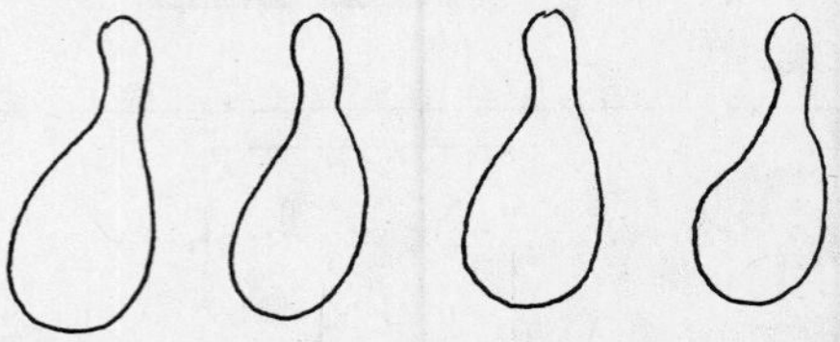

5. Color $\frac{1}{2}$.

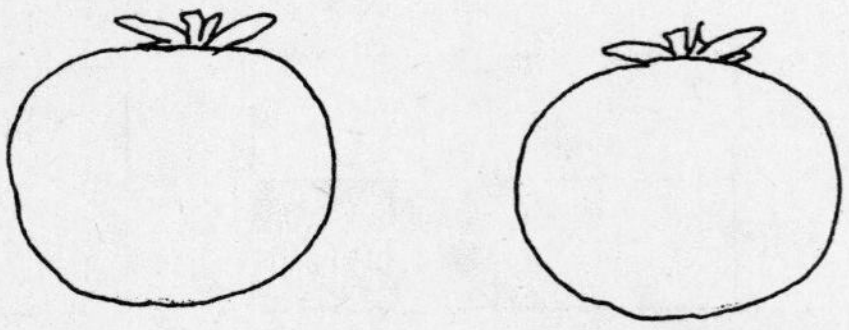

6. Color $\frac{1}{3}$.

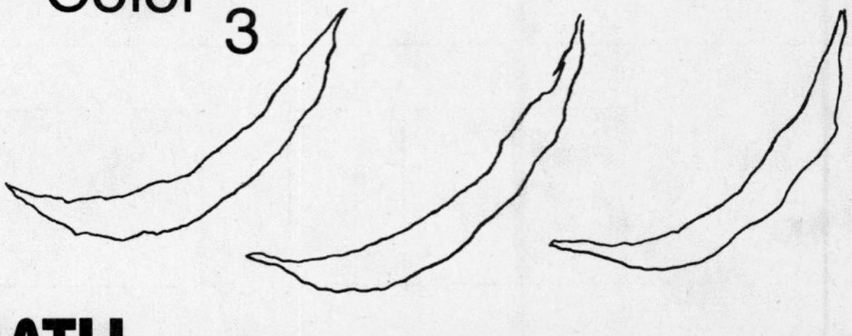

THINK MATH

$\frac{1}{2}$ of the dogs are inside.

$\frac{1}{2}$ of the dogs are outside.

How many dogs are there in all?

_____

Fractional parts of sets

__4__ inches

Inches

4 inches

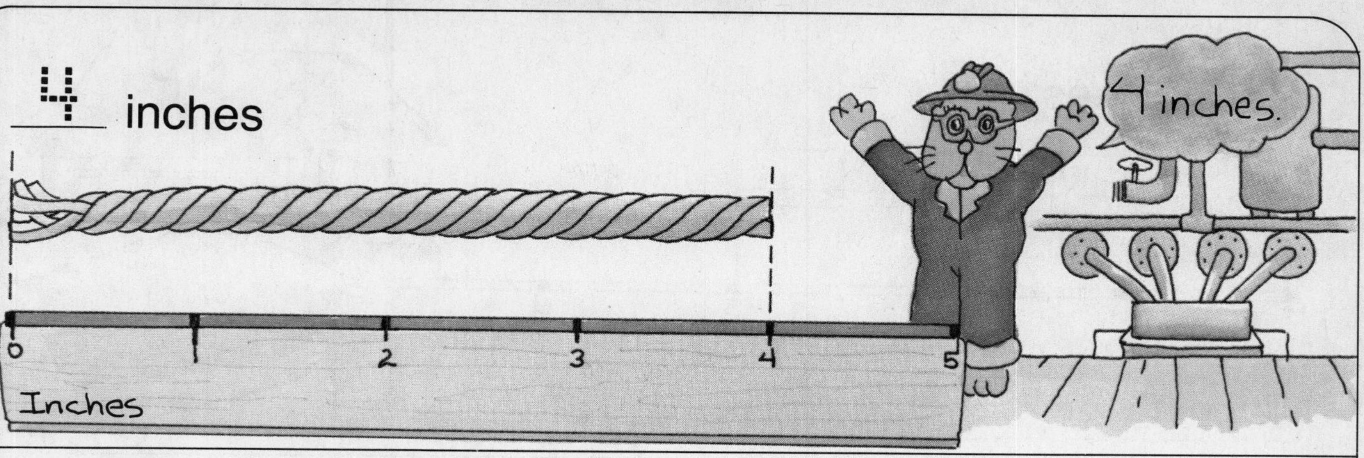

Write the number of inches.

1.

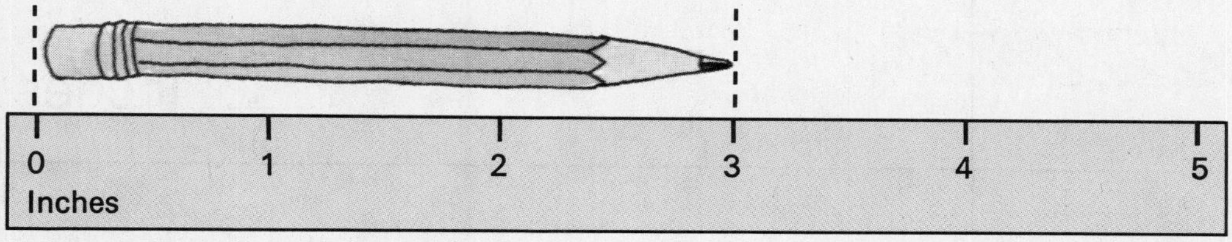

0 1 2 3 4 5
Inches

___3___ inches

2.

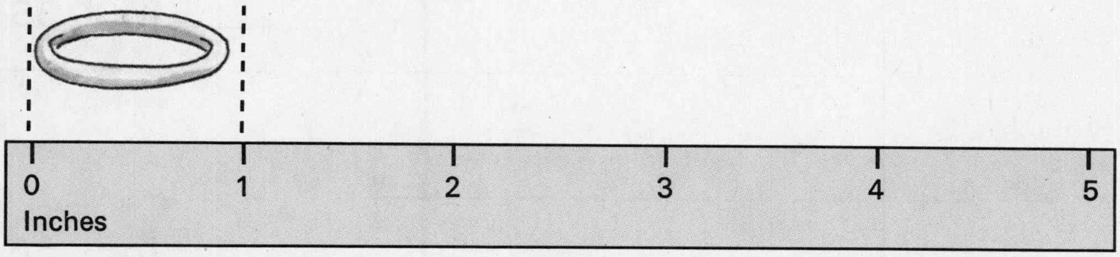

0 1 2 3 4 5
Inches

_____ inch

3.

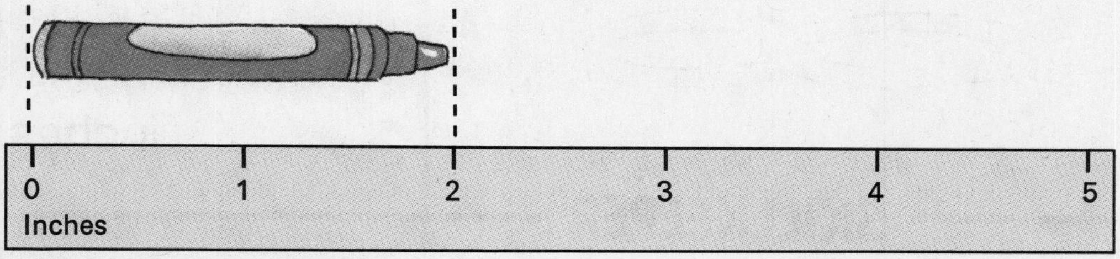

0 1 2 3 4 5
Inches

_____ inches

4.

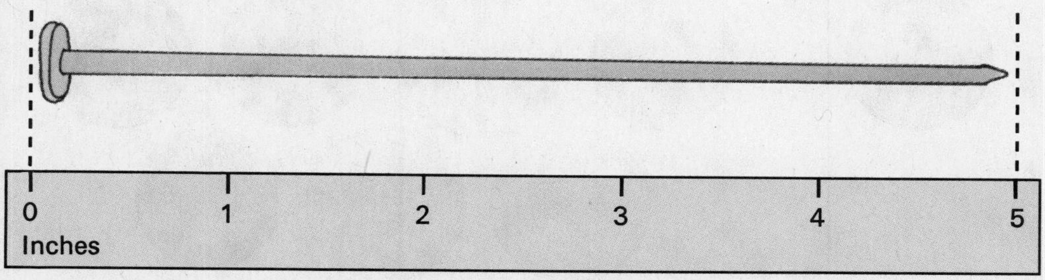

0 1 2 3 4 5
Inches

_____ inches

Measuring length—reading an inch ruler

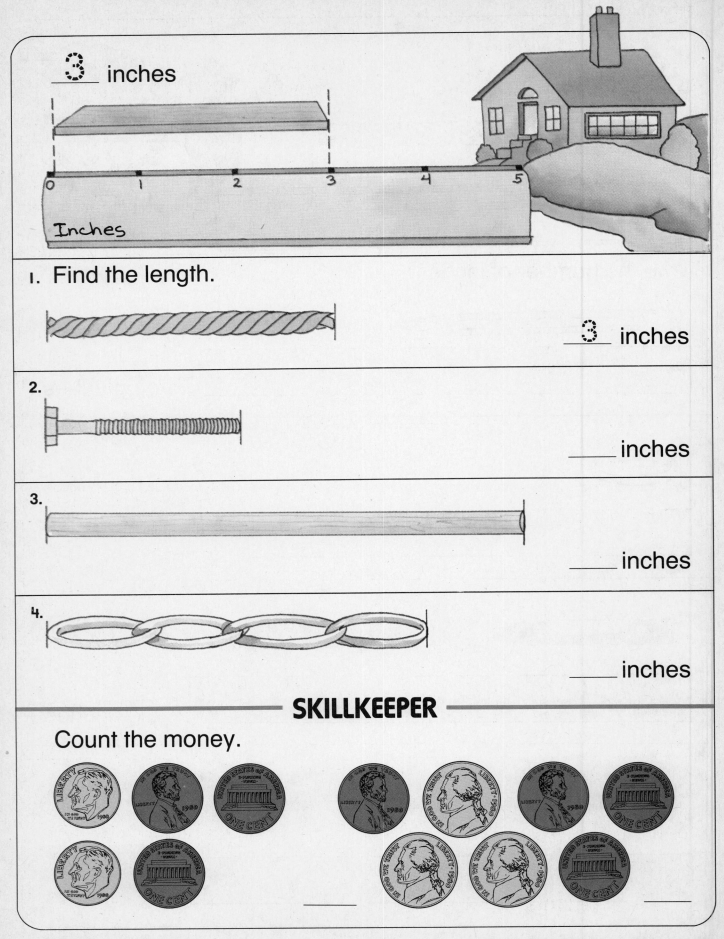

3 inches

Inches

1. **Find the length.**

_____ **3** inches

2.

_____ inches

3.

_____ inches

4.

_____ inches

SKILLKEEPER

Count the money.

_____   _____

Measuring length—using an inch ruler

Name _____

1 pint

Color the cups you can fill.

1.

1 pint

2.

2 pints

3.

3 pints

4.

4 pints

Capacity—cups and pints

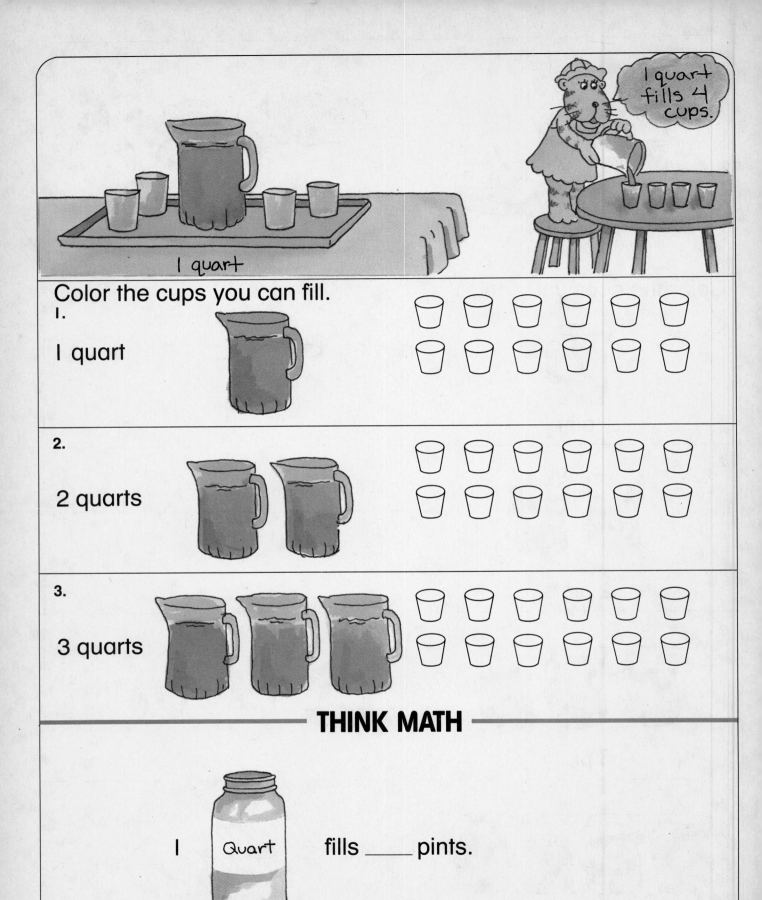

Color the cups you can fill.

1.

1 quart

2.

2 quarts

3.

3 quarts

THINK MATH

1 Quart   fills ____ pints.

Capacity—cups and quarts

Name _____

1. Ring the objects that weigh more than a pound.

2. Ring the objects that weigh less than a pound.

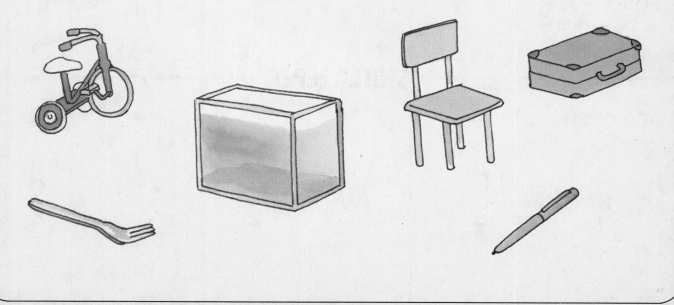

Weight—pounds

Cold Day   Warm Day   Hot Day

Ring the correct one.

1.

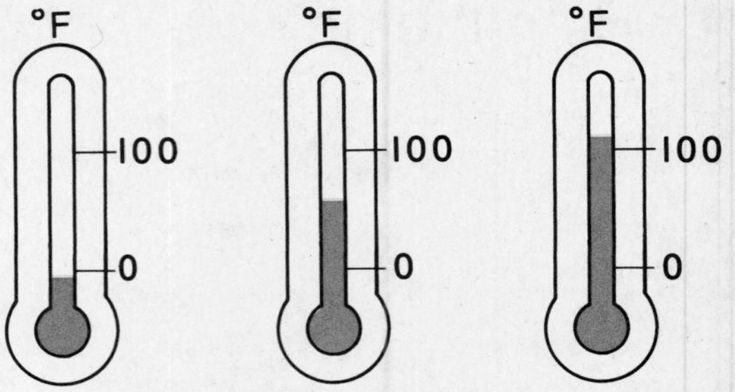

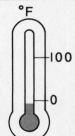

2.

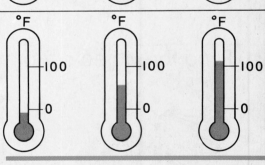

3.

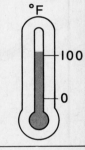

SKILLKEEPER

Add or subtract.

$$6 + 4 \qquad 10 - 2 \qquad 9 + 2 \qquad 11 - 2 \qquad 5 + 3 \qquad 8 - 2$$

Temperature—degrees Fahrenheit

CHAPTER REVIEW/TEST

1. Ring the figure that shows the fraction.

$\dfrac{1}{2}$ $\dfrac{1}{3}$ $\dfrac{1}{4}$

2. Ring the fraction.

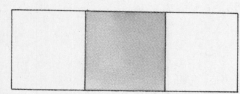

$\dfrac{1}{2}$ $\dfrac{1}{3}$ $\dfrac{1}{4}$

3. Color $\dfrac{1}{4}$.

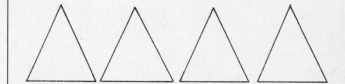

4. Use your inch ruler. Find the length.

_____ inches

5. Color the cups you can fill.

6. Ring the objects that weigh more than a pound.

CUMULATIVE REVIEW

Subtract.

1.
$$12$$
$$-\ 7$$

○ 2
○ 4
○ 5

2.
$$10$$
$$-\ 6$$

○ 4
○ 8
○ 6

3.
$$9$$
$$-5$$

○ 5
○ 6
○ 4

4.
$$11$$
$$-\ 6$$

○ 5
○ 6
○ 7

Add.

5.
$$17$$
$$+12$$

○ 19
○ 25
○ 29

6.
$$46¢$$
$$+22¢$$

○ 68¢
○ 24¢
○ 58¢

Subtract.

7.
$$49$$
$$-18$$

○ 32
○ 31
○ 27

8.
$$78¢$$
$$-56¢$$

○ 22¢
○ 24¢
○ 26¢

9. Solve.

Tony had 9¢.
He spent 4¢.
How much does he have now?

○ 7¢

○ 5¢

○ 9¢

Name _____

ANOTHER LOOK

$\frac{1}{2}$

$\frac{1}{3}$

$\frac{1}{4}$

$\frac{1}{2}$ $\left(\frac{1}{3}\right)$ $\frac{1}{4}$

$\frac{1}{2}$ $\frac{1}{3}$ $\left(\frac{1}{4}\right)$

$\left(\frac{1}{2}\right)$ $\frac{1}{3}$ $\frac{1}{4}$

0   1   2
Inches

__2__ inches

Ring the figure that shows the fraction.

1. $\frac{1}{3}$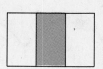

2. $\frac{1}{4}$

3. $\frac{1}{2}$

Ring the fraction.

4. 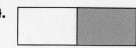 $\frac{1}{2}$ $\frac{1}{3}$ $\frac{1}{4}$

5. $\frac{1}{2}$ $\frac{1}{3}$ $\frac{1}{4}$

6. $\frac{1}{2}$ $\frac{1}{3}$ $\frac{1}{4}$

Use your inch ruler. Find the lengths.

7.  _____ inch

8.  _____ inches

ENRICHMENT

1. Show halves. Color $\frac{1}{2}$.

 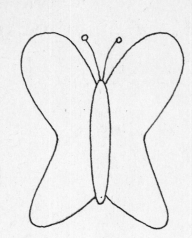 

2. Show thirds. Color $\frac{1}{3}$.

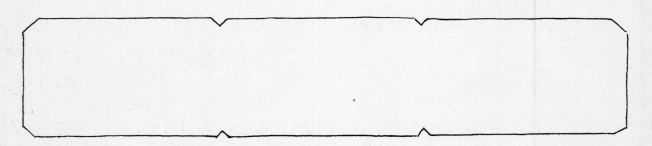

3. Show fourths. Color $\frac{1}{4}$.

  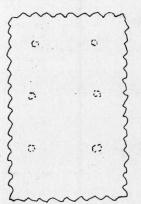

Enrichment—drawing fractional parts

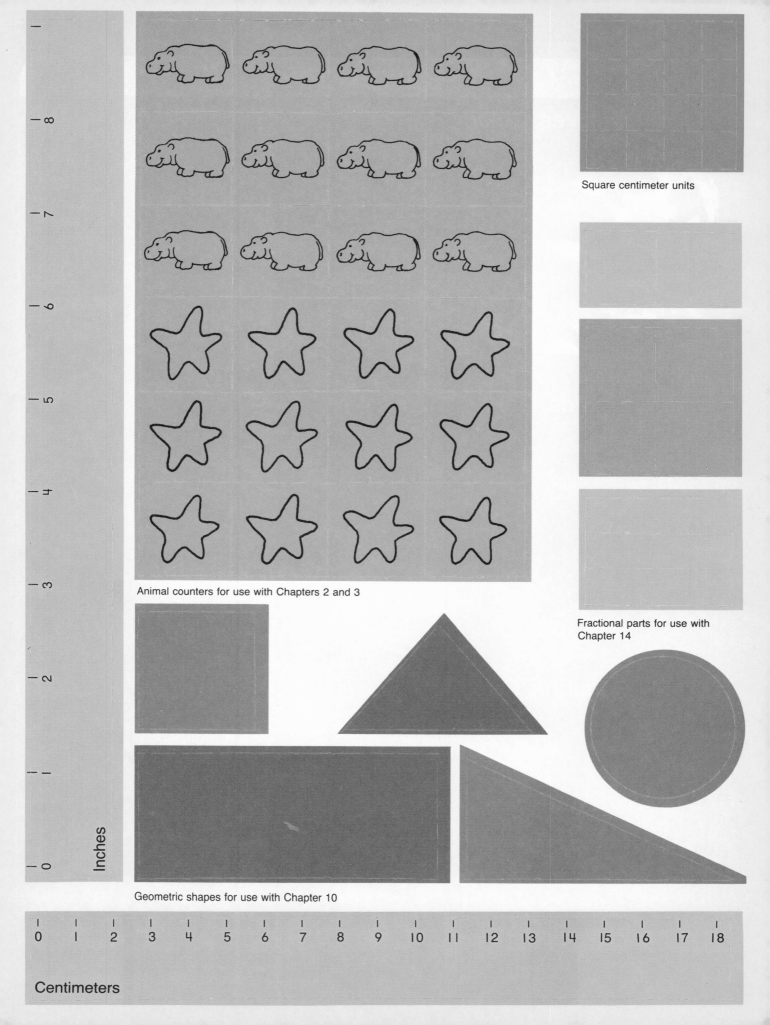

Square centimeter units

Animal counters for use with Chapters 2 and 3

Fractional parts for use with Chapter 14

Geometric shapes for use with Chapter 10

Inches

Centimeters

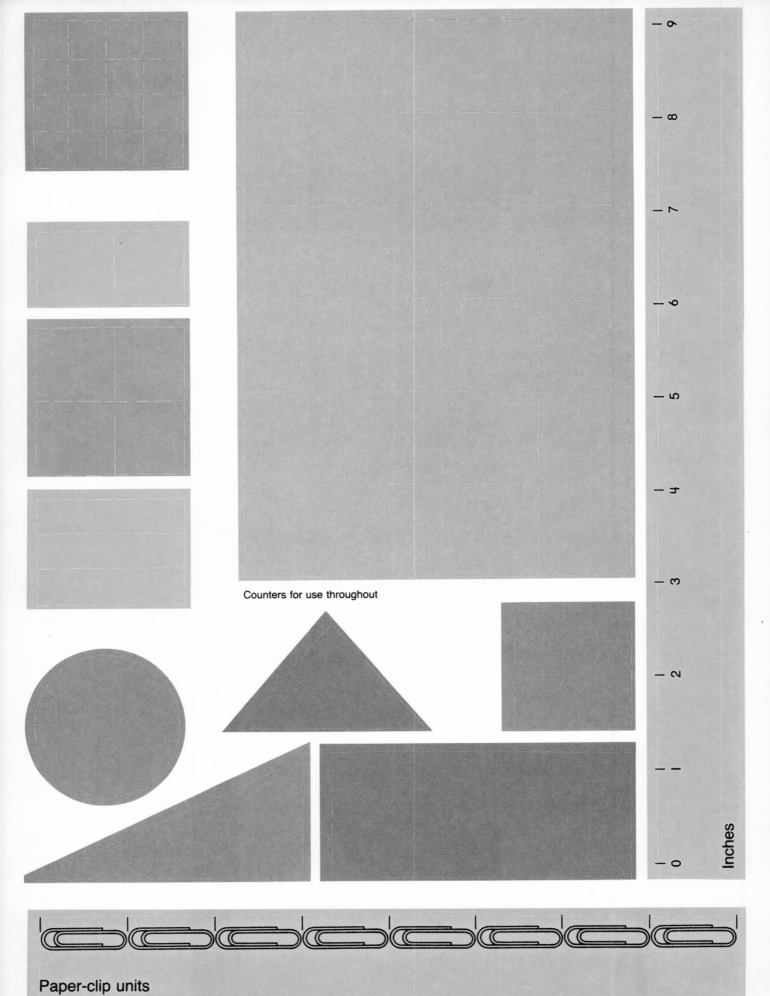

Counters for use throughout

Inches

Paper-clip units